THE LEGAL, MEDICAL AND CULTURAL
REGULATION OF THE BODY

Medical Law and Ethics

Series Editor
Sheila McLean, Director of the Institute of Law and Ethics in Medicine,
School of Law, University of Glasgow

The 21st century seems likely to witness some of the most major developments in medicine and healthcare ever seen. At the same time, the debate about the extent to which science and/or medicine should lead the moral agenda continues, as do questions about the appropriate role for law.

This series brings together some of the best contemporary academic commentators to tackle these dilemmas in a challenging, informed and inquiring manner. The scope of the series is purposely wide, including contributions from a variety of disciplines such as law, philosophy and social sciences.

Other titles in the series

Bioequity – Property and the Human Body
Nils Hoppe
ISBN 978-0-7546-7280-7

Altruism Reconsidered
Exploring New Approaches to Property in Human Tissue
Michael Steinmann, Peter Sýkora, and Urban Wiesing
ISBN 978-0-7546-7270-8

The Child As Vulnerable Patient
Protection and Empowerment
Lynn Hagger
ISBN 978-0-7546-7252-4

Disclosure Dilemmas
Ethics of Genetic Prognosis after the 'Right to Know/Not to Know' Debate
Edited by Christoph Rehmann-Sutter and Hansjakob Müller
ISBN 978-0-7546-7451-1

Critical Interventions in the Ethics of Healthcare
Challenging the Principle of Autonomy in Bioethics
Edited by Stuart J. Murray and Dave Holmes
ISBN 978-0-7546-7396-5

The Legal, Medical and Cultural Regulation of the Body
Transformation and Transgression

Edited by

STEPHEN W. SMITH
University of Birmingham, UK

RONAN DEAZLEY
University of Glasgow, UK

ASHGATE

Published by
Ashgate Publishing Limited
Wey Court East
Union Road
Farnham
Surrey, GU9 7PT
England

Ashgate Publishing Company
Suite 420
101 Cherry Street
Burlington
VT 05401-4405
USA

www.ashgate.com

British Library Cataloguing in Publication Data
The legal, medical and cultural regulation of the body : transformation and transgression.
-- (Medical law and ethics)
  1. Human body--Law and legislation. 2. Human body--Social
  aspects. 3. Human reproductive technology--Law and
  legislation. 4. Human reproductive technology--Moral and
  ethical aspects. 5. Self-mutilation--Law and legislation.
  I. Series II. Smith, Stephen W. III. Deazley, Ronan.
  344'.04194-dc22

Library of Congress Cataloging-in-Publication Data
The legal, medical, and cultural regulation of the body : transformation and transgression /
[edited] by Stephen W. Smith and Ronan Deazley.
    p. cm. -- (Medical law and ethics)
  Includes index.
  ISBN 978-0-7546-7736-9 (hardback) -- ISBN 978-0-7546-9465-6 (ebook)
  1. Human body--Law and legislation--Great Britain. 2. Human reproduction--Law and
legislation--Great Britain. 3. Human reproductive technology--Law and legislation--
Great Britain. 4. Human body--Law and legislation. 5. Human body--Moral and ethical
aspects. I. Smith, Stephen W., 1973- II. Deazley, Ronan.
  KD667.H85L44 2009
  344.4104'194--dc22

                                                                        2009031064

ISBN 978-0-7546-7736-9 (hbk)
ISBN 978-0-7546-9465-6 (ebk)

Mixed Sources
Product group from well-managed
forests and other controlled sources
www.fsc.org Cert no. SGS-COC-2482
© 1996 Forest Stewardship Council
FSC

Printed and bound in Great Britain by
TJ International Ltd, Padstow, Cornwall

Contents

List of Contributors

Helen Beebee is a Professor of Philosophy at the University of Birmingham and the Director of the British Philosophical Association.

Margot Brazier is a Professor of Law at the University of Manchester and the author of *Medicine, Patients and the Law*, 4th Edition (Penguin, 2007).

Ronan Deazley is a Professor of Law at the University of Glasgow.

Mary Ford is a Lecturer in Law at the University of Strathclyde.

Marie Fox is a Professor of Law at the University of Keele.

Sonia Harris-Short is a Reader in Law at the University of Birmingham .

Kate Ince is a Reader in French Film and Gender Studies at the University of Birmingham.

Claire McIvor is a Lecturer in Law at the University of Birmingham.

Mr Justice Munby was appointed to the High Court (Family Division) in 2000.

Victoria Pitts-Taylor is Professor of Sociology at Queens College and the Graduate Center of the City University of New York.

Robert Smith is a surgeon based at the Falkirk Royal Infirmary and a co-author of *Apotemnophilia: Information, Questions, Answers and Recommendations about Self-Demand Amputation* (Authorhouse, 2000).

Stephen W. Smith is the Director of the Institute of Medical Law at the University of Birmingham.

Robert Song is a Senior Lecturer in the Department of Theology and Religion at the University of Durham.

G.R. Sullivan is a Professor of Law at University College London.

Colin Warbrick is an Honorary Professor of Law at the University of Birmingham.

Heather Widdows is a Professor of Global Ethics at the University of Birmingham and the Lead Editor of the *Journal of Global Ethics*.

Preface

The origins of this collection lie in a conversation in June 2007 about tattoos, body art and body modification, and in particular about the legal rights and claims (if any) that might subsist in relation to the same – not the body as property, but body adornment as intellectual property. As the conversation progressed, its focus shifted from intellectual property concerns to the various other ways in which the body, and the use of the body, is prescribed and regulated – not just in law, but medically and culturally also. From that conversation grew the idea for a one-day conference in September 2008, coordinated by the University of Birmingham's *Institute of Medical Law*, which conference in turn gave rise to this edited collection.

As the editors of this collection, we would like to take this opportunity to thank a number of people without whom this work would not have been brought to press. In the first place, we would like to thank the various speakers who contributed to the conference in 2008. When we began planning for that event we drew up a short list of academics and professionals – drawn from a range of disciplines – that we were interested in hearing give papers at the same. Remarkably, everyone we approached agreed to participate, and willing so. We are truly grateful for their time and effort in contributing to what was a thoroughly enjoyable conference and what we hope will prove to be a thoroughly engaging collection. Thanks are also due to the University of Birmingham's Collaborative Research Network fund for supporting the conference financially, to Emer McKernan and June Firth for their help and support in organizing that event and to Paul Mora who provided invaluable editorial assistance in preparing this collection for publication.

Particular thanks are due to Professor Margot Brazier. From the start we were certain that we wanted to end the conference with a keynote address, and from the start we were certain that we wanted Margot to deliver the same. As with the other contributors, Margot has been more than generous with her time and support. Moreover, on the day of the conference, as we sat listening to Margot deliver her concluding address, drawing together the various themes from each of the papers with such skill, and intelligence, and wit, we realized how redundant it would be to try to replicate that feat in writing our own introduction to this collection. And so, Margot's concluding address morphed into an Introductory Essay. Although unplanned, we thought that particular transformation particularly clever.

Stephen W. Smith
Ronan Deazley

Introduction
Being Human: Of Liberty and Privilege

Margaret Brazier

Introduction

This paper began as an ending and is transformed into a beginning.[1] The editors of this fascinating collection invited me to sum up at the conclusion of the day on which all the papers that follow were originally presented and debated, debated I should say with vigour. The task of summing up at the end of such a conference always sounds easier than it proves to be. My euphoria at not having to write a whole paper of my own for September soon evaporated. The papers began to arrive on my desk, and on 8 September 2008, I listened to the presentations through the day. Each was, and is, so packed full of thought and insight that I cannot in what is now an introductory essay respond to all of the speakers, or to any of them, in the depth that their work merits. Moreover, each section of the book has gained its own focused Introduction. So if I say little about some of the papers that follow, I trust that the authors will forgive me. I do no more than offer a 'taster' for some of what is to follow.

In the metamorphosis that this paper has undergone in its positioning in the collection, one may espy a rich metaphor connecting the publication to its subject matter of the body. For the nature of animal life, human and non-human, is that we struggle to draw boundaries asking when does life begin, when does it end. Yet life is a continuum. Gametes are living organisms even when ova are hidden deep in the body of a female fetus. Our organs may live on in others long after we are no more. The more science has to teach us about the biological organisms that house our identity, the more exciting and troubling the possibilities of bodies become.

Why do Bodies Matter?

Scientific advances in transplant medicine, fertility treatment and, most recently, stem cell therapies have added a new dimension to ethical, social and legal[2] debates

---

1   For a more complete explanation of how this concluding essay became an introductory essay, please see the Preface to this volume.

2   For an excellent analysis of law's neglect of 'embodiment', see Fletcher, R., Fox, M. and McCandless, J. (2008), Legal Embodiment: Analysing the Body of Healthcare Law,

about the body. Today our own bodies hold the potential to offer therapies to us and to others.[3] Science has joined faith and culture in claiming a stake in living and dead bodies at all stages in life's continuum. It has even blurred the boundary between human and non-human animal life. However rather than start with such 'grand' questions, reading the draft papers for this collection over the summer prompted me to reflect on the myriad ways we consider our bodies (and the bodies of others) in everyday life. So as will be apparent, I do not follow the order of the book with its nice journey from the start of life, but rather I begin with what may seem to be more mundane questions about what bodies mean to their inhabitants.

In her essay on cosmetic surgery, Victoria Pitts-Taylor notes how '[B]ody practices are increasingly positioned in various ways as expressing, reflecting or revealing various aspects of the self.'[4] She writes, not of the use of bodies for transplant or 'medicine', but of the importance of the exterior to many people, of the body as a 'project'. Had I been asked 12 months ago, 'do you spend much time thinking about your own body, Margot?' my answer would (I think) have been 'no, not much unless it isn't working properly.' Dysfunction reminds us of the body. However, had I answered 'no, not much' I would unconsciously have lied, for, of course, I think a lot about my body. And I do so in a range of contexts every day. I give just a few examples. It is my primary *vehicle*, getting me up each day, conveying me downstairs for breakfast when I begin to fill it with fuel for the day. It is a crucial *instrument* for my day – an instrument that switches on the toaster and bends to pet and feed my puppy. It is part of my *clothing* (*or adornment*) as I style my hair and (when I can be bothered) put on make-up.

And above all for me, as for all of the authors of these essays, it is my means of *financial support*. Reader, do not panic! I am not about to reveal a tawdry past in glamour modelling or worse, in selling my body in the tabloid sense. I sell my *brain* (such as it is). That organ of my body is crucial to my ability to persuade the University of Manchester to pay for my services. Yet it can only function as part of the whole. Dysfunction of the lowly bowels can impair the function of the lofty brain. When commodification of body parts is discussed, all too often we leave out the living brain *in situ*. Those who like me are concerned about the sale of kidneys or commercial surrogacy have to find an answer to why it acceptable for us to hire out our brains, but not for a woman to rent her womb.[5]

Medical Law Review 16, 321–345; and see other papers in that Special Issue (Volume 16:3) of the *Medical Law Review*.

3   See Brazier, M. (2006), Human(s) (as) Medicine(s), in MacLean, S. (ed.), *First Do No Harm*, (Ashgate), at pp. 187–202.

4   See Pitts-Taylor, V., Medicine, Governmentality and Biopower in Cosmetic Surgery, below at pp. 159–170.

5   For a nuanced discussion of bodies and their uses see Dickenson, D. (1997), *Property, Women and Politics*, (Cambridge Polity Press), at pp. 160–165; and see Dickenson, D. (2007), *Property in the Body: Feminist Perspectives*, (Cambridge University Press).

I want to suggest that is the range of functions and symbolisms inherent in bodies, living or dead, human or non-human, that make the body such a vexing ethical, legal and social question. Staying just for a moment longer with the adult, living, human body, consider how varied individual perceptions (and prejudices) are about the functions of the body. Take the body as *clothing* (*or adornment*). Place a value of 1 (virtually nil) to 10 (most important thing in your life) on that function. Be honest. Now think about those who would give clothing/adornment a value of 9/10. Would you think them vain, or even a little odd?[6] Would you judge men differently from women, or the pensioner of 82 differently from the youth of 21?

Altering Bodies

How we look can be an integral part of who we are, even if we score a low value to clothing/adornment. How we look will often be the first way in which others begin to define us. Asked to describe Stephen Smith for someone due to meet him for the first time, I will begin with a physical description, not an account of his considerable intellect. Unless his new acquaintance is blind, how Stephen looks is how he will initially be defined. Appearance is individual, yet because we live as a community – and are to an extent pack animals – throughout history attempts have been made to prescribe appearance. So long hair for men at the court of Charles I was the norm. Long hair for men in the 1950s was curtailed, often coercively. No junior lawyer or doctor could be seen with hair on his shoulders.

In Western society, are we more liberal now? Or have we just shifted the boundaries a little? So in 2009 in Britain, whether we are male or female, long or short hair (or no hair) is fine. A middle-aged woman can access Botox to smooth out her wrinkles without charges of excessive vanity. But are there still limits? Does chopping off a limb to complete the individual's body image remain beyond the pale, even though, as Robert Smith has shown in his formidable essay,[7] the impact on the individual for a person with Body Integrity Identity Disorder of constraining his or her bodily choices is much greater than any decision by an ageing female law professor about whether to go for Botox or not. Or do I trivialize the Botox dilemma? Does society still play a commanding role in how some of us should look? The ageing woman becomes invisible. Her younger sister is instructed by her employers to wear discreet make-up. Victoria Pitts-Taylor notes that cosmetic medicine and surgery inscribe 'hierarchies of race and gender onto the body'.[8] I would add a hierarchy of age to her list. The challenge for liberals is does it matter or should we simply rejoice at transformations that make the individual happier? Should we join Pitts-Taylor in rejecting simplistic assumptions that the individual

---

6　I confess I would think them both vain and misguided.
7　Smith, R.C., Less is More: Body Integrity Identity Disorder, below at pp. 147–157.
8　Pitts-Taylor, *op. cit.* at p. 166.

seeking to alter his or her appearance is somehow a 'victim' of the cosmetic (surgery) industry rather than simply exhibiting a care of self?[9] Remember the broad definition of health offered by the WHO: 'a state of complete physical, mental and social well being and not merely the absence of infirmity'. For the older woman, or man, preserving the exterior illusion of youth may enhance the internal conviction that age is a state of mind, not being. I might regret that appearance should matter so much to my 'sisters' and see them as vulnerable to the influence of the media and the cosmetic industry but am I equally influenced by the blue stocking environment in which I grew up and lead my life? As John Harris[10] has so cogently argued, there is no such thing as a fully autonomous choice and when we scrutinize the choices of others to assess whether they are maximally autonomous we are ourselves heavily influenced by outcomes.[11]

At what point might we move from transformation to transgression? The voluntary amputee sets us a test.[12] Amputation of a limb and excision of a healthy eye are perceived as so far outside the norm that at best the individual must be seen as *ill*, and if complying with his wishes is lawful at all, it is as treatment. Medicalizing Body Integrity Identity Disorder is a prerequisite of rendering the choice valid. But paradoxically, once we medicalize the condition we start to doubt the choice. Is this ill person competent to give consent?[13]

Where boundaries are drawn is troubling. Robert Smith noted that surgery for gender identity disorder is seen as 'currently justified'[14] yet removal of womb and breasts constitutes riskier and more major surgery than amputation below the knee. There are those who tattoo their whole body surface and pierce every orifice. They can do so (if adults) without troubling the medical or legal professions.

What we allow people to do to themselves, what we allow others to do to them, what we allow surgeons to do, is an age-old dilemma. And just as adornment of the body has fashions so, as Robert Arnott has shown,[15] does medicine. Consider bleeding, once the physician's remedy of choice, though carried out by less elevated

---

9   See also Latham, M. (2008), The Shape of Things to Come: Feminism, Regulation and Cosmetic Surgery, *Medical Law Review* 16, 437–457.

10   See for example, Harris, J. (1985), *The Value of Life*, (Routledge and Kegan Paul), at pp. 195–203.

11   Some argue that the Court of Appeal took this outcome-based approach in *Re T (Adult: Refusal of Treatment)* [1992] 4 All ER 649. Ian Kennedy and Andrew Grubb commented that the court may well have 'adopted the undue influence approach out of its desire that the patient should not die'; Kennedy, I. and Grubb, A. (2000), *Medical Law*, 3rd Edition (Butterworths), at p. 757.

12   Elegantly explored in MacKenzie, R. (2008), Somatechnics of Medico-Legal Taxonomies: Elective Amputation and Transableism, *Medical Law Review* 16, 390–412.

13   See Elliott, T. (2009), Body Dysmorphic Disorder: Radical Surgery and the Limits of Consent, *Medical Law Review* 17 (forthcoming).

14   Smith, *op. cit.* at p. 152.

15   Robert Arnott provided a talk on the day of the conference entitled Transforming the Body: Rights and Power about Cranial Trepanation which has not been included in this edited

barber-surgeons.[16] Cranial trepanation has antiquity, but a mixed pedigree. Arnott suggests that today there are limited therapeutic uses for trepanation in proper hands, but notes that shamanistic trepanation continues across the world, and that, as with body integrity identity disorders, some people actively seek relief that they believe will come from having a hole drilled in their skull.

Assume I join their ranks. I seek trepanation to enhance my brainpower, to release the 'inner me'. No reputable surgeon in the UK is likely to see my request as therapeutically indicated. Yet amateur neurosurgery risks my life and were a layfriend to help me out, she would be likely to face prosecution for causing grievous bodily harm, regardless of my consent. Bizarre choices need medical validation. 'Reasonable surgery' transforms assault into a lawful act.[17] So at what point should all the non-medics rise up to condemn the paternalism of state and the surgeons? Our bodies – our choices, we cry. Liberty should endorse any choice of a competent adult.

Transgression and the Criminal Law

Bob Sullivan addresses this thorny question in his rich and complex essay. I am fascinated by the line drawn between gladiatorial combat and *R v Brown*.[18] He exposes the fallacy of the easy way out, that is to claim that the individual seeking amputation of a limb or deliberately seeking to contract an STD lacks mental capacity. Regret does not negate choice. Bizarre, even morally repugnant, choices do not conclusively indicate lack of capacity.[19] Sullivan argues for robust liberalism, at least in the context of sexual conduct, and rules out legal moralism as a means of overruling choices that are *prima facie* self-harming and others abhor. But, bravely, he puts the case for limited paternalism. He contends that there may be a case for state intervention 'where an agent proposes to do something to herself or have something done to her which threatens to end a life potentially worth living or an immediate, serious and permanent setback to the core interest of her physical health or soundness with no offsetting gain remotely commensurable with the loss'.[20] Even in such cases, Sullivan would eschew the criminal law[21] and

---

collection. For a further discussion on cranial trepanation, see Arnott, R., Finger S. and Smith, C. (eds) (2003), *Trepanation: History, Discovery, Theory*, (Swets and Zeitlinger).

16 See Brazier, M. (2008), The Age of Deference: A Historical Anomaly? in Freeman, M. (ed.), *Law and Bioethics: Current Legal Issues*, Volume II (Oxford University Press), at pp. 464–475.

17 See Elliott, *op cit*.

18 [1994] 1 AC 212.

19 *St George's Healthcare NHS Trust v S* [1998] 3 All ER 673, at 692.

20 Sullivan, G.R. Liberalism and Constraining Choice: The Cases of Death and Serious Bodily Harm, below at pp. 205–233, 232.

21 As does Elliott, *op. cit.*

suggests some form of civil commitment to prevent self-harm. We must be sure that the 'intervention will advance the long-term interests of the agent' and that the process has 'robust review and release procedures'.[22]

Sullivan offers a neat solution to the question posed by Smith.[23] Would the argument that he (Smith) advances for performing single below the knee amputations hold good for the man who seeks to be a double amputee or to have his eyes put out? The answer no could be justified by Sullivan's formula that by so disabling yourself, you threaten your core health and soundness. He may offer us an escape from medicalization. It does not seem that Sullivan insists that only a qualified and licensed doctor could comply with a request for bodily mutilation, if it fell short of the threshold he sets that there be no impact on the person's core interests, although opting to have an unqualified person 'operate' on you may both increase the risk to your core health and the likelihood that your mental capacity may be questioned. There still remain two issues. (1) Civil commitment still deprives me of my liberty and so, should Sullivan's proposal ever be implemented, the devil would be in the detail determining exactly when I forfeit the liberty to decide my own interests. (2) Must I ever consider weighing my interests against others? As I have noted elsewhere, autonomy has in popular debate become 'I want therefore must have'.[24]

Refining in Autonomy

Before considering wants and demands, and essaying the murky waters of reining in autonomy, we should be clear, as Sir James Munby[25] is in his paper, that doctors do owe a duty to treat those whom they accept as their patients, and that a key question in modern health care law has become whose views take precedence if the patient's judgement of his own best interests conflict with that of his doctors. Such a conflict arose in the tragic case of Leslie Burke. Claire McIvor[26] mounts a vigorous defence of the Court of Appeal.[27] Their Lordships were clear that patients had no right to demand treatment – and now we are considering orthodox medical treatment, not holes drilled in the skull. In defending the Court of Appeal, McIvor notes a number of problems with any notion of autonomy as driving demand. To me, one the hardest tasks is to reflect on how one might view Burke in a Utopian world where financial resources were not a problem. Would we still be constrained

---

22   Sullivan, *op. cit.* at p. 232.

23   Smith, *op. cit.*

24   Brazier, M. (2006), Do No Harm – Do Patients Have Responsibilities Too?, *Cambridge Law Journal* 65, 397.

25   Munby, J., A Duty to Treat? – A Legal Analysis, below at pp. 179–182.

26   See McIvor, C., Bursting the Autonomy Bubble: A Defence of the Court of Appeal Decision in *R (On the Application of Leslie Burke) v GMC*, below at pp. 183–203.

27   *R (On the Application of Leslie Burke) v GMC* [2005] 3 WLR 1132.

by professional integrity[28] and some kind of broader responsibility to others? Consider a demand for IVF and multiple embryo transfer made by a woman who already has six children under 10 – an example not a million miles away from the case in the USA of the woman who gave birth to octuplets in January 2009.[29] She knew, and her doctors knew, that she herself might die and that a multiple pregnancy might result in disability to her babies – did she act wrongly? I suggest that she did for she ignored her obligations to her existing offspring, as well as to the possible future children. McIvor presents a compelling case that no doctor has any obligation to comply with her demands. But has the law the legitimate claim to stop her if she can find a compliant doctor and pay for all her treatment? After all, I have an unfettered right to refuse treatment. The possible paradox in endorsing a right to say no, yet refusing a claim to insist on implementing every yes, requires that we follow the lead of Nicky Priaulx[30] and John Coggon[31] in recent papers where they dissect what the judges mean when they speak of autonomy. Does the core legal value remain bodily integrity?

Embryonic Bodies

So far I have focused on the adult human body and the papers that address such bodies. Three papers consider our bodies in their earliest stages. Why do we bother at all about the human embryo, a microscopic bundle of cells invisible to the human eye? That we do is proven by the millions of words written about, and the substantial jurisprudential attention devoted to, the embryo. Even those who espouse the view that embryos are nought but a cluster of cells care deeply about them.[32] The current debate about human admixed embryos addressed by Robert Song[33] and Marie Fox[34] delves into the heart of the main question surfacing in all our papers within this collection, why do bodies (and in particular human bodies) matter at all?

Song quotes Baroness O'Cathain speaking in the debate on the Human Fertilisation and Embryology Bill in the House of Lords in 2007. She affirmed that 'God created man in his own image', and so 'a clear definition between the

---

28   See Draper, H. and Sorrell, T. (2002), Patients' Responsibilities in Medical Ethics, *Bioethics* 16, 335.

29   See Mother had 'multiple IVF' although she already had six children, *The Times*, 31 January 2009.

30   Priaulx, N. (2008), Rethinking Progenitive Conflict: Why Reproductive Autonomy Matters, *Medical Law Review* 16, 169–200.

31   Coggon, J. (2007), Varied and Principled Understandings of Autonomy in English Law: Justifiable Inconsistency or Blinkered Moralism, *Health Care Analysis* 15, 235–255.

32   Consider the proportion of John Harris's published work devoted to the embryo, an entity he declares lacks moral value.

33   Song, R., Human-Monsters, Monstrous Humans? Humanity, Divinity and Interspecies Embryos, below at pp. 127–141.

34   Fox, M., Legislating Interspecies Embryos, below at pp. 95–125.

species must remain'.[35] His paper is complex and the richer for that complexity. He questions the trend to instrumentalize and compartmentalize the body and to make *health* the be all and end all of existence. Just to say transgressing species boundaries will benefit medicine is not good enough. The ability to do X should not be the only determinant of the liberty to do X.

Mixing bodies is in itself a teasing question. We do it now in inserting human genes in pigs, in transplanting porcine heart valves into humans, and even in drinking cows' milk. To test our views on creating truly admixed embryos with human and non-human genes, I suggest we should check our ethical stance were such an enterprise carried out in a context very different to the cause of advancing medicine via stem cell therapies.

Let us say that I would like to create a chimpanzee/human cross-breed[36] because I think it would be cute or make a good servant. I will call her Rose, treat her with great care and she will have a better life than a chimp in a zoo. Her limited intelligence will mean she is happy as a 'slave'. I suspect that you will all from different perspectives be condemning the wrongness of my conduct for I am meddling now with a sentient being. My wrongdoing may lie for those who are content to permit the creation of admixed embryos in the laboratory, not in the creation of the thing, the cluster of cells in the Petrie dish, but in the development of the 'animal'. Proponents of personhood may be content to allow me to engineer my new species, but then assign personhood to 'my' servant thus granting her rights that undermine her use for me. In this paragraph, I deliberately muddle my use of pronouns for the essence of the question I pose is this: is Rose 'it' or 'she'? As Fox notes, those who are comfortable with our current relationship with non-human animals will object to the moral confusion engendered by 'Rose'. Fox forces us to think about the other body of opinion among those who consider the status quo 'deeply problematic'.

Mary Ford vividly illustrates the immense difficulty of achieving compromise on how we view the embryo.[37] She does a convincing 'hatchet job' on the Warnock concept of 'special status' for the embryo. Few readers will now remember the debates on Options A and B in the course of the first Human Fertilisation and Embryology Bill in 1989.[38] The attempt to ban embryo research altogether only just failed. Yet even that prohibitive option was a compromise that would not have stopped the destruction of embryos surplus to need in fertility treatments. And if embryos should have the same moral status as born humans they cannot simply

---

35   Song, *op. cit.* at p. 128.

36   Though note the discussion in Fox about whether any such 'true hybrid' would develop beyond fertilization, see Fox, *op. cit.*

37   Ford, M., Nothing and Not-Nothing: The Law's Ambivalent Response to Transformation and Transgression at the Beginning of Life, below at pp. 21–46.

38   See Brazier, M. (1989), The Challenge for Parliament: A Critique of the White Paper on Human Fertilisation and Embryology, in Dyson, A. and Harris, J. (eds), *Experiments on Embryos*, (Routledge and Kegan Paul), at p. 142.

be so sacrificed. Much of the debate in the passage of the Human Fertilisation and Embryology Act still focused on this same issue – the status of the embryo. It is not stem cell therapies that are problematical – to put it crudely, for opponents it is whether we can 'kill' to develop such therapies. As Song says, unease about admixed embryos was much milder among those who supported the 1990 compromise on the status of the embryo than among those who continue to regard the embryo 'as a human being possessed of dignity'.[39]

Heather Widdows[40] considers embryology and liberty in a somewhat different context. Should we limit our capacity to intervene to prescribe the form of the bodies of our children, say, to order a boy who will captain Lancashire and England cricket teams, or, to use a more realistic example, to resort to Pre-Implantation Genetic Diagnosis (PGD) to seek a child who will be deaf like her parents? The rights and wrongs of such particular choices of so-called designer babies have been much debated. But Widdows has a much more general concern to air. Will allowing such choices result in a more commodified attitude to all children? Could an unlimited capacity to tamper with the bodies of our future children alter our human love for our young? A tricky question here (reflected in many of the other papers) is the role of medical science. For all of recorded history, people have sought to influence the shape of their families and the nature of their children. Think how hard Catherine of Aragon, the first of Henry VIII's six wives, must have prayed for a healthy son. When her successor Anne Boleyn produced a daughter, I am not sure the odious Henry was any less disappointed than, in this age of the reproductive technologies, Heather Widdows's example of parents who end up with a 'dark, ugly girl'[41] after sex selection via PGD would be. Can we justify prohibiting medicine from achieving what hope and prayer fail to deliver?

The bodies of women have always been the object of social control by Church and State. At the centre of society's concern lay woman's ability to gestate. Without a woman's womb, no heir could be forthcoming. Therefore, her body must be monitored to ensure that no false heir gestated in that womb. Yet wombs were also, in a sense, a woman's greatest asset. And as society freed women from some of the social constraints of past times, so women became the gender in control of reproduction. A woman in England can choose to conceive, not to conceive, to abort, not to abort and her choice trumps any preference of male partners[42] unless she has to resort to New Reproductive Technologies (NRTs). Once the embryo

---

39   Song, *op. cit.* at p. 128.

40   Widdows, H., Persons and their Parts: New Reproductive Technologies and Risks of Commodification, below at pp. 77–87.

41   *Ibid.* at p. 80.

42   So neither as the putative father of the child or as the woman's husband can the male partner in 'natural reproduction' challenge a decision to carry out an abortion, see *Paton v BPAS* [1979] QB 276; *Paton v UK* [1980] 3 EHHR 409; *C v S* [1987] 1 All ER 1230.

is outside her body, as Sonia Harris-Short[43] shows, women may have to share power over procreation.[44] The man's reproductive liberty entitles him to say no, that embryo will not become *my* child. But she argues *Evans v UK*[45] is wrong in not allowing an exception in 'cases where the embryos genuinely represent the last chance for one of the gamete providers to have their own genetically related child'.[46]

Whether you agree with Harris-Short or not, the plight of Natallie Evans and the argument that *Evans* is wrong provides another strand to the themes of this book, the importance of physicality. The desire for a child who shares our genes, a desire that for many people (not all) is different in quality from the desire for a child to nurture, remains strong. Humans seek a connection with their young. Experiments in collective parenting on the model of the Israeli *Kibbutz* and its children's houses seem doomed to fail. Although the English are an exception with their readiness to pack children off to boarding school!

Bodies Are Us!

We cannot as yet escape our bodies, or the bodies of those we love either as lovers or parents. Practical liberty depends on the body in that dysfunction increases the likelihood of dependence. Freedom to live life within your own world view depends on the body; unwanted intrusion on the body hurts, not just the flesh, but the ability to control your own life. Thus the common law placed an apparently high premium on bodily integrity, prohibiting even the least touching.[47] How far that was for centuries mere rhetoric rather than reality must be doubted and bodily inviolability was expressly denied to married women and in practice meant little to the average subject of the Crown. In many ways until recently it was the bodies of the dead[48] and the not yet born[49] who (which) were better protected by the law. In 2009, there are those who contest value in the body at all, investing value only in persons and granting persons undiminished control over those bodies.[50] The body

---

43   Harris-Short, S., Regulating Reproduction: Frozen Embryos, Consent, Welfare and the Equality Myth, below at pp. 47–75.

44   And see Jackson, E. (2008), Degendering Reproduction, *Medical Law Review* 16, 346–368.

45   [2007] 2 FCR 5 (Grand Chamber).   -

46   Harris-Short, *op. cit.* at p. 48.

47   *Cole v Turner* [1704] 6 Mod Rep 149.

48   See Richardson, R. (2000), *Death, Dissection and the Destitute*, 2nd Edition, (The University of Chicago Press).

49   See the *magnum opus* of Dellapenna, J. (2006), *Dispelling the Myth about Abortion History*, (Carolina Academic Press). Whether or not you agree with Dellapanna's conclusions, his work shows the extent of legal engagement with the embryo and fetus across the ages.

50   See Harris, *op. cit.* at pp. 7–21.

in that context is simply an instrument, to be used, or disposed of at its owner's behest.

I would want to contest the view that only some bodies have value and argue that the human organism has itself a value from conception to decay.[51] But that does not mean that embryos are necessarily sacrosanct or that no uses may be made of the bodies of the dead or parts of the living.[52] We need to reflect on the privilege our bodies confer on us. I doubt that debate about what our bodies *are* can on its own help us address the questions raised within this collection. I wonder if we should reflect more both on what our bodies can *do* for us and for others, and the sense in which we are but tenants of this flesh. Herring and Chau[53] have argued powerfully (*inter alia*) that our bodies are 'interconnected and interdependent with the bodies of others'. Unless we are brought up by wolves and live as hermits, so are our lives. The body that I inhabit depended on my parents' genes and my mother's nourishment before and after birth. And later this body nourished another. In each day our bodies receive and do services for others even if only at the mundane level of pouring a cup of coffee. We tend our young and sick and should tend our elderly. But do we need more attention to what we owe to others, to reconsider duties to rescue absent from the common law? And if we do, must we also think about the marvels of what the physical body itself can do?

References

Arnott, R., Finger S. and Smith, C. (eds) (2003), *Trepanation: History, Discovery, Theory*, (Swets and Zeitlinger).

Brazier, M. (1989), The Challenge for Parliament: A Critique of the White Paper on Human Fertilisation and Embryology, in Dyson, A. and Harris, J. (eds), *Experiments on Embryos*, (Routledge and Kegan Paul).

Brazier, M. (2006), Do No Harm – Do Patients Have Responsibilities Too?, *Cambridge Law Journal* 65, 397.

Brazier, M. (2006), Human(s) (as) Medicine(s), in MacLean, S. (ed.), *First Do No Harm*, (Ashgate).

Brazier, M. (2008), The Age of Deference: A Historical Anomaly? in Freeman, M. (ed.), *Law and Bioethics: Current Legal Issues*, Volume II, (Oxford University Press).

Coggon, J. (2007), Varied and Principled Understandings of Autonomy in English Law: Justifiable Inconsistency or Blinkered Moralism, *Health Care Analysis* 15, 235.

---

51   See McGuinness, S. and Brazier, M. (2008), Respecting the Living Means Respecting the Dead Too, *Oxford Journal of Legal Studies* 28, 297–316.

52   See Brazier, *op. cit.*, 'Human(s) (as) Medicine(s)'.

53   Herring, J. and Chau, P.-L. (2007), My Body, Your Body, Our Bodies, *Medical Law Review* 15, 34–61.

Dellapenna, J. (2006), *Dispelling the Myth about Abortion History*, (Carolina Academic Press).

Dickenson, D. (2007), *Property in the Body: Feminist Perspectives*, (Cambridge University Press).

Dickenson, D. (1997), *Property, Women and Politics*, (Cambridge Polity Press).

Draper, H. and Sorrell, T. (2002), Patients' Responsibilities in Medical Ethics, *Bioethics* 16, 335.

Elliott, T. (2009), Body Dysmorphic Disorder: Radical Surgery and the Limits of Consent, *Medical Law Review* 17 (forthcoming).

Fletcher, R., Fox, M. and McCandless J. (2008), Legal Embodiment: Analysing the Body of Healthcare Law, *Medical Law Review* 16, 321.

Harris, J. (1985), *The Value of Life*, (Routledge and Kegan Paul).

Herring, J. and Chau, P.-L. (2007), My Body, Your Body, Our Bodies, *Medical Law Review* 15, 34.

Jackson, E. (2008), Degendering Reproduction, *Medical Law Review* 16, 346.

Kennedy, I. and Grubb, A. (2000), *Medical Law*, 3rd Edition, (Butterworths).

Latham, M. (2008), The Shape of Things to Come: Feminism, Regulation and Cosmetic Surgery, *Medical Law Review* 16, 437.

MacKenzie, R. (2008), Somatechnics of Medico-Legal Taxonomies: Elective Amputation and Transableism, *Medical Law Review* 16, 390.

McGuinness, S. and Brazier, M. (2008), Respecting the Living Means Respecting the Dead Too, *Oxford Journal of Legal Studies* 28, 297.

Priaulx, N. (2008), Rethinking Progenitive Conflict: Why Reproductive Autonomy Matters, *Medical Law Review* 16, 169.

Richardson, R. (2000), *Death, Dissection and the Destitute*, 2nd Edition, (The University of Chicago Press).

PART I
REGULATING REPRODUCTION

Chapter 1
Introduction to Part I

Helen Beebee

The chapters in this section address, in different ways, the 'transgressive' status of human embryos and foetuses. English law treats embryos and foetuses neither as persons nor as property: they lack the rights accorded to persons, but they are not mere 'commodities' that are owned by one or both of the biological parents or gamete providers or prospective social parents who have paid for surrogacy. This transgressive status raises a host of difficult moral and legal questions, which are forced into particularly sharp relief by advances in reproductive technology. Frozen embryos may lack rights, but they may nonetheless have interests: what are these interests, and how important are they when weighed against other relevant considerations? How are the interests of a frozen embryo connected with issues concerning the welfare of the person they have the potential to become? Should disputes about the use or disposal of frozen embryos engage with the interests of the embryo itself, or merely with the rights and/or interests of the gamete providers? Under what circumstances is the selection of genetic traits acceptable; and again, are the relevant concerns the interests of the embryo, the welfare of the potential person, and/or the rights and interests of the gamete providers (or those who wish to use the gametes)? Or should the wider societal implications of the commodification of children be taken into account?

Answers to these questions are difficult partly because they require a balancing act between considerations of quite different sorts: the rights, interests, and welfare of the involved parties, and also the interests of society at large. But they are also difficult because it is not always even clear what the relevant considerations are. For example, philosophically speaking, it is difficult to justify the claim that embryos have interests at all; certainly we cannot simply infer that they actually have interests merely from the fact that they will, or may, later become persons with interests. What, exactly, is the 'right' to procreative liberty (which might, for example, be thought to conflict with any restriction on the selection of genetic traits)? Do biological differences between men and women accord them different rights? Does the right to procreative liberty include all, or just some, of the right to pass on one's genes, the right to choose which of one's genes one passes on, the right to be a gestational mother, and the right to perform the social role of a parent?

The chapters in this section shed light on questions in this area, though in very different ways. Mary Ford argues that embryos and foetuses rightly belong in the postmodern category of the 'gothic self' – a category that cannot be subsumed under the category of the 'liberal self' that the law presupposes. Thus it is unsurprising that the 'special status' accorded to embryos and foetuses in English law cannot be justified from within the confines of existing legal categories. Sonia Harris-Short argues that in disputes about the disposition of frozen embryos, the interest of the female gamete provider in biological motherhood should, in some circumstances, be allowed to tip the legal balance that currently exists between the procreative rights of both gamete providers. And Heather Widdows argues that the selection of genetic traits should be limited, on the grounds that doing so would limit the commodification of children.

Ford argues that the 'special status' accorded to embryos and foetuses cannot be justified by appeal to arguments about respect for interests, relationships, dignity or potentiality. Ford argues that the problematic status of embryos and foetuses within the law stems from the liberal notion of the self with which the law operates, according to which legal subjects are free, autonomous, independent, rational and self-interested. She argues that foetuses and embryos can be subsumed under the postmodern category of the 'gothic' or 'monstrous' self – 'disordered, leaky and lacking in self-sovereignty' – and that it is the fact that the embryo/ foetus falls within this category, and not a legal argument that implicitly rejects such a category, that explains and justifies its 'special status'.

Ford's chapter raises interesting questions about what the consequences of such a reconceptualization of the unborn would be. A proposal endorsed by Ford is to strive to resist the language of what Julia Kristeva calls 'abjection', 'a kind of casting-out', as Ford puts it, 'characterised by the ambivalence that results from existing between categories'. Ford notes in particular the judgement in the case of *Re A*, involving the proposed separation of conjoined twins. (Both twins would die if left in their conjoined state; one, 'Mary', would inevitably die on the operating table if the operation were to proceed.) In considering the advantages the operation would hold for Mary, the judgement cited the 'bodily integrity which is the natural order for all of us', and one judge said that 'the proposed operation would give these children's bodies the integrity which nature denied them'. Thus the operation would be beneficial to Mary – despite the fact that it would kill her – because it would allow her to achieve the 'natural' physical state of the liberal self, as opposed to consigning her to a (short, but nonetheless longer) life in an abject state. The proposal would thus be to be wary of such arguments, given their presuppositions about the intrinsic desirability of features of the liberal self (in this case the physical separateness of the body).

This proposal raises a question, however. As Ford notes, a central feature of the gothic self or body is the ambivalence that it engenders in our responses to it: the gothic self is a self we regard both as deserving – we feel an affinity with the gothic 'Other', because they are nearly, but not quite, one of us – and threatening, 'thus inviting us to repel it'. Indeed, Ford says, '[i]t would be strange if the embryo/ foetus were able to avoid [responses of abjection], given how readily it maps onto the concepts of the monstrous and the abhuman.' This suggests that abjection is in fact an appropriate response to the foetus/embryo: not a response we should try to avoid (as suggested by the proposal described above), but a response that is in fact entirely appropriate to its object. After all, if the category of the gothic is a *bona fide* category, into which the embryo/foetus genuinely falls, and it is constitutive of something's being a member of that category that it invites responses of abjection, then it seems that to counsel against such responses is tantamount to claiming that the embryo/foetus does not really belong in that category at all. Thus, while accepting the gothic character of the embryo/foetus may provide us with a better understanding of our responses to it, and a better explanation for its 'special status', it would not deliver any positive proposal as to how, morally or legally, it ought to be treated.

On the other hand, the benefits of simply better understanding our responses should not be underestimated. As Widdows notes in her chapter, the 'yuk factor' – whereby a medical procedure is rejected as 'repugnant', 'repulsive' or 'grotesque' without appeal to further argument – has played a major role in bioethical debates, for example in the debate about cloning. Insofar as such a response plays a similar role in debates about the embryo/foetus, conceiving it as a case of abjection might help to shed light on the role the 'yuk factor' ought to play in bioethical disputes. One might argue on this basis, for example, that while the response itself is a legitimate response to the 'abhuman' (so that the force of the 'yuk factor' is not simply ignored or rejected as inappropriate), the rejection of the procedure is not morally justified purely on the basis of the response, since this would be to assume that the abhuman, or the gothic self/body, does not have a legitimate place in nature.

The problematic status of embryos as neither persons nor property is raised in Sonia Harris-Short's chapter through the consideration of the case of *Evans v Amicus Healthcare and Others*. Natallie Evans required urgent medical treatment involving the removal of her ovaries and fallopian tubes, and she and her partner therefore embarked upon IVF treatment. However, after she had undergone the medical treatment, Evans and her partner separated, and her ex-partner (Johnson) withdrew his consent (as he was legally entitled to do) to Evans' use of the embryos, thus removing any possibility of her becoming a genetic mother. The initial legal judgement, subsequently confirmed by the Court of Appeal and the European Court of Human Rights, was that the rights to procreative liberty balanced, in that while Article 8 of the European Convention protected Evans' right to decide to become a genetic parent, it equally protected Johnson's right not to become a genetic parent. Hence there were no grounds for revoking Johnson's withdrawal of consent.

Harris-Short regards the outcome of the case as unjust on broadly feminist grounds: given that in fact many women 'still invest a great deal more in reproduction and parenting than men', the principle of gender equality underpinning the legal framework should not be held to be sacrosanct, since this ignores the special interest that some women have in biological motherhood. Harris-Short argues that two amendments to the Human Fertilisation and Embryology Act 1990 (HFE Act 1990) would solve the problem: first, the parties should be allowed to reach their own agreement at the outset concerning the fate of frozen embryos; for example, they should be allowed to give irrevocable consent to future use of the embryos. Second, in those rare cases of dispute where some unexpected supervening event undermines the assumptions on the basis of which the original agreement was made (for example one gamete provider unexpectedly becoming infertile), referral to the courts should be permitted so that the (new) interests of the involved parties can be reconsidered.

Harris-Short's response to the *Evans* case raises interesting questions about the status of embryos. She notes that, while the statutory regime enshrined in the HFE Act 1990 is founded on the 'twin pillars' of welfare and consent, 'in the context of disputes over frozen embryos it is however the single pillar of consent which dominates'. She notes that the second proposed amendment would allow for the interests of the embryo to play a role; for example, the interest of the embryo in being born, while it perhaps should not be given much weight, might be enough to tip the balance in favour of the woman in a case like *Evans*. Questions about what interests (if any) embryos have, what those interests are, and how much weight should be accorded to them would need to be seriously considered here, given the status of embryos as non-persons – as would questions concerning the connection between the intrinsic interests of the embryo and the future welfare of the embryo *qua* potential person.

Harris-Short's chapter also raises questions about a fundamental disagreement amongst feminist writers concerning the legitimacy of the politics of difference: is it legitimate, or desirable, for the law to be sensitive to contingent cultural differences between men and women concerning their desire for, or the extent to which their self-conceptions are tied to, parenthood? And again, advances in reproductive technology force new questions upon us. Even if we accept the legitimacy of enshrining such differences in law, is the relevant desire or interest one that attaches, in the case of the woman, to genetic parenthood, or to pregnancy and giving birth, or merely to raising a child from birth or near-birth? For example, in the *Evans* case, Evans in principle was still able to achieve parenthood in the latter two senses (she could, for example, undergo IVF with an embryo that came from different gamete-providers).

Heather Widdows' chapter argues that new reproductive technologies may result in a more commodified conception of children. Widdows argues that there is an analogy between the commodification of persons that – she argues – results from the trading of transplant organs and the commodification of children that results from the selection of characteristics, such as intelligence and attractiveness (for example by choosing egg or sperm donors with these characteristics). Widdows notes that, in the context of a loving family raising the child with the chosen traits, the risk of commodification might be seen as a relatively minor ethical concern. However, she stresses that the issue is broader than simply the attitudes and relationships of the particular people concerned in any given case: 'at a societal level we should resist the gradual normalising of practices which make commodification more likely', since 'encouraging commodificatory attitudes may ultimately result in a collectively more commodified attitude not only to particular children but to all children'. Hence potentially commodifying practices – in the selection of traits no less than in organ transplantation – should be resisted unless there are ethically pressing reasons not to.

Widdows' chapter raises difficult philosophical and moral questions about the connection between the selection of traits and commodification. For example, supposing that Widdows is right that the relatively unconstrained selection of traits would have a negative effect on our collective attitude towards children in general, how crucial is it to this negative effect that the selection of those traits is paid for? One can imagine people donating their eggs or sperm in an act of charity – to help to increase the number of beautiful or intelligent people, say. This would render the selection of traits more akin to organ donation than to organ-selling, the former clearly being less commodificatory than the latter. Should such a state of affairs be regarded as better than one in which the selection of traits is paid for? If not, then it would appear that our ethical worries are not, at bottom, worries about commodification per se.

Also, Widdows' claim that there is a connection between the selection of traits of particular (potential) children and the commodification of children in general is one that deserves exploring in depth. At first sight, this is a point at which the analogy with organ sale breaks down since it is unclear that organ-trading amongst a relatively small number of people results in a more commodificatory attitude, within society at large, towards persons in general (as opposed to such an attitude merely amongst those who are involved in organ-trading, say). On the other hand, a commodificatory attitude towards children in general is surely easier to imagine than such an attitude towards persons in general, since some mainstream parental behaviour arguably tends towards the commodificatory in any case. Consider, for example, the amount of money some parents are prepared to spend on designer clothes for babies. One might worry that a baby togged out in the latest designer gear plays a similar role, in some contexts at least, as an expensive designer handbag or the latest mobile phone.

The chapters in this section raise as many questions as they answer, as is usual with texts that touch on philosophical issues. But each chapter advances the debate in interesting and important ways, and contains arguments that will repay close scrutiny and further discussion.

Chapter 2

Nothing and Not-Nothing: Law's Ambivalent Response to Transformation and Transgression at the Beginning of Life

Mary Ford[1]

Introduction: The Embryo and Foetus as Sites of Transformation/ Transgression

If we take 'transformation' straightforwardly to mean a process of changing, or becoming, and 'transgression' to mean a state of non-compliance with familiar or existing norms and categories, we can see immediately how these apply to human embryos and foetuses. Taking transformation first, then admittedly, *frozen* embryos are not 'transforming' for as long as they remain frozen. The transformative process is interrupted or suspended – perhaps never to be resumed. Nevertheless, they are entities whose destiny – if they have one at all – is further transformation. Any future existence will consist, primarily, of a process of transforming. The theme of transformation applies even more straightforwardly to embryos and foetuses *in vivo*. From the moment of fertilization onwards, the entity moves through a rapid succession of stages in which cells divide, implantation occurs and physiological changes take place so that the appearance and complexity of the entity alters at a rate which is perhaps unequalled at any time throughout its development after birth. The moment of birth is the occasion for another incredibly important transformation – and although this particular transformation involves no *intrinsic* changes to the entity itself, it is at this point that the entity undergoes a *legal* transformation, and acquires the status of 'legal person'.

As far as transgression is concerned, embryos and foetuses are paradigms of non-compliance. They exist as liminal entities, at the boundaries of categories, and as interstitial entities – across and between categories. Those that are located inside the body are alive, but they lack independent life. They are human, but not part of the 'human community'. From a certain point onward, they look human,

1 Lecturer in Law, University of Strathclyde. The author wishes to thank Stephen W. Smith and Jamie Lee for reading and commenting on a draft version of this chapter, and the participants at the Symposium for discussion of the issues.

but not yet human enough. As Marie Fox has commented, frozen embryos also transgress other boundaries: they are organic entities with the potential for life, yet are created and stored in a laboratory and are, until the point of implantation, utterly dependent on technology.[2] Perhaps the ultimate transgression is that, as we shall see, embryos and foetuses are neither legal entities nor absolute legal nonentities – neither fully legally-present nor fully legally-absent.

The Law's Response

The law's response to the embryo/foetus seems paradoxical. Quite apart from the ambivalent statements in the case law (discussed below), each of the two relevant *statutory* frameworks regulating treatment of embryos and foetuses in the UK also seems to embody contradictions. As Sonia Harris-Short observes elsewhere in this volume, 'both the HFE Act 1990 and the Abortion Act 1967 are premised on the principle that the embryo/foetus, as a potential person, has a special status under English law worthy of protection'.[3] Yet these statutes also operate to allow the destruction of embryos and foetuses by permitting, respectively, embryo experimentation and abortion.

The Report of the Warnock Committee on Human Fertilisation and Embryology, which established the ethical framework for the 1990 Act, contains one of the most arresting examples of an ambivalent response to the embryo/foetus.[4] The Committee notes that 'the human embryo ... is not, under the present law of the UK accorded the same status as a living child or an adult', and adds that 'nor do we necessarily wish it to be accorded that same status'. However, the Committee is 'agreed that the embryo of the human species ought to have a special status'.

The Committee declines to specify what this 'special status' is, or how it is to be justified. The brief consideration, a few paragraphs earlier, of some of the 'moral principles' which lead some people to oppose embryo research mentions two objections, based respectively on the embryo's 'potential for human life' (discussed later) and on fears about eugenics and 'tampering with the creation of human life' (the familiar concerns about 'playing God'). Whether these considerations form any part of the justification for the 'special status' recommended by the Committee, however, is unclear. Nevertheless, having recommended 'special status' for the human embryo without explaining *either* what form it is to take *or* how it is to be

---

   2   Fox, M. (2000), Pre-Persons, Commodities or Cyborgs: the Legal Construction and Representation of the Embryo, *Health Care Analysis* 8, 171.

   3   Harris-Short, S. (2009), Regulating Reproduction – Frozen Embryos, Consent, Welfare and the Equality Myth, pp. 47–75.

   4   Warnock, M. (1985), *A Question of Life: The Warnock Report on Human Fertilisation and Embryology*, (Basil Blackwell).

justified, the Committee proceeds to claim that such status is in fact 'a matter of fundamental principle which should be enshrined in law'.[5]

In the next paragraph the equivocation continues, as the Committee advises that its previous acknowledgment that the embryo's special status is 'a matter of fundamental principle' 'does not entail that this protection may not be waived in certain specific circumstances'.[6] The Warnock Committee's response to the embryo represents, in a sense, a microcosm of wider cultural uncertainty and ambivalence about how such entities ought to be regarded.

John Seymour has described how the law tries to respond to the foetus 'in a way that recognizes its distinctiveness and intrinsic value'.[7] He writes:

> When asking how the law views the fetus, the courts' starting-point has frequently been to determine whether the fetus is a "person". The most widely accepted view is that it is not. This conclusion, however, is unhelpful. While the law is adept at indicating what the fetus is *not*, it throws little light on what the fetus *is*. It is clear that it is not a non-entity. Whatever it is, in the words of the English Court of Appeal, it is "not nothing".[8]

This refers to the judgement of the Court of Appeal in the famous case of *St George's Healthcare NHS Trust v S*: 'whatever else it may be a 36-week foetus is not nothing: if viable it is not lifeless and it is certainly human'.[9]

Neither, in the eyes of the law, is an embryo or foetus a 'mere thing'. In the limited litigation over frozen embryos in the UK, the courts here have made clear that they will not entertain the idea that frozen embryos might be property: in Wall J's judgement in the High Court in the *Evans* case,[10] anti-property rhetoric abounds, and was not contradicted on appeal by the higher courts. For example, the judgement declares that: 'there is no property in an embryo, but in contrast to a foetus, both gamete donors have an interest in, and rights over, the embryos they have created';[11] that 'of course, there was no "property" in the embryos created';[12] and that '[embryos] are different from mere property'.[13]

In a landmark United States case involving the disposal of frozen embryos – *Davis v Davis*[14] – the Tennessee Supreme Court decided that frozen embryos

---

5   *Ibid.*, at para. 11.17.

6   *Ibid.*, at para. 11.18.

7   Seymour, J. (2000), *Childbirth and the Law*, (Oxford University Press), at p. 184.

8   *Ibid.*, at p. 183.

9   [1998] 3 WLR 936, at 952.

10   *Evans v Amicus Healthcare Ltd and Others, Hadley v Midland Fertility Services Ltd and Others* [2003] EWHC 2161 (Fam).

11   *Ibid.*, at para. 178.

12   *Ibid.*, at para. 280.

13   *Ibid.*, at para. 219.

14   842 S.W.2d 588 Tenn., 1992.

'occupy an interim category [between personhood and property] that entitles them to special respect because of their potential for human life'.[15] If a frozen embryo, which is in a suspended, technically lifeless state ought to be regarded as having some kind of 'special status', does this not imply an even *stronger* status for the embryo or foetus *in vivo*, engaged in a transformative process and moving inexorably toward birth and so towards membership of the human community.

'Special Status': A Meaningless Notion?

So embryos and foetuses have variously been described as 'not nothing', as deserving of 'special status' or as possessing 'distinctiveness and intrinsic value'. But statements of this kind raise questions. First, what could be the *source* of any 'special status' the embryo/foetus might possess? Another question arises when we try to imagine what the 'special status' of the embryo or foetus, or a recognition of its 'distinctiveness and intrinsic value', might mean in practice. How, practically speaking, does one 'value' a foetus?

In addressing these problems, I will briefly examine what seem to me to be the possible sources of any duty to ascribe 'special status' to the embryo/foetus – the notions that status arises from potentiality, from interests, from relationships, and finally, from notions of human dignity.[16] I will argue that each of these possibilities is too problematic as a basis for according special status, and that in any case, even if we were able to justify the notion of special status in the abstract, it seems meaningless in practice.

Special Status based on Potentiality

To argue that respect or status ought to be assigned on the basis of potentiality is to make the claim that an entity should be accorded a degree of value on the basis that it has the potential to become something else, *if certain conditions are fulfilled*. With regard to the embryo/foetus, this type of argument generally involves the claim that it is morally significant that the embryo or foetus has the potential, if certain conditions prevail, to become a being with full moral status (expressed variously as 'human person' or 'human being').

In the beginning-of-life context, one of the first obstacles encountered by arguments from potentiality is the twofold problem that (i) not *all* embryos/foetuses have the potential to become beings with full moral status; and (ii) not *only* embryos and foetuses have such potential. Some embryos and foetuses lack the potential to develop into born human beings with full moral status because

---

15   *Ibid.*, at 597.

16   Human dignity and potentiality for personhood were explicitly cited by the Grand Chamber of the European Court of Human Rights in *Vo v France* [2004] 2 FCR 577 at paragraph 84 as possible justifications for extending protections to the embryo/foetus.

they are affected by abnormalities so severe that they will not survive to be born. Very early embryos also have the potential to divide and thus develop into more than one human being. Conversely, it could be said that sperm and ova, as well as embryos and foetuses, have the potential to become beings with full moral status, such that we ought also to treat *these* as having a degree of 'special status' on the basis of their potentiality. Against this, Rosalind Hursthouse has appealed to the notion of 'natural development' to argue that, while a fertilized ovum, embryo or foetus will *naturally develop* into a fully developed being, the human sperm or ovum will not, unless another event intervenes (fertilization).[17] This appeal to 'natural development' is unconvincing, however. Hursthouse herself acknowledges that the 'natural development' argument must contend with a 'general scepticism about relying on any sense of "nature" or "natural"'; for some, Hursthouse admits, notions such as 'natural development' are inherently 'dubious'.[18]

Another problem for 'natural development' arguments is that it is not only fertilization, but also implantation and successful gestation that must intervene to take the sperm or ovum to birth and full legal status; two of these must also intervene in the case of the fertilized ovum, and one in the case of the embryo/ foetus. This is close to a point made by John Harris in responding to claims that sperm and ova can be excluded from potentiality arguments:

> It is sometimes objected that it is only the fertilised egg that has all the necessary potential present in one place, so to speak, and it is this that is crucial. It is only when the egg has been fertilised, so the argument goes, that a new unique entity exists that itself has all the potential necessary to become a new human being. This seems plausible enough until we remember that something had the potential to become that fertilised egg; and whatever had that potential, had also the potential to become whatever it is that the fertilised egg has the potential to become![19]

This notwithstanding, the law *does* differentiate between the status of the embryo/foetus and that of gametes. As noted above, the judgement in *Evans* makes clear that frozen embryos (and thus presumably embryos and foetuses *in utero*) are not 'mere things';[20] by contrast, the Court of Appeal held, in the recent case of *Yearworth & Ors v North Bristol NHS Trust*,[21] that stored sperm samples *were* the property of the men who had produced them. Although it is often assumed that potentiality is the reason for recognizing 'special status' in the case of the embryo/foetus,[22] and so for making this kind of differentiation between embryos

---

17 Hursthouse, R. (1987), *Beginning Lives*, (Basil Blackwell), at pp. 81–82.
18 *Ibid.*, at p. 82.
19 Harris, J. (1985), *The Value of Life* (Routledge), at p. 12.
20 See *Evans v Amicus Healthcare Ltd and Others*, *op. cit.* n. 10.
21 [2009] EWCA Civ 37.
22 See, for example, Harris-Short, *op. cit.* n. 3.

and gametes, considerations like those discussed by Harris give us cause to doubt whether this is indeed a sound basis on which to make such a distinction.

One of the most compelling problems with arguments from potentiality is the difficulty of establishing why potentiality should be regarded as morally significant at all. In our dealings with entities in the here-and-now, it could be argued, we should accord them the status appropriate to what they currently *are*, rather than to what they may one day be. We should focus, for example, on the appropriate way to value the embryo/foetus as an *actual embryo/foetus*, rather than a potential something-else. If we hold human personhood or membership of the human moral community in high regard, the appropriate way to respond to this is simply to ascribe high levels of moral value to these attributes when we encounter them. Indeed, it could even be claimed that to ascribe value to beings on the explicit basis that we value certain properties *which they do not possess* is incoherent.

Relatedly, such arguments encounter the difficulty that it is usually impossible confidently to assess the potential that a particular entity has. Beings may have the potential for a variety of different futures, and some of those futures, if actualized, would affect the way we treat the being in question, or the status we accord it. For example, an embryo/foetus might have the potential to become a violent criminal, a mother, or an adult with incapacity. But we do not take any of this into account when deciding how we ought to treat it. As John Harris has memorably observed, we are all potential corpses: 'We will all inevitably die, but that is, I suppose, an inadequate reason for treating us now as if we were dead'.[23] This notwithstanding that death is inevitable; birth, for the embryo/foetus, is not.

To Harris's point, it might be responded that those who argue for special respect for the embryo/foetus on the basis of its potentiality are not necessarily arguing that we should, to paraphrase Harris, treat the embryo/foetus *now* as if it were a person. Rather, they may be arguing for some lesser acknowledgement which is cognizant of the absence of the 'ultimate' rank of personhood itself (or some variation thereof), but which honours the future possibility of it. But this serves only to highlight another problem with arguments from potentiality; namely, that they are normatively contentless. As Rosalind Hursthouse has pointed out, arguments from potentiality can lead us either to conservative *or* to liberal conclusions:

> There are hardly any consequences concerning the rights and wrongs of abortion, foetal research, *in vitro* fertilization, etc., which follow *directly* from taking [the] view of the foetus [as potential human being or person] … someone who holds this view can, quite consistently, rank any potential human being over any animal and very close to an actual human being; hence moving very close to the conservative position. Or they can, quite consistently, rank any potential human being very low, below many if not all animals and quite close to a bit of human

---

23   Harris, *op. cit.* n. 19, at p. 11.

tissue; hence moving close to an extreme liberal position. Or they can take up a variety of positions in between.[24]

Of course, as Hursthouse acknowledges, the point of making an argument from potentiality is usually to emphasize the *humanness* of the embryo/foetus rather than to make the more negative point that the entity has *nothing but* potential. Nevertheless, the point is well made that arguments from potentiality fail to provide any practical guidance, and can be vehicles for whatever normative content the holder's pre-existing ethical dispositions incline her to.

So even if we can say, with confidence, that 'X is a potential Y', this in itself means little, ethically-speaking. If we wish to make the argument that morally relevant qualities like personhood exist in degrees, and that it is appropriate to ascribe varying degrees of status/respect to entities on the basis that these beings possess (for example) personhood to a greater or lesser extent, then we are free to attempt an argument along those lines; however, this is a different kind of argument from arguments based on potentiality. A 'degrees of personhood' argument is an argument for valuing the *actual* possession of an attribute (albeit only a degree of it) unlike a potentiality argument, which argues that status ought to be ascribed although it acknowledges that the attribute in question may not be present to *any* degree (and indeed may never materialize).

Given the range of problems with arguments from potentiality (of which I have provided only a sample here), such arguments cannot be regarded as providing a persuasive justification for according the embryo/foetus 'special status' in law.

Special Status as 'Respect for Interests'

Another possibility is that 'special status' could be accorded on the basis that the embryo/foetus has *interests* of some sort which ought to be respected. An immediate problem with this is that it would be difficult to establish that embryos or foetuses have interests at all. Scientists disagree about the gestational age at which foetuses become sentient, i.e. capable of experiencing pleasure or pain. There is a range of views, ranging from those who believe that sentience may be present in the first trimester,[25] to those who doubt that foetuses are sentient at all during pregnancy,[26] but the majority view appears to be that sentience emerges late in the third trimester, on the basis that no sentience is possible without a cortical structure in place, and that that is only in place sometime between 30 and 35 weeks'

---

24 Hursthouse, *op. cit.* n. 17, at p. 73.

25 An example of such an approach is contained in a 1996 report by the United Kingdom Parliament's All Party Pro-Life Group, entitled Foetal Sentience and published in the *Catholic Medical Quarterly* XLVII, no. 2 November 1996, 6.

26 See, for example, the view expressed in Derbyshire, S. (1999), Locating the Beginnings of Pain, *Bioethics* 13:1, 1.

gestation.[27] So unless and until a foetus is sentient, it might be argued, it can have no interests which could be respected. If this is accepted, then on the majority view of foetal sentience (the third trimester view), respect for foetal interests doesn't even become a possibility until extremely late in pregnancy and it is difficult to think of any practical way in which we could 'respect' any interests it has.

A possible exception is that if the foetus were either demonstrated, or assumed, to be sentient at any point during gestation, we could respect foetuses of that gestational age and older by refraining from causing them unnecessary pain. This would mean using anaesthesia during foetal surgery procedures and during any procedure to terminate pregnancy.

Now a response to all this might be to say that 'having interests' need not necessarily depend upon sentience at all. A being may not be able to feel pleasure or suffer pain, but it may, nevertheless, still be possible to harm or benefit that being. In other words, *having* interests does not necessarily depend upon consciously *experiencing* those interests. If that is accepted, then there is less of a problem with the idea that embryos and foetuses could have the kinds of interests that might be deserving of respect. But what kinds of interests might these be? It is difficult to imagine any such interests as being particularly sophisticated. It is difficult, in fact, to imagine embryos/foetuses having any interests at all beyond a basic interest in not being harmed or destroyed. Note that here, we are proceeding on the assumption that interests can exist in the absence of any conscious awareness of harm or benefit. But even if we are prepared to concede this for argument's sake, it is difficult to get further than an unconscious interest in not being harmed or destroyed – and within the framework of the current law, such interests cannot be 'respected', since they are often simply outweighed by the interests of legal persons.

Another possibility is that the special status of the embryo/foetus might be founded *not* in the need to respect the interests of the individual entity itself, but in the wider interest society has in preserving the 'dignity' of human life generally. This will be discussed separately, below.

Special Status Based on Relationships

Another way of trying to figure out the conundrum of the supposed 'special status' of the embryo/foetus might be to dig beneath the 'rights and interests' rhetoric which so often appears on the surface of debates about pregnancy, and to look instead at the underlying relationships involved. Some feminist writers and others have argued that, instead of taking notice only when we see a formal 'right' or 'interest' appear on the landscape, we ought to be looking at the whole landscape

27   See, for example, Burgess, J.A. and Tawia, S.A. (1996), When Did You First Begin To Feel It? – Locating the Beginnings of Human Consciousness, *Bioethics* 10:1, 1.

of relationships within which rights and interests occur.[28] On such a view, any understanding of the 'special status' of an entity would have to take in the whole context of the relationships involving that entity; it cannot be simply a matter of noting that 'entity X has crossed threshold Y' and so acquires a particular status as a result of possessing (enough of) a certain attribute.

Could this 'whole relationship' approach help us understand the need to respect and value the embryo or foetus? Unfortunately, not very much. Obviously, embryos –whether frozen or otherwise – and foetuses do not 'have' relationships in any sort of active way. There are relationships *in respect* of them; in other words, they may be objects of the relationships between others. As entities which do not form one side of any relationship, they are, at best, the passive recipients of the ethical behaviour of others – perhaps even 'moral patients', if we assume that they can be harmed. But the existence of relationships is taken to be important for moral status because it is claimed to be morally significant that we, as humans, enter into emotional and caring bonds with one another, which can take a variety of complex and subtle forms and variations. To the extent that the embryo/foetus cannot (yet) do this, it is difficult to see how it could be entitled to any special respect on the basis of relationships.

Special Status Based on Dignity

The concept of 'human dignity', the criticisms of it, and the possible defences to these criticisms, cannot be explored in any detail here. I will focus on just one of the reasons why an approach which accords special status to the embryo/foetus on the basis of its inherent 'dignity' may be problematic. The idea that membership of the human species is in itself enough to deserve respect has been criticized for being 'speciesist', that is, for assuming that being human is something special, without justifying what exactly is special about it. To justify the idea that simply being human gives us any special status, we would have to show that there was something morally relevant that all humans have in common, and that *only* humans have in common, apart from the biological fact of our being human individuals. In fact, no one has yet been able to come up with any property other than humanity itself which is shared by all humans and only humans, let alone a property that justifies privileging humans above other species, without resorting to faith-based claims about souls, and the like.[29]

---

28 Writers who have asserted the ethical priority of relationships and 'caring' over rights and 'justice' include Noddings, N. (2003), *Caring: A Feminine Approach to Ethics and Moral Education*, 2nd Edition, (University of California Press); Held, V. (2006), *The Ethics of Care: Personal, Political, and Global*, (Oxford University Press); and Slote, M. (2007), *The Ethics of Care and Empathy*, (Routledge).

29 A classic discussion of speciesism is that in Singer, P. (1993), *Practical Ethics*, 2nd Edition, (Cambridge University Press), Chapter 3, 'Equality for Animals', at pp. 55–82. For

Yet we may doubt that 'speciesism' need necessarily be regarded as problematic. The protections of international human rights law and European human rights law are confined to members of the human species, after all, and at a theoretical level it can be argued that there is nothing inherently wrong with showing greater concern for our own species than for others. As noted already, some commentators have argued that ethical principles should not be too abstract. Rather, in adopting ethical positions, we should take into account the reality of the relationships and caring bonds that exist between fellow humans, and acknowledge that we owe a richer ethical duty to one another than we do to members of others species. Noddings, for example, while acknowledging that humans have certain limited ethical obligations toward animals, does not regard these obligations as being coextensive with the obligations human beings have toward one another.[30]

There *is* a problem with this, however, in that it raises the uncomfortable issue of whether, if I can justify preferring my own species, I can also justify preferring my own race. What about someone from my own town? While it may be possible to justify 'local preferences' at a species level, on the basis that there are distinctively 'human' relationships, and also at the *very* local level of our own families – because of the particularly strong relationships involved at that level – this leaves open the more troublesome question of what happens in between. If it is morally permissible for me to prefer my own species to other animals, and to prefer my own family to other humans, what makes it impermissible for me to give a job to a white woman instead of a Chinese woman, or to treat a colleague from Glasgow preferentially to one from Edinburgh? Obviously, there are laws against the most extreme examples of such behaviours, but what makes them immoral? Whenever we begin to thaw towards speciesism, we need to take care that we are not undermining the standards that prevent intra-species discrimination as well. To summarize this first problem: the 'human relationship' argument certainly provides a reason to prefer humans, but I would argue that we should be careful only to adopt standards that provide reasons to prefer them all *equally*.

So I think there are grounds for resisting the idea that we owe the embryo/ foetus special respect on the basis of notions of 'human dignity'. But even if we could avoid the problem mentioned above (for example, if we were members of a religious faith that provided us with a basis for accepting that humans shared a special status and shared it equally (so that there was no danger of racism)), we would still run into the familiar problem of what 'special status' might mean in practice. It is difficult to think of anything practical that we can actually *do* to respect or value the embryo/foetus.

---

a brief overview of the argument from speciesism, see Warren, M.A. (1997), *Moral Status: Obligations to Persons and Other Living Things*, (Clarendon Press), at pp. 67–68.

30 Noddings, *op. cit.* n. 28, at pp. 155–157.

Indeed, it is difficult, if not impossible, to imagine valuing it at all, except by avoiding harming or destroying it.[31] Assuming that those who make statements about the 'special status' of the embryo/foetus do not mean to make termination of pregnancy illegal, to restrict access to it or to reverse the series of decisions which puts beyond doubt the equal rights of pregnant women to refuse medical treatment,[32] then once again the rhetoric of 'special respect' seems meaningless, in practical terms. Unless a particular embryo or foetus 'benefits', indirectly, from the statutory restrictions on embryo experimentation or termination of pregnancy built into the 1990 and 1967 Acts, it can be destroyed: there is no middle position. Some academic commentators have suggested that even if the embryo/foetus were to be accorded the status of 'person', this would not automatically preclude the taking of any action which causes its death.[33] This view is given succour by the decision of the Grand Chamber of the ECHR in *Vo v France*[34] that even if a foetus falls within the scope of the 'right to life' in Article 2, in the case of the foetus the right would be 'implicitly limited by the mother's rights and interests';[35] in other words, even an ascription of personhood to the embryo/foetus would not necessarily entail any greater degree of legal protection than that already afforded under the present laws of the United Kingdom.

A Clash of Selves

The Liberal Self of Law

In the liberal, humanist philosophy of the Enlightenment, a view of the self emerges (sometimes called the 'liberal humanist subject', or the 'modern bourgeois subject')[36] which emphasizes human capacities for autonomy and rationality, and understands the self as free, independent and self-interested.[37] This self is

---

31 An argument might be made along the lines that the law has attempted to 'show respect' to foetuses, for example, by prosecuting the 'foetus earrings' case (*R v Gibson* [1991] 1 All ER 439); however the offence prosecuted in this case was the common law offence of 'outraging public decency', so that it was the feelings of the public, rather than the inherent dignity of the foetus, which the law was supposedly intervening to protect.

32 See *St George's Healthcare NHS Trust v S, op. cit.* n. 9); and *Re MB (Adult: Medical Treatment)* [1997] 2 FLR 426.

33 See, for example, Thomson, J. (1971), A Defence of Abortion, *Philosophy and Public Affairs* 1:1, 47–66; and McDonough, E. (1996), *Breaking the Abortion Deadlock: From Choice to Consent*, (Oxford University Press).

34 [2004] 2 FCR 577.

35 *Ibid.*, at para. 80.

36 Hurley, K. (1996), *The Gothic Body: Sexuality, Materialism and Degeneration at the Fin de Siècle*, (Cambridge University Press), at p. 8.

37 The view of the self as a 'rational, autonomous agent' is central to Kantian ethics; as such it is prominent in Kantian-influenced theories such as the liberal political theory

an autonomous individual with the potential for full self-knowledge. Critical theorists have observed that the law defines and approaches its subjects in a way that presupposes the liberal, modernist model of selfhood.[38] 'Legal liberalism', according to the claims of critics, focuses on the subject's capacities for rationality, autonomy and self-sovereignty, and privileges discourses which revolve around liberal values such as rights, justice and legitimacy.

On this view, law's understanding of the self is characterized by abstract individualism. The subject is conceived as an 'individual' in the sense of being independent and free to act, but not as a *distinct* individual, since little heed is paid to individual differences in terms of abilities, needs, interests and circumstances. This is, perhaps, understandable, given mainstream liberalism's broad favouring of a neutral role for law and state, and its broad acceptance of the notion that law should confine itself to the role of keeping order, and should leave individuals as free as possible to pursue the values and projects of their own choosing with minimal interference.

It is possible to justify this claim that the self of law is identifiably liberal by pointing to some of the key features or functions of law. In the context of the criminal law, for example, courts confront questions such as 'where are the limits of individual responsibility?'[39] A major task of law, according to one leading commentator on 'the gothic' in literature, is to 'isolate the individual as a legal entity and thus begin questions about blame, guilt and innocence'.[40] Furthermore,

---

of Rawls, J. (1971), *A Theory of Justice* (Clarendon Press); but other strains of liberalism – contractarianism and ultilitarianism – can also be argued to conceptualize the subject as individualistic, self-interested and/or rational (for example, contractarianism seems to depend on the notion of the self as 'bargainer', and utilitarianism, although oft-criticized for paying insufficient attention to the self as individual, seems nevertheless to encourage an atomistic view of selfhood, ignoring the plethora of complex interconnections between my happiness and yours. The 'harm principle' in particular appears to presuppose a view of the subject as rational, self-determining and 'private'. The 'preference utilitarianism' of Peter Singer goes further and explicitly values 'personhood' – a status which depends upon the possession of sufficient degrees of rationality and self-consciousness – above all other forms of existence.

38   For an early (Marxist) example of such critique, see Pashukanis, E. (1978), *Law and Marxism: A General Theory*, Einhorn, B. (trans.), Arthur, C. (ed.) (Ink Links). Writing in 1924, Pashukanis identified the legal subject as an aritificial, impersonal construction, detached from what we might call the 'natural' subject. He wrote that legal subjecthood 'is definitively separated from the living concrete personality, ceasing to be a function of its effective conscious will and becoming a purely social function. The capacity to act is itself abstracted from the capacity to possess rights' (at p. 115). As a Marxist, Pashukanis traced this construction of subjecthood, ultimately, to capitalist modes of production (see Letwin, S. (2005), *On the History of the Idea of Law*, (Cambridge University Press), at p. 231).

39   Punter, D. (1998), *Gothic Pathologies: The Text, The Body and The Law*, (Macmillan), at p. 15.

40   *Ibid.*, at p. 16.

constructs like the 'reasonable man test', 'reasonable doubt' and 'reasonable belief' seem to point to a liberal model of selfhood wherein individual behaviour is measured against objective standards of rationality.

Consider, too, the requirement of non-discrimination: the need, in law, to 'treat like cases alike' and unalike cases differently. This obviously requires clear categories and boundaries – or at the very least, it requires that we be able to make things (scenarios, selves, and actions) fit, to a greater or lesser extent, into recognized and pre-existing categories in order that the law knows what to do with them.

Another feature of law that supports the claim that the self of law is liberal is the centrality of rights. The whole notion of rights – and of legal status more generally – presupposes: (i) that individuals are capable of choosing, and are entitled to have their choices respected; and (ii) the view of the self as self-contained and capable of excluding others. Many (if not all) areas of law are concerned with enabling the individual to achieve self-containment and exclusivity by policing the boundaries of the self and the body. Some obvious examples are to be found in the law of tort (particularly in the area of trespass to the person), the criminal law (particularly with regard to crimes such as battery and rape), and medical law (wherein the principle of patient autonomy is paramount). Patient autonomy provides the basis for wide-ranging rights to consent to or refuse medical treatment (Lord Donaldson famously stated in *Re T* that competent patients have the right to refuse treatment for rational, irrational or unknown reasons or for no reason at all[41]), and regularly trumps other foundational principles of bioethics, such as beneficence.

Autonomy has even been regarded (by Lord Hoffman in the landmark *Bland*[42] judgement) as capable of trumping so supposedly fundamental a principle as the sanctity of life.[43] Again, this analysis presupposes the ideal of the bounded, individuated subject. Finally, and crucially, the law presumes that the subject is able and competent, i.e. that it can act and choose, as well as being a recipient of the actions and choices of others.[44]

The Gothic/Monstrous Self

In recent years, a literature has emerged which evaluates the fictional trope of the 'gothic' – characterized by 'ambivalence and uncertainty'[45] – as a counterpoint to liberalism, and explores the concepts of the 'gothic self' and the 'monster' (explained below) as literary precursors to, as well as contemporary examples of, the postmodern Other. In parallel, a strand of critique has flourished within

---

41　*Re T (Adult: Refusal of Treatment)* [1993] Fam 95, at 113.

42　*Airedale NHS Trust v Bland* [1993] AC 789.

43　*Ibid.*, at 827.

44　The legal presumption of capacity is now statutory in England and Wales, under s. 1(2) of the Mental Capacity Act 2005.

45　Botting, F. (1996), *Gothic*, (Routledge), at p. 3.

postmodern feminist theory which challenges the idea that vulnerability,[46] volatility,[47] and even 'monstrosity'[48] are necessarily negative, arguing that such qualities are inescapable features of humanity, and can be understood, and honoured, as conditions of transformative power.

If the liberal self is characterized by autonomy, rationality, order, balance, harmony, stability, self-sovereignty and boundedness, the gothic self is everything that this liberal self is not. As Paul Atkinson notes, 'the gothic body ... stands in stark contrast to the bourgeois, bounded "body of modernity".'[49] Whereas the liberal self is autonomous, the gothic self is dependent. Whereas the liberal self is rational, the gothic self is irrational. We find disorder and chaos in place of order and stability, imbalance and excess instead of balance and harmony. On the one hand, then, we see the bounded, individuated, self-contained 'liberal self', capable of retaining that which is self and excluding that which is other. On the other hand, we have the gothic self – disordered, leaky and lacking in self-sovereignty. These two models of selfhood are in clear opposition to one another.

Just as the gothic stands in opposition to the liberal, so it also stands in opposition to the legal (as one would expect, given the seeming identity between the two). David Punter puts it succinctly when he writes that gothic represents 'freedom from the law';[50] 'the gothic', he notes, 'is indeed extra-legal'.[51]

A key concept in the gothic, and one which has been drawn upon in recent postmodernist writing on selfhood, is the notion of monstrosity. There are clear parallels between the gothic figure of the monster and the postmodern Other. The monster fulfils the same function as the Other in that 'we stake out the boundaries of our humanity by delineating the boundaries of the monstrous',[52] making it 'a concept we need in order to tell ourselves what we are *not*'.[53] More specifically, though, monstrosity in gothic horror is closely linked to the concept of the 'abhuman'. Given that the prefix 'ab-' means a loss of, or a move away from, we can define the concept of the abhuman as involving a loss of, or a move away from, humanness.

Kelly Hurley writes that '[t]he abhuman subject is a not-quite human subject, characterized by its morphic variability, continually in danger of becoming not-

---

46   See, for example, Shildrick, M. (1997), *Leaky Bodies & Boundaries: Feminism, Postmodernism and (Bio)ethics*, (Routledge).

47   See, for example, Grosz, E. (1994), *Volatile Bodies: Toward a Corporeal Feminism*, (Indiana University Press).

48   See, for example, Shildrick, M. (2002), *Embodying the Monster: Encounters with the Vulnerable Self*, (Sage), and the discussion of 'monstrous corporeality' therein.

49   Atkinson, P. (2005), Review: Gothic Imaginations, *Social Studies of Science* 35:4, 653–664, at p. 660.

50   Punter, *op. cit.* n. 39, at p. 12.

51   *Ibid.*, at p. 200.

52   Hanafi, Z. (2000), *The Monster in the Machine: Magic, Medicine and the Marvelous in the Time of the Scientific Revolution*, (Duke University Press), at xiii.

53   *Ibid.*, at p. 218.

itself, becoming other'.[54] This quality of 'almost, but not quite' is close to what Freud meant by 'the uncanny' (*'unheimlich'*)[55] – the peculiar fearfulness that brings to mind the familiar – and it invites responses of abjection (distancing, casting-out), disgust, shame and revulsion.[56]

An example to illustrate this comes from the gothic short story *The Crew of the Lancing* by William Hope Hodgson, discussed by Kelly Hurley in her 1996 book *The Gothic Body*.[57] In the story, the *Lancing*, a ship adrift in the tropics, is boarded by mysterious sea-monsters who eat its crew. Alerted by a strange noise 'with a horribly suggestive human note ringing through it', the narrator of the story, a member of the crew of another ship, boards the *Lancing* and discovers the creatures crawling on the decks. The language of abhumanness abounds as he describes the horror he finds, telling us first that 'there was something familiar about them', then saying that 'they were like nothing so much as men', in fact, 'fearsome parodies of humans'. He experiences 'an extraordinary feeling of horror and revulsion' and concludes that these are 'the most horrible creatures I had ever seen'.[58] The source of the horror here is not the fact that the creatures have *no* human-like qualities; rather, it is the fact that they seem to exist liminally, at the margins of the category 'human', and interstitially, across or between categories and 'conform[ing] cleanly to none of them'.[59]

The response of the narrator in *The Crew of the Lancing* is a classic response of abjection. Julia Kristeva, in *Powers of Horror: An Essay On Abjection*,[60] discusses abjection as a kind of casting-out, characterized by the ambivalence that results from existing between categories. In *Bodies That Matter*,[61] Judith Butler describes 'the abject' as designating 'those "unlivable" and "uninhabitable" zones ... populated by those who do not enjoy the status of the subject but whose living under the sign of the "unlivable" is required to circumscribe the domain of the subject'.[62] In law, too, we find 'abjection' responses. Medical law cases, particularly end-of-life cases and any cases involving severe disability, provide a particularly rich seam of the language of abjection. Wherever quality of life and

---

54 Hurley, *op. cit.* n. 36, at pp. 3–4.

55 Freud, S. (2003), *The Uncanny*, (Penguin Classics), at p. 124.

56 Isabel Karpin has applied the concept of 'the uncanny' to *ex utero* embryos (and to foetuses and children that develop from them) – see Karpin, I. (2006), The Uncanny Embryos: Legal Limits to the Human and Reproduction Without Women, *Sydney Law Review* 28, 599; here, however, I will argue that *all* embryos and foetuses are uncanny/ gothic/monstrous, perhaps even *more* so if located inside the body of a woman.

57 Hurley, *op. cit.* n. 36, at pp. 23–25.

58 Quoted *ibid.*, at p. 23.

59 *Ibid.*, at p. 24.

60 Kristeva, J. (1982), *Powers of Horror: An Essay On Abjection*, (Columbia University Press).

61 Butler, J. (1993), *Bodies That Matter: On The Discursive Limits of Sex*, (Routledge).

62 *Ibid.*, at p. 3.

the limits of tolerability and liveableness are discussed, we find certain conditions and predicaments portrayed as abject.

One stark example is the language of the judgements in the famous case of *Re A*.[63] This case concerned the proposed surgical separation of conjoined twins who would both die if left in their conjoined state. If they were separated, the stronger twin ('Jodie') had a reasonable chance of survival, but the weaker twin ('Mary') would inevitably die on the operating table. In *obiter dicta* in that case, all three judges alluded to the liberal ideal of the bounded, individuated, sovereign self. Ward LJ stated that 'the only gain I can see [for Mary] is that the operation would, if successful, give Mary the bodily integrity and dignity which is the natural order for all of us',[64] though he qualified this by calling that a 'wholly illusory goal' since Mary would die before she could derive any benefit from it. Brooke LJ was less guarded: he said that '[t]he doctrine of sanctity of life respects the integrity of the human body. The proposed operation would give these children's bodies the integrity which nature denied them.'[65]

In a similar vein, Walker LJ wondered whether 'the mere fact of restoring [Mary's] separate bodily integrity, even at the moment of death, can be seen as a good in itself and as something which ought to be achieved in the best interests of Mary as well as Jodie'.[66] He concluded that the operation would be in Mary's best interests because 'for the twins to remain alive and conjoined in the way they are would be to deprive them of the bodily integrity and human dignity which is the right of each of them'.[67] Underpinning all of this is a typically liberal view of subjecthood: 'Every human being's right to life carries with it, as an intrinsic part of it, rights of bodily integrity and autonomy – the right to have one's own body whole and intact.'[68]

So abject and illicit was the twins' anomalous, ambiguous physicality, it seems, that it would be better to be separate and dead than alive and conjoined: as Punter notes, 'the law cannot permit ... the exceptional body ... the existence of a monster thus poses the utmost threat to the law'.[69] The gothic body, says Punter, is 'perpetually unamenable to the rule of law'.[70]

Postmodernist/critical writers have challenged the dominance of liberal notions of the subject in order to debunk conventional narratives around female,[71]

---

63   *Re A (Children) (Conjoined Twins: Surgical Separation)* [2001] Fam 147.

64   *Ibid.*, at 184.

65   *Ibid.*, at 240.

66   *Ibid.*, at 251.

67   *Ibid.*, at 258.

68   *Ibid.*, at 259.

69   Punter, *op. cit.* n. 39, at p. 45.

70   *Ibid.*, at p. 46.

71   There is a vast literature on female embodiment and subjecthood. See, for example, Young, I. (2005), *On Female Body Experience: 'Throwing Like a Girl' and Other Essays*, (Oxford University Press); Price, J. and Shildrick, M. (eds) (1999), *Feminist Theory and the Body: A Reader*, (Edinburgh University Press). In the legal context, see, for example,

disabled,[72] vulnerable[73] and transgender[74] persons and their bodies, as these occur both in wider culture and in the healthcare setting, and to argue for a recalibration of our perceptions, informed by an appreciation of the artificiality of prevailing discourses and constructs. The fact that these beings are the result of, or are engaged in, processes of transformation which transgress modernist, liberal norms is, according to this strand of critique, the cause of their marginalization in mainstream discourse. In effect (though this claim is not always made explicitly), they are the objects of abjection-responses – horror responses. To understand this, and to understand, too, that we ought to regard the 'conventional ethics' of liberal normativity and its truth-claims as highly suspect and problematic, is to appreciate why mainstream accounts of femaleness, disability, intersexuality and disease/illness ought urgently to be replaced with narratives free from liberal ideological assumptions.

What is striking, however, is that this powerful critique is rarely extended to the embryo/foetus, notwithstanding that it would be difficult to find a more paradigmatic case of transformation and transgression in the human context than that of the human embryo/foetus. I want to remedy that here by claiming that the embryo/foetus appears before the law as a gothic, perhaps even a monstrous entity, and that it deserves to be considered in postmodernism's challenging of liberal constructions of what it means to be a human subject or self. I will seek to establish the gothic nature of the embryo/foetus in two stages: first, by arguing that the embryo/foetus acquires a gothic character by virtue of its origins and associations; and second, by reconsidering the 'hallmarks' of gothic selfhood/monstrosity, and claiming that the embryo/foetus is an almost perfect embodiment of each of them.

The Foetus as Gothic Self

Origins and Associations

Origins　Embryos and foetuses are created either by desire, by violence or by science. Desire and science are parts of human existence that we cannot do without; like violence, however, they are forces which, if not controlled, threaten to endanger, and subvert, our familiar modes of existence. Even among those

---

Bridgeman, J. and Millns, S. (1998), *Feminist Perspectives on Law: Law's Engagement with the Female Body*, (Sweet & Maxwell).

72　See, for example, Leach Scully, J. (2008), *Disability Bioethics: Moral Bodies, Moral Difference*, (Rowman & Littlefield).

73　Again, a voluminous literature exists: see, for example, Shildrick, *op. cit.* nn. 46 and 48; Grosz, *op. cit.* n. 47.

74　See, for example, Sharpe, A. (2002), *Transgender Jurisprudence: Dysphoric Bodies of Law*, (London: Routledge-Cavendish).

who would regard subversion of existing orders and norms as a benign, welcome or even necessary development, however, the majority favour incremental or controlled change, rather than chaotic or cataclysmic revolution; our survival and flourishing as individuals and as a species require that the pace of change does not outstrip the pace at which we are able to adapt. A degree of conservatism is part of our evolutionary hardwiring. Since embryos and foetuses are created by processes which inspire fear, then, as much as they inspire awe, the embryo or foetus – every embryo or foetus – is a subversive, a fearsome creature. Indeed, the power of sex and science to threaten us is due, in no small part, precisely to the power of these institutions to create (or thwart) life. Sex also threatens us physically, as a potential vehicle for the transmission of disease, and, existentially, as a focal point of narcissism, self-loathing and despair. Science, for its part, threatens to change the world too radically, or not to change it enough. It burdens us with knowledge that creates dilemmas or obligations for us, or exposes us to information about threats to our health. Embryos and foetuses have their origins in one or other (or both) of these profoundly exciting, but profoundly troubling institutions, so that they are, from their very inception, ambivalent and challenging beings.

Associations   Cultural perceptions of embryos and foetuses are also rendered problematic by the various negative associations which these entities can never fully avoid. Two such associations, as noted already, are sex and science. In addition, I want to claim that there is an inescapable association between embryos, foetuses and female bodies. Why are these associations negative? Taking science first, the narrative of science remains as much a narrative of vagueness, ignorance, error and speculation as of conquest, achievement, knowledge, proof and certainty. All scientific inquiry is motivated by lack of knowledge, and much of it progresses, tentatively and messily, toward an incomplete account which merely lessens our ignorance. Often, the knowledge thus gained is troubling rather than reassuring. Sex, too, is threatening: intercourse can be messy, noisy, even painful, and can involve extremes of sensation and emotion; invariably, it involves blurring and intruding upon bodily boundaries, and in some cases, might also represent a transgression of norms of conventional or personal morality..

The inevitable association between the embryo/foetus and the female body which usually surrounds it compounds its negative perception still further. A wealth of feminist critique exists which exposes the negativity of mainstream perceptions of femaleness, and, particularly, female corporeality. Some of it has been noted already.[75] In disciplines as diverse as cultural theory, ethics, and law, the archetype of the 'monstrous feminine' has been laid bare and challenged by feminists writing in a broadly postmodernist vein. Barbara Creed, in her book, *The Monstrous Feminine*,[76] makes the case that the female reproductive body is the

---

75   See, *op. cit.* nn. 46–48.

76   Creed, B. (1993), *The Monstrous-feminine: Film, Feminism, Psychoanalysis*, (Routledge).

prototype of monstrosity in the realm of popular culture. In the bioethical context, too, it has been claimed that the strong association between the female and the monstrous has led to women being perceived as inherently diseased or deficient.[77] Michael Thomson has argued that, within the regulatory framework of the Human Fertilisation and Embryology Act 1990, the already prevalent association of the female (and, Thomson says, particularly the maternal) with the monstrous is exacerbated in the context of new reproductive technologies because the notion of the 'monstrous feminine' combines with anxieties over technology to produce a construction of the woman as 'an object of horror and fascination'.[78]

This literature makes us alert to the caricature of woman as emotionally and physically weak, vulnerable, unstable and dependent; yet with a body which is also powerful and threatening, capable of containing the male both in intercourse and in pregnancy, and of performing hidden and profound transformations. If perceptions of embryos and foetuses really are inextricably bound up with prevailing contemporary (mis)understandings of female corporeality, as I claim they are, then the former will surely absorb some of the dread and discomfort inherent in the latter.

Here, two points must be made. First, because the focus of this chapter is on embryos and foetuses as sites of transformation and transgression, my interest now is in how negative perceptions of women and their bodies might impact upon perceptions of embryos and foetuses, through the association (which I claim is inevitable) of one with the other. Clearly, any impact on the embryo or foetus is far from being the *most* troubling or problematic effect of this kind of damaging construction of women's bodies; however the primary object of concern – that of the harms such constructions must mean for women themselves – is already well-theorized. The 'otherness' of women is by now familiar; the otherness of the foetus, on the other hand, is often overlooked (or compounded).

Second, feminists have argued that narratives of pregnancy often exclude or ignore the personhood of the pregnant woman, instead imagining the foetus in isolation, 'floating freely'. This may seem to mean, contrary to what I am claiming here, that the association of the embryo or foetus with the woman is *not* inescapable, since (according to this particular feminist argument) the two can be separated in the cultural imaginary to such an extent that the woman is routinely excluded from the picture. Cynthia Daniels, for example, has cited foetal imaging technology, and the fact that it is increasingly possible to treat the foetus, medically, as something like a 'separate patient', as factors which have contributed to the public perception of the foetus as separate and independent from the woman.[79] Technology has enabled us to gaze at the foetus *in utero* in a way that makes pregnancy a 'public

---

77   See, for example, Shildrick, *op. cit.* n. 46; see also Grosz, *op. cit.* n. 47.

78   Thomson, M. (1997), Legislating for the Monstrous: Access To Reproductive Services and the Monstrous Feminine, *Social & Legal Studies* 6:3, 401–424.

79   Daniels, C. (1993), *At Women's Expense: State Power and the Politics of Fetal Rights*, (Harvard University Press), at pp. 19–22.

event', and the public image is that of a foetus 'autonomous from the woman'.[80] As Rachel Roth has noted, this perception of 'autonomy' results in the public construction of the foetus not only as an *independent*, but as an '*innocent* third party',[81] an image which has been exploited in anti-abortion literature, where, Daniels tells us, 'the fetus is visually severed from the mother, presented as an autonomous free-floating being ...', with the result that 'the pregnant woman [begins] literally to disappear from view'.[82] The severing of foetus and woman is part of the reason why, according to Lynn Morgan and Meredith Michaels, '[s]ince [the 1960s and 1970s], the social organization of reproduction in the United States has unfolded in a way that routinely erases women from the picture and naturalizes the presence of fetuses ... [a]s fetuses in their "maternal environments" become ubiquitous, women seem to vanish.'[83]

All of this seems to indicate that, at least in the view of these feminist commentators, the pregnant woman–foetus association is far from ubiquitous; indeed, it is precisely because that association can be, and *has* been, severed in the public imagination, they argue, that women are often excluded from their proper place in the cultural and political processes by which reproduction is organized. Nevertheless, while I would agree with these writers that the challenging notion of the 'woman as person' is conveniently ignored in many accounts of pregnancy, I would argue that the association between embryos/foetuses and women's bodies (the 'maternal environment', to use the pernicious phrase quoted by Morgan and Michaels) remains strong, feeding into our overall consciousness of embryos/foetuses and shaping our understandings of what they are.

By virtue of their origins in, and associations with, science, sex, and the female body, then, embryos and foetuses are already firmly associated with danger, subversion and transgression even before we consider the specifics of their nature, and their intrinsic characteristics.

Intrinsic Features

Even if it could be separated from the origins and connotations which associate it so decidedly with the transgression of liberal standards, the embryo/foetus would nevertheless be an *intrinsically* gothic entity; its very body, and existence, refute and transgress liberal norms of subjecthood. It is, as Seymour notes, an 'inchoate being'.[84] When we consider the various hallmarks of the gothic – monstrosity, abhumanness, liminality, an existence which invites responses of abjection – we

---

80   *Ibid.*, at p. 22.

81   Roth, R. (2000), *Making Women Pay: The Hidden Costs of Fetal Rights*, (Cornell University Press), at pp. 185–186 (emphasis added).

82   Daniels, *op. cit.* n. 79, at p. 21.

83   Morgan, L. and Michaels, M. (eds) (1999), *Fetal Subjects, Feminist Positions*, (University of Pennsylvania Press), at p. 4.

84   Seymour, *op. cit.* n. 7, at p. 135.

see that the embryo/foetus is a model of each. It 'offers the spectacle of a body metamorphic and undifferentiated … in place of a unitary and securely bounded human subjectivity [we find] one that is both fragmented and permeable'.[85] These words were in fact written as a description of *fin de siècle* gothic, but they could just as easily serve as a description of the embryonic/foetal body.

The embryo/foetus *in vivo* is engaged in a continuous and radical process of transformation, rapidly traversing a series of identities – fertilized ovum, zygote, embryo, foetus – and embodying the 'transgressively transformational' quality that, according to Atkinson, so defines the gothic.[86] The embryo/foetus, like all that is gothic, is 'always on the point of dissolving into something else'.[87] Moreover, the instability of the embryonic/foetal body unquestionably maps it on to the central gothic concepts of monstrosity and the abhuman. The abhuman body is 'the human body whose humanness is tenuous, incomplete, at all moments liable to regression'.[88] Recall Hurley's observation that: 'the abhuman subject is a not-quite-human subject, characterized by its morphic variability, continually in danger of becoming not-itself, becoming other'.[89] From these definitions, it is relatively straightforward to posit the embryonic/foetal body as a paradigm of the abhuman.

The embryo/foetus can also be seen to reflect the essence of monstrosity, since the horror of the monstrous 'lies in the undifferentiation of the monstrous body'.[90] Moreover, as Hanafi notes, monstrosity taps into:

> [O]ur confusion at understanding what constitutes a human being: are we flesh or are we spirit? Are we body or are we soul? And what is the relation between the two? It would seem that the human condition is fraught with dangers: both to lapse into pure 'body-hood' and to become indistinguishable from mechanically-animated matter are pervasive threats.[91]

In other words, narratives of monstrosity highlight the precariousness of the balance between mind and body. The dangers of the human condition are characterized here as being (i) to (col)lapse into 'pure body-hood' and (ii) to merge with technology to the point where human distinctiveness is lost. The latter danger brings to mind Marie Fox's discussion of cryopreserved embryos.[92] The former captures one of the features of *all* embryos and foetuses which renders them 'gothic': the fact that they are bodies without developed minds, existing in what seems to be close to a condition of 'pure body-hood'.

---

85   Hurley, *op. cit.* n. 36, at p. 3.
86   Atkinson, *op. cit.* n 49, at p. 657.
87   Punter, *op. cit.* n. 39, at p. 200.
88   Hurley, *op. cit.* n. 36, at p. 113.
89   *Ibid.*, at pp. 3–4.
90   *Ibid.*, at p. 23.
91   Hanafi, *op. cit.* n. 52, at p. 96.
92   Fox, *op. cit.* n. 2.

The fluid, unstable corporeality of the embryo/foetus is precisely the kind of threatening embodiment which we should expect to invite classic responses of abjection. Like the creatures on the deck of the *Lancing*, embryos and foetuses possess human qualities, but abstracted from the context in which we would normally encounter them. Also like the creatures on the *Lancing*, the embryo/foetus is a liminal/interstitial entity, overlapping across recognizable categories in typically gothic fashion without belonging fully to any one of them.[93] This *uncanny* juxtaposition of the familiar and the unfamiliar produces the dual elements of abjection: revulsion and recognition. That odd mixture of distaste and sympathy we feel when we come across something which is so unlike us in situation and appearance, and yet in which we recognize characteristics that we ourselves share, is the heart of the abjection-response.

Given the identifiably gothic character of the body of the embryo/foetus – its undeniable Otherness – we might expect the broad postmodernist critique of the liberal self to include, somewhere, an acknowledgment that, along with the bodies of women, intersex and transgender people, people with disabilities and so on, the embryonic/foetal body, too, is gothicized by modernist liberal dogma. Yet the critique which has been made so eloquently and influentially in these other contexts is largely silent on the question of the embryo/foetus.

The gothic potential of the embryo/foetus has not been entirely lost on academic commentators. The few who have noted gothic or monstrous representations of the foetus, however, have not done so in order to challenge as suspect the assumptions underpinning such portrayals; on the contrary, they appear to adopt them. One of the earliest examples of 'gothic pregnancy' in the bioethical literature must surely be the famous 'violinist' scenario presented by Judith Jarvis Thomson in her 1971 article, 'A Defense of Abortion'.[94] Thomson sketches a nightmarish scenario, intended as an analogy to pregnancy, in which a sleeping subject is kidnapped and forcibly connected to a famous violinist to save the violinist's life. Her point is to argue that terminating pregnancy is morally permissible because, just as the sleeper in the imagined scenario has no moral responsibility for the welfare of the violinist, the pregnant woman has no such responsibility towards her foetus.

Another commentator, Ernest Larsen, has written of 'the fetus as monster', imagining that pregnancy might *often* feel like 'an invasive experience of the monstrous'.[95] He writes: '[t]hat which is unknown or unknowable, unnamed or unnamable, unstable but ever more insistent, hidden from sight yet imperiously

---

93   Contrary to Lord Mustill's suggestion, in *Attorney-General's Reference (No 3 of 1994)* [1998] AC 245 (at 255), that the foetus is 'an organism *sui generis*' (in a category of its own), my claim here is that it is the foetus's overlapping of categories, and its presence just outside the thresholds of categories, that defines it.

94   Thomson, J. (1971), A Defense of Abortion, *Philosophy and Public Affairs* 1:1, 47–66.

95   Larsen, E. (1999), The Fetal Monster, in Morgan, L. and Michaels, M. (eds), *Fetal Subjects Feminist Positions*, (University of Pennsylvania Press), at p. 240.

present to the body, is that thrilling territory of fear that marks out the site of horror. And all these qualities mark the fetus, *every fetus*, as a potential monster.'[96] Again, Larsen's point is not that the foetus *appears* gothic or monstrous, because it is viewed (as are we all) through the prism of liberal ideology; rather, he takes 'the popularity of such images of the fetus as monster' (he is referring here to the numerous portrayals of pregnancy and childbirth in cinematic horror narratives) as 'a repeated confirmation' of what pregnancy might 'often' feel like.[97]

Conclusion

It might be claimed that all of the foregoing is undermined by a fundamental contradiction: that, while a central claim of this chapter has been that the natural response of the liberal law to the gothic self (and therefore to the embryo/foetus) will be to reject it or 'cast it out', the examples provided near the beginning of this discussion appear to demonstrate the contrary. That is, all of the examples given seem to show *favourable* responses to the embryo/foetus – responses which speak of special status/respect, of distinctiveness, or of intrinsic value.

To this, it can be responded that the existence of seemingly positive statements is not incompatible with an abjection-response. To regard apparent approval as incompatible with abjection is to misunderstand the nature of abjection itself: abjection, as noted earlier, is by definition an *ambivalent* response. It consists predominantly in fear and revulsion, certainly, but with an accompanying sense of identification with, and sympathy for, the abject entity. That the law recognizes something familiar or sympathetic in the embryo/foetus is entirely compatible with abjection, therefore.

Moreover, although the law may occasionally speak the language of 'special status/respect', it declines to provide any grounding for it. Several possible justifications for 'special status' were considered earlier, and none were satisfactory; in any case, the exercise was necessarily speculative, since the law's own approach to the embryo/foetus is ad hoc, and lacking in reasons. It is also notable that, despite the rhetoric, 'special status' has few practical implications (particularly in the case of the embryo/foetus *in vivo*). If acknowledging the 'special status' of the embryo/foetus does not oblige us to act or refrain in any way – if it does not translate into concrete protection, in other words – it may be regarded as purely rhetorical.

Finally, it should be noted that despite the existence of a few dicta, by far the overwhelming response of the law to the embryo/foetus is to ignore it. As a legal non-person, the embryo/foetus rarely falls to be considered by the courts at all; the 'positive' dicta come from cases where, for one reason or another, such entities have been more visible than usual. This visibility before the law is likely

---

96   *Ibid.*, at pp. 240–241.
97   *Ibid.*, at p. 240.

to decrease in future, however. Because the law regarding the right of pregnant women to refuse medical treatment has now been clarified,[98] refusals of medical treatment by a pregnant woman are unlikely to be the subject of much (if any) litigation in future. While this clarification is overdue and certainly welcome, a corollary of it is that the embryo/foetus is likely to slip further out of sight of the law.

In light of Punter's observation that the gothic body is 'perpetually unamenable to the rule of law', the overwhelming invisibility of the embryo/foetus ought hardly to be surprising. Indeed, such a 'casting out' of the legal landscape conforms to what we should expect of a classic abjection-response. It leaves us with little (and diminishing) evidence of the law's ongoing response to the embryo/foetus; nevertheless, the evidence we can glean from other sources – for example, from the case of *Re A* and other cases where issues of quality of life and tolerability are discussed – supports the view that *the embryo/foetus embodies the* opposite *of everything the law requires of its subjects.*

What ought to be done? For a start, instead of *embedding* the notion of the foetus as 'monstrous' or as 'outcast', as narratives like Judith Thomson's and Ernest Larsen's do, or excluding discussion of the embryo/foetus altogether as most postmodernist discourses on corporeality and subjecthood do, we ought to be alive to the parallels between the body of the embro/foetus and other 'monstrous' bodies. We ought to be willing to acknowledge the possibility that the embryo/foetus invites responses of abjection – from academic commentators and judges, as well as from ordinary members of the moral community. It would be strange if the embryo/foetus were able to *avoid* such responses, given how readily it maps onto concepts of the monstrous and the abhuman. As such, any notion that the incomplete, unstable body of the embryo/foetus can be excluded from serious attempts to critique liberal subjecthood, particularly in the bioethical context, must be regarded as problematic.

Of course, postmodern feminism must respond ambivalently to the risky suggestion that the embryo/foetus be allowed the status of Other and be accommodated within postmodernist understandings of what it means to be human. Ambivalence is the appropriate response, since the embryo/foetus is simultaneously deserving (thus inviting our sympathy) and threatening (thus inviting us to repel it).

In the end, the law is ill-equipped to respond satisfactorily to life before birth. The kind of 'special status' which best befits the 'inchoate' embryo/foetus, therefore, is one that reflects the law's failure to make sense of it, and the reasons for that failure: the status of the postmodern Other. Of course, this kind of status cannot be conferred by law. Whether postmodernist theory will develop in a way that embraces the Otherness of the embryo/foetus remains to be seen.

---

98   See *St George's Healthcare NHS Trust v S* and *Re MB (Adult: Medical Treatment)*, *op. cit.* n. 32.

References

Atkinson, P. (2005), Review: Gothic Imaginations, *Social Studies of Science*, 35:4, 653.

Botting, F. (1996), *Gothic*, (Routledge).

Bridgeman, J. and Millns, S. (1998), *Feminist Perspectives on Law: Law's Engagement with the Female Body*, (Sweet & Maxwell).

Burgess, J.A. and Tawia, S.A. (1996), When Did You First Begin To Feel It? – Locating the Beginnings of Human Consciousness, *Bioethics* 10:1, 1.

Butler, J. (1993), *Bodies That Matter: On The Discursive Limits of Sex*, (Routledge).

Creed, B. (1993), *The Monstrous-feminine: Film, Feminism, Psychoanalysis*, (Routledge).

Daniels, C. (1993), *At Women's Expense: State Power and the Politics of Fetal Rights*, (Harvard University Press).

Derbyshire, S. (1999), Locating the Beginnings of Pain, *Bioethics* 13:1, 1.

Fox, M. (2000), Pre-Persons, Commodities or Cyborgs: the Legal Construction and Representation of the Embryo, *Health Care Analysis* 8, 171.

Freud, S. (2003) *The Uncanny*, (Penguin Classics).

Grosz, E. (1994), *Volatile Bodies: Toward a Corporeal Feminism*, (Indiana University Press).

Hanafi, Z. (2000), *The Monster in the Machine: Magic, Medicine and the Marvelous in the Time of the Scientific Revolution*, (Duke University Press).

Harris, J. (1985), *The Value of Life*, (Routledge).

Harris-Short, S. (2009), Regulating Reproduction – Frozen Embryos, Consent, Welfare and the Equality Myth, in Smith and Deazley (eds), *The Legal, Medical and Cultural Regulation of the Body: Transformation and Transgression*, (Ashgate).

Held, V. (2006), *The Ethics of Care: Personal, Political, and Global*, (Oxford University Press).

Hurley, K. (1996), *The Gothic Body: Sexuality, Materialism and Degeneration at the Fin de Siècle*, (Cambridge University Press).

Hursthouse, R. (1987), *Beginning Lives*, (Basil Blackwell).

Karpin, I. (2006), The Uncanny Embryos: Legal Limits to the Human and Reproduction Without Women, *Sydney Law Review* 28, 599.

Kristeva, J. (1982), *Powers of Horror: An Essay On Abjection*, (Columbia University Press).

Larsen, E. (1999), The Fetal Monster, in Morgan, L. and Michaels, M. (eds), *Fetal Subjects Feminist Positions*, (University of Pennsylvania Press).

Leach Scully, J. (2008), *Disability Bioethics: Moral Bodies, Moral Difference*, (Rowman & Littlefield).

Letwin, S. (2005), *On the History of the Idea of Law*, (Cambridge University Press).

McDonough, E. (1996), *Breaking the Abortion Deadlock: From Choice to Consent*, (Oxford University Press).

Morgan, L. and Michaels, M. (eds) (1999), *Fetal Subjects, Feminist Positions*, (University of Pennsylvania Press).

Noddings, N. (2003), *Caring: A Feminine Approach to Ethics and Moral Education*, 2nd Edition, (University of California Press).

Pashukanis, E. (1978), *Law and Marxism: A General Theory*, Einhorn, B. (trans.), Arthur, C. (ed.) (Ink Links).

Price, J. and Shildrick, M. (eds) (1999), *Feminist Theory and the Body: A Reader*, (Edinburgh University Press).

Punter, D. (1998), *Gothic Pathologies: The Text, The Body and The Law*, (Macmillan).

Rawls, J. (1971), *A Theory of Justice*, (Clarendon Press).

Roth, R. (2000), *Making Women Pay: The Hidden Costs of Fetal Rights*, (Cornell University Press).

Seymour, J. (2000), *Childbirth and the Law*, (Oxford University Press).

Sharpe, A. (2002), *Transgender Jurisprudence: Dysphoric Bodies of Law*, (Routledge-Cavendish).

Shildrick, M. (1997), *Leaky Bodies & Boundaries: Feminism, Postmodernism and (Bio)ethics*, (Routledge).

Shildrick, M. (2002), *Embodying the Monster: Encounters with the Vulnerable Self*, (Sage).

Singer, P. (1993), *Practical Ethics*, 2nd Edition, (Cambridge University Press).

Slote, M. (2007), *The Ethics of Care and Empathy*, (Routledge).

Thomson, J. (1971), A Defence of Abortion, *Philosophy and Public Affairs* 1:1, 47–66.

Thomson, M. (1997), Legislating for the Monstrous: Access To Reproductive Services and the Monstrous Feminine, *Social & Legal Studies* 6:3, 401–424.

Warnock, M. (1985), *A Question of Life: The Warnock Report on Human Fertilisation and Embryology*, (Basil Blackwell).

Warren, M.A. (1997), *Moral Status: Obligations to Persons and Other Living Things*, (Clarendon Press).

Young, I. (2005), *On Female Body Experience: 'Throwing Like a Girl' and Other Essays*, (Oxford University Press).

Chapter 3

Regulating Reproduction: Frozen Embryos, Consent, Welfare and the Equality Myth

Sonia Harris-Short

Introduction

The case of *Evans v Amicus Healthcare Ltd and Others*[1] brought the question of who should exercise control over the storage and use of frozen embryos firmly into the public eye. The case eventually found its way to the Grand Chamber of the European Court of Human Rights in Strasbourg where the consent-based 'bright-line' approach adopted in the Human Fertilisation and Embryology Act 1990 (HFE Act 1990) was found to be consistent with Articles 2, 8, 12 and 14 of the European Convention.[2] The case, which was the first of its kind in the UK, attracted considerable media attention. Although there was considerable sympathy for the plight of Natallie Evans, the outcome divided commentators – some arguing that the courts were right to uphold the equal right of Mr Johnston, Natallie Evans's former partner, to choose not to become a genetic parent; others seeing the destruction of the embryos which represented Ms Evans's last chance to have a genetically related child as a grave violation of her reproductive rights.[3]

The *Evans* case was particularly tragic. Ms Evans was undergoing routine investigations for continuing fertility problems when it was discovered that she had serious borderline tumours in both ovaries. This necessitated the almost immediate removal of her ovaries and fallopian tubes. However, she was advised that in order to try to preserve her capacity to have her own child she could undertake one round of IVF treatment before surgery. Within hours of receiving the diagnosis, Ms Evans and her then partner Mr Johnston signed the relevant consent forms and embarked upon the first stages of IVF. This successfully resulted in six embryos which were placed in storage whilst Ms Evans underwent treatment for the ovarian cancer. Although she made a complete recovery, she was advised not to attempt an embryo transfer for two years. Unfortunately, just a few months later Ms Evans and Mr Johnston separated and later that year he wrote to the clinic withdrawing his consent to the continued storage, and thereby future use, of the embryos. Under the current statutory regime this meant that the embryos would have to be

---

1   [2004] EWCA Civ 727, [2005] Fam 1.
2   *Evans v UK* [2006] 1 FCR 585 (Chamber); [2007] 2 FCR 5 (Grand Chamber).
3   For a summary of the media's response see: Sheldon 2004a, 310–11.

destroyed. Ms Evans initiated legal proceedings in an attempt to prevent the clinic destroying the embryos and to allow her to be able to use the embryos in future treatment.

Undoubtedly, the *Evans* case had a particular poignancy because the embryos represented Ms Evans's last chance to have a genetically related child. It is, however, unlikely to be unique. Whilst by no means commonplace, disputes over the storage and use of frozen embryos will almost certainly constitute a growing problem. Obtaining exact figures for the number of embryos in storage in the UK is difficult, but in 1996 it was estimated that the number stood at approximately 52,000 (Boulton 1996).[4] Given the increasing number of couples turning to fertility treatment, that number will have grown considerably. IVF can be very stressful and treatment may take many months, even years. The enormous strain it places on all those involved makes separation during the course of the treatment a real possibility. Whenever separation occurs, difficult questions will inevitably arise as to who should have the right to decide over the continued storage and future use of any frozen embryos which have resulted from previous treatment.

The purpose of this chapter is thus to examine the approach which is taken to the storage and use of frozen embryos in the UK as enshrined within the HFE Act 1990. It will be argued that whilst, in the majority of cases, the 'bright-line' approach adopted in the HFE Act 1990 is fair and reasonable, its failure to admit of exceptions can be the cause of serious injustice. In particular, it renders invisible important considerations such as the impact of infertility on people's lives – a factor which can impact particularly seriously on women – as well as the potentially significant factor of the embryos' own independent interests. It will thus be suggested that to alleviate the potentially harsh effects of the current statutory regime two amendments are required. First, parties undertaking fertility treatment should be able to contract out of the statutory regime enshrined in Schedule 3 and determine for themselves, at the outset of treatment, how any future dispute over the disposition of frozen embryos should be resolved. Second, in the absence of such an agreement, the statutory regime would continue to apply, but subject to a residual discretion vested in the courts or the Human Fertilisation and Embryology Authority (HFEA) to carry out a genuine balancing of the parties' and the embryos' respective interests where the embryos in question represent the last chance of one of the gamete providers to become a genetic parent.[5] In a small

---

4   In 2006, there were 7,862 frozen embryo transfers in the UK. See, Human Fertilisation and Embryology Act (2007), *A long term analysis of the Human Fertilisation and Embryology Authority Register data (2001–2006)*, table 16. Available at <hfea.gov. uk/docs/Latest_long_term_data_analysis_report_91-06.pdf>.

5   Under the current statutory regime, the HFEA and the courts would not be able to authorize what would otherwise be a criminal offence by the clinic (storage and use of embryos and gametes without effective consent). The statute would therefore need to be amended to confer this power on the authorities. Conferring such a power on the HFEA is, however, perfectly possible. It was confirmed by Charles J in *L v the Human Fertilisation*

number of cases, depending on the strength of the various considerations in play, this balancing of interests should permit the courts or the HFEA to override the lack of a gamete provider's consent to the continued storage and future use of any embryos resulting from the use of his or her sperm or eggs.

The Current Legal Framework for Resolving Disputes over Frozen Embryos

In the UK, fertility treatment involving *ex vivo* embryos is subjected to detailed statutory regulation. The HFE Act 1990 established a system of licensing whereby it is an offence for any person to bring about the creation of an embryo *in vitro* or to keep or use an embryo except in pursuance of a licence issued by the Human Fertilisation and Embryology Authority.[6] The storage or use of an embryo can only lawfully take place in accordance with the requirements of the licence, and a clinic failing to observe these requirements faces revocation of their license and/ or criminal prosecution.[7] This statutory regime is founded on what have come to be termed the 'two twin pillars' of welfare and consent.[8] Within the context of disputes over frozen embryos it is however the single pillar of consent which dominates. It is a condition of every licence that the terms of Schedule 3 of the Act are complied with.[9] Schedule 3 deals with the necessary 'effective consents' to the use and storage of gametes and embryos. Pursuant to paragraph 6(3), an embryo, the creation of which was brought about *in vitro*, must not be used for any purpose unless there is an effective consent by each person whose gametes were used to bring about the creation of the embryo to the use of the embryo for that purpose. The embryo must be used strictly in accordance with those consents.

---

and Embryology Authority; Secretary of State for Health [2008] EWHC 2149, that the HFEA can issue a special direction amending the terms of a clinic's license to permit storage of gametes or embryos without effective consent where the applicant is seeking permission from the HFEA to export the gametes or embryos for treatment abroad. This power would, however, appear to be derived from and thereby limited to cases of export under s. 24(4) of the HFE Act. There is no general power conferred on the HFEA to amend the terms of licenses to permit storage and use of gametes without effective consent. In the *Evans* case, Natallie Evans did not seek to export the embryos for treatment abroad so the Court of Appeal did not consider whether s. 24(4) could have been applied to confer power on the HFEA to permit, by special direction, the storage and export of the embryos for her to undertake such treatment. It is, however, indicated by Charles J in *L v HFEA; Secretary of State for Health* that different considerations would probably apply where the gamete provider was not permanently incapacitated as in the instant case and the earlier case of *R v HFEA ex parte Blood* [see esp. para. 113].

6   HFE Act 1990, s. 41.
7   HFE Act 1990, ss. 18 and 41.
8   *Evans v Amicus Healthcare Ltd and others* [2004] EWCA Civ 727, at [23].
9   HFE Act 1990, s. 12(c).

Paragraph 2(1) provides the purposes for which consent may be given: (a) providing treatment services to the person giving consent, or that person and another specified person together; (b) providing treatment services for others; (c) for the purposes of research.[10] Paragraph 8(2) of Schedule 3 goes on to provide that an embryo created *in vitro* must not be kept in storage unless each person whose gametes were used to bring about the creation of the embryo consents to the storage and the embryo is stored in accordance with those consents. Paragraph 2(2) further provides that consent to the storage of embryos must specify the maximum period of storage and state what is to be done with the gametes or embryo if the person who gave the consent dies or is unable because of incapacity to vary the terms of the consent or to revoke it. The consent may also specify conditions subject to which the gametes or embryos may remain in storage.[11] Crucially, to be effective the consent of the gamete provider must not have been withdrawn. Paragraph 4 specifically provides that the terms of any consent to the use of an embryo may be varied or withdrawn at any point until the embryo has been used in the provision of treatment services or for the purposes of research. Anyone providing consent under Schedule 3 must be advised of this right to vary or withdraw.[12]

Schedule 3 thus creates a 'bright-line' approach. The consent of the gamete provider to the continued storage or use of any embryo created using his or her gametes is an absolute requirement. The bright-line is placed at the point of embryo transfer.[13] That means that until the embryo is used in treatment the gamete provider has an unqualified right to withdraw that consent. If the consent of the gamete provider is withdrawn there is no other option than for the embryo to be destroyed; the statutory framework does not permit of any discretion. Such an approach has the clear benefit of promoting transparency and legal certainty, avoiding in the words of Thorpe LJ and Sedley LJ the 'arbitrariness and inconsistency' that a more flexible, fact-specific regime would introduce.[14] Certainty does, however, come at a price. The inflexibility of the current regime has the potential to cause great injustice in difficult cases.

These strict requirements on consent are not relaxed by the Human Fertilisation and Embryology Act 2008.[15] The new legislation makes only one change to the current statutory regime which is to introduce a 12-month 'cooling off' period following withdrawal of consent by one of the gamete providers. A clinic will thus be able to continue to store the embryos lawfully for a further 12 months following notice of withdrawal being received, thereby creating space for the other interested

---

10   HFE Act 1990, Sched. 3, para. 2(1).

11   HFE Act 1990, Sched. 3, para. 2(2).

12   HFE Act 1990, Sched. 3, para. 3(2).

13   This interpretation of the phrase 'used in providing treatment services' was confirmed by the Court of Appeal in *Evans v Amicus Healthcare Ltd and others* [2004] EWCA Civ 727, at [33].

14   *Evans v Amicus Healthcare Ltd and others* [2004] EWCA Civ 727, at [69].

15   The new legislation was given Royal Assent on 13 November 2008.

parties to be notified and, if possible, agreement reached on the future disposition of the embryos.[16]

The 'Bright-Line' Approach – A Cause of Injustice?

Promoting legal certainty in the field of assisted reproduction is clearly important. In this most sensitive of areas people need to know where they stand: both what the risks are that they are undertaking and what legal protection they have. However, as recognized by the government, legal certainty is not the only important consideration guiding the regulation of fertility treatment in the UK. In the evidence presented to Wall J at first instance in the *Evans* case, the Secretary of State for Health identified a number of policy considerations underpinning the 1990 Act:

> (1) [T]he female right of self-determination in relation to a pregnancy; (2) the primacy of consent accorded in the modern age to the need for freely given and informed consent to medical intervention; (3) the period over which IVF takes place; (4) the special significance of parenthood; (5) the interests of the child; (6) equality of treatment between the parties; (7) the promotion of the efficacy and use of IVF and related techniques; and (8) clarity and certainty in relations between partners.[17]

Despite these numerous considerations, the government's key objectives underlying Schedule 3 of the Act are clear: primacy has been accorded to the need for legal certainty and equality of treatment between the parties.[18] However, not only is it strongly questionable whether legal certainty over the storage and use of frozen embryos should be secured at the expense of all other relevant considerations, such as a meaningful analysis of the welfare of the child and the special significance of parenthood to the parties in question, but whether Schedule 3 actually achieves one of the government's two overriding objectives: equality of treatment between the parties.

---

16 Human Fertilisation and Embryology Act 2008, Sched. 3, para. 7.

17 *Evans v Amicus Healthcare Ltd and others* [2003] EWHC 2161 (Fam), at [186]. The government repeated this position before the Grand Chamber of the European Court of Human Rights: *Evans v UK* [2007] 2 FCR 5, at [68].

18 *Evans v Amicus Healthcare Ltd and others* [2003] EWHC 2161 (Fam), at [187]. See in particular the arguments presented on behalf of the Secretary of State for Health considered by Wall J in *Evans* at [236]–[244].

Gender Equality in Reproductive Decision-Making

Searching for Equality in Parenting and Beyond   The inflexibility of the absolute consent requirements in Schedule 3 of the HFE Act 1990 were challenged by Natallie Evans in the Evans litigation on the grounds that they were incompatible with her rights to procreative liberty and non-discrimination under Articles 8 and 14 of the European Convention.[19] It was held by Wall J at first instance that the Article 8 rights of Ms Evans were engaged. This conclusion was subsequently confirmed by the Court of Appeal and the European Court of Human Rights, the jurisprudence of the latter on this issue now being clear: the right to respect for private life includes a right to procreative liberty at the heart of which is the right to decide whether or not to become a genetic parent.[20] It was further held that the government's statutory regime, which had the effect of preventing Ms Evans from using the embryos to fulfil her dream of becoming a genetic parent, constituted a prima facie interference with her rights under Article 8(1).[21] However, in determining whether such interference could be justified, it was the unanimous view of Wall J, the Court of Appeal and the Grand Chamber of the European Court of Human Rights in Strasbourg that the Article 8 rights of Mr Johnston were also engaged and that Article 8 afforded equal protection to his procreative liberty, in particular his decision not to become a genetic parent with Ms Evans against his will. In balancing the competing Article 8 rights of Ms Evans and Mr Johnston, it was also agreed at all levels that the government had been justified in adopting a bright-line approach which afforded primacy to the need for the continuing consent of both gamete providers. Underpinning this conclusion was the perceived need to ensure equal respect for the Article 8 rights of both the male and female gamete providers; rights which they all agreed were not only of equivalent weight and importance but 'entirely irreconcilable'.[22] In terms of the balancing exercise demanded by Article 8, the competing rights were thus regarded as simply cancelling one another out.[23] The principle of gender equality underpinning this approach has been strongly endorsed by Tim Annett:

---

19   The arguments on the points of statutory construction were never strong – Schedule 3 being clear and unambiguous in its terms.

20   *Evans v Amicus Healthcare Ltd and others* [2003] EWHC 2161 (Fam), at [182]; *Evans v Amicus Healthcare Ltd and others* [2004] EWCA Civ 727, at [60]; *Evans v UK* [2007] 2 FCR 5, at [71]. The right was conceptualized by the European Court not as the right to become a mother (which Evans could still do through egg donation or adoption), but as a right to become a genetic parent. See *Evans v UK* at [72]. Evans's 'obsession' with becoming a genetic parent may well be criticized given alternative means of becoming a mother were still available to her. For discussion, see Lind 2006.

21   *Evans v Amicus Healthcare Ltd and others* [2003] EWHC 2161 (Fam), at [183]; *Evans v Amicus Healthcare Ltd and others* [2004] EWCA Civ 727, at [60].

22   *Evans v UK* [2007] 2 FCR 5, at [73].

23   *Evans v Amicus Healthcare Ltd and others* [2004] EWCA Civ 727, at [110]–[111]. See also *Evans v UK* [2007] 2 FCR 5, at [73] and [89]. This endorsed the Chamber

For an argument that there is no equivalence between the male and female gamete providers to be convincing it would have to be shown that Mr Johnston's interest in not having a child is inferior to Ms Evans's interest in having a child. Although with natural conception a male gamete provider has no right of veto prior to implantation, the 1990 Act aims to treat both parties equally even though this does not mirror nature. Whilst some mothers may have greater involvement in the upbringing of their children than do some fathers, it would hardly be acceptable to suggest that a father's interest in his child (whatever that might be) is or should be any less than the mother's. If the genetic link shared by male and female gamete providers is important in terms of parenthood, we would need to explain whether this link has the same significance for men and women before reaching any conclusions. (Annett 2006, 430)

Interestingly, the question of gender equality was not examined under Article 14 of the Convention, as the non-discrimination arguments were made on alternative grounds.[24]

The appeal made throughout the *Evans* decisions to the need to ensure gender equality in reproductive decision-making has a certain intuitive appeal.[25] Despite the obvious sympathy for Ms Evans's plight, many liberal feminist scholars would strongly agree with the equality objectives underpinning the courts' approach. The search for gender equality in both private and public life has led to calls by leading feminist commentators for gender neutrality to be entrenched into every aspect of family life (Okin 1989; McGlynn 2001, 326–330). Indeed, the importance of 'egalitarian family life' and 'gender neutral parenting' has become a rallying cry for some liberal feminist scholars (Okin 1989, esp. Chapter 8; McGlynn 2001). In the words of Okin:

A just future would be one without gender. In its social structures and practices, one's sex would have no more relevance than one's eye color or the length of one's toes. No assumptions would be made about 'male' and 'female' roles; childbearing would be so conceptually separated from child rearing and other family responsibilities that it would be a cause for surprise, and no little concern, if

---

judgement where the Court held that it '[did] not accept that the Article 8 rights of the male donor would necessarily be less worthy of protection than those of the female; nor [did] it regard it as self-evident that the balance of interests would always tip decisively in favour of the female party'. *Evans v UK* [2006] 1 FCR 585, at [66].

24   Wall J (infertile women as opposed to healthy women); Thorpe LJ and Sedley LJ (women whose partners have withdrawn their consent as opposed to women whose partners have not); and Arden LJ (women who can conceive naturally as opposed to women using assisted reproduction).

25   For a good critique of the gender equality arguments see Sheldon 2004a and Lind 2006.

men and women were not equally responsible for domestic life or if children were
to spend much more time with one parent than the other (Okin 1989, 171).

In accordance with this approach, a woman's reproductive and mothering roles are
given no greater value or significance than those of her male partner.

Popular discourses on fatherhood reinforce feminist calls for equality and
gender neutrality in modern family life. Securing a meaningful role for the father
in contemporary family life has become a major preoccupation of government.
In recent years, legal and political rhetoric on fatherhood (if not in the lived
realities of contemporary family life) has come to be dominated by the image
of the 'hands-on' father – a man who is no longer emotionally detached from his
family and whose role is narrowly defined as 'bread-winner' and 'disciplinarian',
but as fully engaged 'active parent' providing full-time care and nurture for his
children alongside the mother (Collier 2003). As Caroline Morris points out, this
image of fatherhood is reflected in the *Evans* case (Morris 2007, 997–998).[26] The
Court of Appeal describes Mr Johnston's objection to fathering a child where he
would not be in a position 'to play a full or proper paternal role, whilst at the
same time remaining financially liable to maintain the child'[27] as a 'fundamental'
rather than a 'purely financial' objection.[28] The gender neutrality of this egalitarian
model of family life in which parenting, in the words of Morris, is regarded as a
'joint and extended enterprise' (Morris 2007, 998) has had a significant impact on
family law, most notably residence and contact disputes over children. However,
its influence in regulating intimate family relationships extends much further.

The goal of achieving gender equality in family life extends naturally into the
sphere of reproductive decision-making. If parenthood is not a gendered activity,
then neither should be decisions over whether or not to become a parent. Again
the logic of the argument is convincing: if both prospective parents will be equally
affected by decisions over reproduction then why should they both not have an

---

26   It should also be noted, however, that this is at the same time a profoundly illiberal,
conservative vision of family life with its emphasis on the raising of children within
heterosexual two-parent families based on genetic and marital ties – a concept of family
which continues to exert a strong ideological hold over the regulation of reproductive-
decision-making and families.

27   *Evans v Amicus Healthcare Ltd and others* [2003] EWHC 2161 (Fam), at [252].

28   *Evans v Amicus Healthcare Ltd and others* [2004] EWCA Civ 727, at [32]. Note
that in many cases the male partner's ability to absolve himself from legal fatherhood (and
thereby financial responsibility) for any resulting child may be sufficient to resolve the
dispute. The possibility of Mr Johnston being able to 'transform' himself into a donor was
raised in *Evans*, but not satisfactorily resolved given the facts of the case. However, for
discussion of this point see Sheldon 2004b. There is nothing within the terms of the HFE
Act 1990 that would prohibit such a solution, although the female partner would need to
go through the consent and welfare processes again as a single applicant. It would have
been advantageous if this point on varying consent could have been clarified in the Human
Fertilisation and Embryology Act 2008.

equal voice in making those decisions. Of course, women have traditionally enjoyed absolute control over reproductive decision-making in the context of natural procreation because of the location of the embryo within her body and the embryo's total dependence upon her. Gender equality has thus been precluded in natural procreation by the overriding right of the woman to physical integrity and self-determination over her own body (Sheldon 2004a, 312).[29] It is for this reason that once the act of intercourse has taken place, the male gamete provider loses all decision-making authority over the fate of the embryo/foetus.[30] For the same reason, medical professionals concerned about the health of the woman or the foetus cannot force a course of treatment upon her or prevent her from engaging in potentially harmful behaviour.[31] As was made clear by the Court of Appeal in *St George's Healthcare NHS Trust v S*, although a foetus may have cognizable interests, the woman's autonomy and self-determination over her own body are inviolable principles of English law:

> In our judgment while pregnancy increases the personal responsibilities of a woman it does not diminish her entitlement to decide whether or not to undergo medical treatment. Although human, and protected by the law in a number of different ways … an unborn child is not a separate person from its mother. Its need for medical assistance does not prevail over her rights. She is entitled not to be forced to submit to an invasion of her body against her will, whether her own life or that of her unborn child depends on it. Her right is not reduced or diminished merely because her decision to exercise it may appear morally repugnant.[32]

The fundamental difference in IVF is that the physical separation between mother and embryo makes gender equality in reproductive decision-making perfectly plausible unless an alternative basis for privileging the woman's voice can be found. Against the background of the modern day angst about the disappearing role of the father in modern family life – a fear which reproductive technologies have exacerbated with their potential for further promoting the reproductive choices of single and lesbian women – the reproductive equality achieved in the HFE Act 1990 has been applauded for giving a meaningful voice back to fathers. In the words of Ruth Deech, former Chair of the Human Fertilisation and Embryology

---

29   For discussion of the law's approach to a woman's rights in pregnancy see, Ford 2008. Ford concludes that the Evans decision sets up a hierarchy of rights in which a woman's right to physical self-determination is given much greater weight than her social/ psychological self-determination.

30   *Paton v United Kingdom* (1980) 3 EHRR 408.

31   *Re F (In Utero) (Wardship)* [1988] Fam 122.

32   *St George's Healthcare NHS Trust v S; R v Collins and others, ex parte S* [1998] 2 FLR 728, at p. 746; and see generally pp. 739–746. See also *Re MB (Medical Treatment)* [1997] 2 FLR 426.

Authority, 'the danger with this advanced science of IVF is that men are gradually being cast aside, whether it's cloning or anything else. They are being reduced to a sort of genetic blob and, having done their duty in the laboratory, are no longer necessary ... the principle of equality is very important' (Deech 2006). Indeed, it was submitted in forceful terms on behalf of the Secretary of State for Health in the *Evans* case that to vest exclusive control over a frozen embryo in the woman would amount to serious sex discrimination against men and would clearly run foul of Article 14 of the European Convention.[33]

However, the initial appeal of this approach, based on a particular understanding of gender equality, betrays a more complex reality. It is strongly questionable whether gender equality in reproductive decision-making, even where the embryo is located outside the woman, really means treating men and women the same – as if there were no relevant differences between them. As is well-recognized in equality discourse, if men and women are differently situated, achieving substantive equality between the sexes may well require treating them differently (see, generally, Lind 2006). The equality arguments advanced by the government in *Evans* and uncritically endorsed by both the domestic courts and the majority of the Grand Chamber in Strasbourg are based on the premise, perhaps mistaken, that reproduction and parenting, with the exception of pregnancy, are experienced in the same way and mean the same to both women and men. Yet, there are strong social and psychological reasons, underpinned by empirical observation, for questioning this assumption (see, for example, Smart and Neale 1999). The prevailing reality concerning the gendered nature of family life in the UK raises challenging questions. Does becoming and being a parent generally mean more to women than it does to men? Do women generally invest more in reproduction and parenting than do men? Does infertility (and the IVF process in particular) affect women more profoundly than it does men?

This is difficult terrain for feminist scholars. Questioning the gender neutrality advanced by scholars, such as Okin and McGlynn, to contend that women experience reproduction and parenting differently from men is seen as dangerous and regressive. It risks reinforcing the assumptions and prejudices which liberal feminists have identified as the cause of women's oppression, thereby reversing all that has been achieved in the last 30 years to liberate women from the constraints of their 'naturally pre-ordained' mothering roles (Okin 1989, 4–5). The idea that whereas men are indifferent to children and parenthood, 'all women need to be mothers, that all mothers need their children and that all children need their mothers' (Oakley, cited by McGlynn 2001, 326),[34] was a pervasive feature of twentieth century thinking on family life. This biological determinism gave rise to the strictly defined gendered division of labour that liberal feminists have fought hard to defeat. However, not all feminists see gender neutrality as the way forward. Indeed, strong disillusionment with the limits of formal equality has

---

33   *Evans v Amicus Healthcare Ltd and others* [2003] EWHC 2161 (Fam), at [240].
34   See also Okin's discussion of Bloom: Okin 1989, 35.

seen a renewed interest in the difference of gender and, in particular, the unique nature of motherhood. Fineman argues that women live a gendered existence; that is, women experience life differently from men and are constituted by those experiences, some of which are biologically based, others of which are rooted in culture (Fineman 1995, 48). In her view, reproduction and parenting are thus unique experiences for women (see also Lind 2006) and the path to true equality lies not in a gender neutral society, but in taking those experiences seriously and ending the devaluation of women's distinctive reproductive and mothering roles (discussed in Okin 1989, 68). In short, rather than seeking to obliterate the difference of gender, feminists such as Fineman argue that gender differences should be celebrated and valued.

Belief in the unique nature of the mother–child relationship clearly remains deeply entrenched within Western society.[35] Despite all the rhetoric surrounding the birth of the 'hands-on' father, empirical data suggests that parenting remains a deeply gendered activity (Smart and Neale 1999; *cf* Morris 2007, 997). The question of whether these differences are socially constructed or rooted in nature has caused considerable debate within the feminist literature (Fineman 1995, 34–35).[36] However, as Fineman rightly points out, to a considerable extent the cause of gender difference is of little importance (Fineman 1995, 34). The fact remains that those differences are real and 'have real material effects on women' (Fineman 1995, 35). Gender neutrality in a deeply gendered world can be a significant cause of injustice and to single-mindedly strive for the utopian goal of gender neutrality whilst ignoring the current reality of women's lives risks worsening not improving their legal position:

> Typically, it is women who bear the costs of the expectations associated with such intimate relations [family life] in our society. Women are not compensated for bearing these costs, and in the make-believe world of abstract legal equality they are, in fact, penalized ... Neutral treatment in a gendered world or within a gendered institution does not operate in a neutral manner, however ... There are more and more empirical studies that indicate that mothers' relative positions have worsened in our new ungendered doctrinal world. Ignoring differences in favour of assimilation has not made the differences in gender expectations and behavior disappear. These differences operate to women's disadvantage as the material implications of motherhood, for example, have negative consequences in the context of career development and opportunity. (Fineman 1995, 26)

---

35   Baroness Hale recently emphasized the 'unique' nature of genetic motherhood in a residence dispute between lesbian co-parents: see, *Re G (Children) (Residence: Same-sex partner)* [2006] UKHL 43; [2006] 1 WLR 2305, at [36].

36   If these differences are socially constructed the law can arguably play an important role in bringing about social reform. However, Fineman is sceptical.

Fineman is particularly concerned that, as a result of liberal feminism's suspicion of motherhood, feminism has contributed to the devaluation of motherhood in law whilst fathers have been able to gain important rights 'based on assertions of sameness and rejection of ideas of difference between the social roles of mother and father' (Fineman 1995, 28).[37] In Fineman's view, this elimination of the gendered concept of motherhood, has worked to the considerable disadvantage of women:

> The law's reluctance to recognize and accommodate the uniqueness of Mother's role in child rearing conforms to the popular gender-neutral fetish at the expense of considerations for Mother's material and psychological circumstances. Even if the ultimate goal is gender neutrality, the immediate imposition of rules embodying such neutrality within the family law context is disingenuous. The effect is detrimental to those who have constructed their lives around gendered roles. (Fineman 1995, 88–89)

The insights of feminists such as Fineman warn against an uncritical acceptance of the 'equality' arguments advanced in *Evans*. Whether biologically or socially rooted, 'motherhood' is core to the identity of many women. It is central to what they are or what they hope to become. To be unable to realize such a core aspect of one's imagined identity can be the cause of immense pain. For some women, to be unable to carry, give birth to, and raise their own child is to see their entire life's purpose disappear. The particular importance of motherhood to women was recognized by Arden LJ giving judgement in the Court of Appeal in *Evans*:

> Infertility can cause the woman or man affected great personal distress. In the case of a woman, the ability to give birth to a child gives many women a supreme sense of fulfilment and purpose in life. It goes to their sense of identity and to their dignity ... [M]any women feel parenthood gives them an assurance of their position in society. Parenthood is a very important matter to women, even today.[38]

This is not to say of course that some men do not have similarly strong feelings about fatherhood. However, no matter how laudable our goals of achieving equality through gender neutrality in our private and public lives, the reality with which we live now is one in which our experiences of, and responses to, parenting, reproduction and infertility are deeply gendered. To put it boldly, *many* women do still invest a great deal more in reproduction and parenting than men[39] and whilst

---

37   This has been seen in the courts' changing approach to residence and contact disputes.

38   *Evans v Amicus Healthcare Ltd and others* [2004] EWCA Civ 727, at [81].

39   Some feminist commentators would find such a conclusion deeply problematic. See, for example, Sheldon 2004a, 313.

there is truth in the argument that for the law to differentiate between men and women on this basis will simply reinforce and entrench many harmful societal expectations and assumptions about women, to ignore the current reality of women's lives and the very real pain that life-changing problems such as infertility can cause, is to pursue gender neutrality at an unacceptable cost. A better balance must be found.

Gender Equality and the Consent Requirements in the Human Fertilisation and Embryology Act 1990 In order to achieve true, substantive equality, there is a persuasive argument that the social (and perhaps biological) assumptions and pressures operating particularly strongly upon women need to be accounted for in our legal regulation of reproduction, and infertility treatment in particular. Equality cannot be achieved within this context by some abstract notion of equality of treatment. Yet, the bright-line approach embodied in Schedule 3 of the HFE Act 1990 allows no room for the gendered nature of these issues to be considered. Consequently, although some men may fall victim to the strict consent requirements of Schedule 3, the law, as it currently stands, is likely to impact particularly harshly on women. To remedy this potential injustice, it could be argued, in general terms, that women's greater investment in reproduction and parenting (allied, some would argue, to the greater investment women make in the IVF process in particular) justifies locating control over all embryos whether or not ex vivo in the woman. The bright-line would be fixed, as it is in natural procreation, at fertilization, from which point on control would vest exclusively in the woman. This would address the concern of feminists who observe that reproduction technologies have facilitated the 'conceptual separation of Mother and Child' and allowed men to reassert their control over a woman's reproductive decision-making (Fineman 1995, 217). A man's equal decision-making authority over frozen embryos provides one such example of men regaining control in the sphere of reproduction – a point that Deech's comments on the Evans decision come close to endorsing.

However, whilst the gendered nature of reproduction must be taken seriously, to introduce a blanket provision vesting total control over all frozen embryos exclusively in the woman would be based on generalized, stereotypical assumptions about *all* men and women that would be as harmful to women's equality as the current approach. What is needed is a way for the law, whilst founded on the ideal of gender neutrality, to be able to respond appropriately to the individual circumstances of women. To argue that a woman's greater investment in reproduction and parenting justifies her exclusive control over all frozen embryos is also to misunderstand the nature of the interests at stake. The woman's core interest in motherhood will not usually be entirely vested in the particular embryos at issue. The importance of the frozen embryos lie in what they represent: the chance of motherhood. Where future treatment is possible, allowing the frozen embryos to perish will not deprive the woman of that chance. Her reproductive liberty will not have been destroyed. She can undergo further rounds of IVF treatment with a new partner or using donor sperm. In the majority of disputes over frozen embryos, the woman's interest in using *these particular embryos* to realize her ambition of motherhood will therefore not be sufficiently strong to justify overriding the reproductive rights and interests of her former partner. To put it in Convention terms, her right to procreative liberty under Article 8(1) will have been infringed but not totally negated, making it much harder to sustain the argument that her partner's reproductive rights and interests are not capable of justifying the interference under Article 8(2). In such cases, absent any contrary agreement (see below), insisting on mutual consent to the continued use and storage of embryos as currently required by Schedule 3 will thus produce a fair and just result to both parties.

Evans was, however, different. The removal of Natallie Evans' ovaries meant that the effect of Schedule 3 of the HFE Act 1990 was to deprive her of *any chance* of becoming a genetic parent. And that is what makes the difference. It is these kind of exceptional circumstances to which the law should be able to respond. Whilst it is recognized that fathering a child with whom you do not want a relationship may cause feelings of anguish, guilt and distress,[40] it is difficult to read the *Evans* case without having considerable sympathy with the view that denying Natallie Evans the chance to use the embryos in future treatment had a more devastating impact on her.[41] The reason is not, however, exclusively rooted in general considerations of gender. Whilst undoubtedly underpinned by societal expectations about the role of women and the continuing importance attributed to 'motherhood' in contemporary society, Natallie Evans's greater investment in these particular embryos is rooted in a combination of the general impact of gender and the gendered nature of her infertility in particular.

The bright-line approach of the HFE Act 1990 rendered the particular nature of Natallie Evans's infertility totally irrelevant in the decision-making process. It should not have been. Natallie Evans and her former partner found themselves in this position because of her infertility and because this was the only realistic medical treatment available which could preserve her capacity to become a genetic parent. However, a woman in Natallie Evans's position is made intensely vulnerable by the terms of Schedule 3. As both Sheldon and Lind point out, gender considerations are again particularly important in this context. Whilst we may feel considerable sympathy for an infertile man, infertile women in the position of Evans are particularly disadvantaged because of the lack of alternative options

---

40   See, for example, the comments of Arden LJ in *Evans v Amicus Healthcare Ltd and others* [2004] EWCA Civ 727, at [89]. Many of the male progenitor's concerns would, however, be met if legal fatherhood could be effectively excluded. See the discussion at n. 28 above.

41   This was also the conclusion reached by the four dissenting judges of the Grand Chamber in *Evans v UK*. See *Evans v UK* [2007] 2 FCR 5, at [6] (dissenting judgement).

to embryo freezing (Sheldon 2004a, 313–315; Sheldon 2004b; Lind 2006).[42] Whilst the law should be able to respond to an infertile man finding himself in a similar position to Evans and wanting to use frozen embryos from previous treatment for future treatment with a new partner or surrogate, given the wide availability of sperm freezing, it is unlikely that an infertile man would find himself in this position. This difference in available treatment renders women much more vulnerable under the HFEA's scheme.[43] As things stand, an infertile woman loses control over her ability to become a genetic parent at the point of fertilization. From that point on, her reproductive options are effectively subjected to a male veto. Should that veto be exercised, her reproductive rights vested in the embryos are destroyed. She will have lost her last chance to realise genetic motherhood.[44] Again, to put it in Convention terms, her Article 8 right is not just infringed, its very core is totally negated.[45] Of course it can be argued, looking at it from the man's perspective, that allowing the embryos to be transferred to the woman totally destroys his right to reject genetic fatherhood. However, we are again driven back to the crucial question of whether the interests are really of the same import. In these particular circumstances, given the combination of the gendered nature of infertility treatment, reproduction and parenting in our society, they are not (for the contrary view, see Annett 2006, 428–430). As it was put in the dissenting judgement of the lower Chamber of the European Court:

> Denying the implantation of the embryos amounts in this case not to a mere restriction but to a total destruction of her right to have her own child. In such a case the Convention case-law is clear and does not allow a State to impair the very essence of such an important right, either through an interference or by non-compliance with its positive obligations. We do not think that a legislative

---

42   Whilst the freezing of sperm to preserve male fertility is widely available, egg freezing remains at an experimental stage – although there have been some important recent developments in this field. See, for example, developments reported on BBC News online. <http://news.bbc.co.uk/2/hi/health/6975363.stm>.

43   The dissenting judgement of the Grand Chamber of the European Court of Human Rights endorsed this position in general terms holding: 'a woman is in a different situation as concerns the birth of a child, including where the legislation allows for artificial insemination methods ... different situations require different treatment. We see the circumstances of the applicant in this light not least because of the excessive physical and emotional burden and effects caused by her condition, and it is on this basis that we voted for a violation of Article 14 in conjunction with Article 8'. *Evans v UK* [2007] 2 FCR 5, at [14] (dissenting judgement).

44   See *Evans v UK* [2007] 2 FCR 5, at [6] (dissenting judgement). It is recognized that Evans could still have become a parent through the use of donated eggs or via adoption, but the overriding importance attributed to genetic parentage remains deeply entrenched within our society and should thus enjoy the law's protection. For discussion of our 'obsession' with genetic parentage, see Lind 2006; Morris 2007, 999.

45   See *Evans v UK* [2006] 1 FCR 585, at [2] (dissenting judgement).

scheme which negates the very core of the applicant's right is acceptable under the Convention.[46]

At the very least, the devastating impact of the withdrawal of consent when the embryos constitute the last possible opportunity for a woman to become a genetic parent is of sufficient consequence that exceptions should be possible to the Schedule 3 consent requirements. Bright lines impacting on the Convention rights of individuals should be subjected to particularly careful scrutiny. And whilst in the majority of cases Schedule 3's bright-line approach is a proportionate interference with the reproductive liberty of a gamete provider, it is disproportionate where the frozen embryos constitute the last opportunity for one of the gamete providers to have a genetically related child.[47] In such circumstances, in order to ensure a fair balance has been struck between the competing Article 8 rights of the parties, referral to the HFEA or the court must be possible.[48]

It was argued by the Court of Appeal in *Evans* that such a balancing exercise would be impossible, requiring a judgement based on a 'mixture of ethics, social policy, and human sympathy' and a 'balance to be struck between two entirely incommensurable things'.[49] The Court of Appeal concluded that such an approach would give rise to 'intractable difficulties of arbitrariness and inconsistency'.[50] However, both the HFEA and the family courts are very used to carrying out such difficult balancing exercises engaging social, ethical and philosophical considerations of the most profound kind. A dispute over frozen embryos is, for example, no more imponderable than a dispute over whether the creation of a 'saviour sibling' should be allowed. Indeed, on a number of occasions, courts in the US, in the absence of either statutory regulation or an enforceable agreement between the parties, have successfully carried out this difficult balancing of the parties' respective interests.

It is, however, important to note that the decisions of the US courts emphasize the need for caution in assuming that allowing a residual discretion to the HFEA or the courts will lead to better protection for infertile women such as Natallie Evans.

---

46   *Evans v UK* [2006] 1 FCR 585, at [2] (dissenting judgement).

47   The possibility of referring a dispute to the HFEA or the courts would be available to both gamete providers albeit there are likely to be many more women seeking such relief than men.

48   Where such a balancing of interests was carried out in the Israeli case of *Nachmani v Nachmani* 50(4) P.D.661 (Isr), the Court came down in favour of the infertile woman. In *Davis v Davis*, the Supreme Court of Tennessee came down in favour of the male partner, but, crucially, the female partner wanted to donate the embryos rather than use them in her own treatment. The Court indicated that the case would have been much closer if Ms Davis had wanted to use the embryos herself and could not achieve parenthood by any other means. See *Davis v Davis*, 842 S.W.2d 588, at [108].

49   *Evans v Amicus Healthcare Ltd and others* [2004] EWCA Civ 727, at [66] and [110].

50   *Evans v Amicus Healthcare Ltd and others* [2004] EWCA Civ 727, at [69].

Although none of the US decisions to date have concerned a case such as *Evans* where the embryos represented the last chance for one of the gamete providers to have their own genetically related child,[51] where a balancing of interests has been carried out, the courts have all regarded the right not to procreate or to be forced to become a parent against one's will as the determining factor. This suggests that even allowing exceptions to the Schedule 3 consent requirements and placing discretionary authority in the courts and the HFEA to determine disposition may not be sufficient to protect the interests of vulnerable parties such as Evans. In light of these concerns, an alternative, but hopefully more effective, mechanism for securing the interests of the infertile party will be considered below.

The Rights and Welfare of the Embryo

Before moving on to consider potential alternatives to the current statutory regime on the disposition of frozen embryos, it is important to note that even this relatively minor proposed amendment to allow exceptions to the Schedule 3 consent requirements and permit a more meaningful, individualized decision-making process in a few exceptional cases will have a further important advantage. Under the current statutory regime, and despite the welfare of the child purportedly being one of the 'twin pillars' of the legislation, the rights and interests of the embryo simply fall out of the equation where there is a dispute between the gamete providers as to the embryo's future storage and use. This is relatively unproblematic where the gamete providers are in agreement as to disposition, as the interests of the embryo would never be sufficiently strong to justify overriding the united reproductive rights and interests of the 'parents'. However, within the context of a dispute, the interests of the embryo are a potentially important consideration in determining the most appropriate outcome. To permit of exceptions to the bright-line approach entrenched in Schedule 3 of the HFE Act 1990 would thus have the additional advantage of providing space for the rights and interests of the embryo to be brought back within the decision-making process.

It is clear under English law that an embryo/foetus does not have independent legal personality and cannot be the holder of rights.[52] Although Strasbourg has been somewhat reticent to entirely exclude the legal personhood of the embryo, it has made it clear that the position taken in the UK is well within the State's margin of appreciation and is thus entirely consistent with the European Convention.[53]

---

51   It was noted in *Davis v Davis* that this would make the balancing exercise much closer. See *Davis v Davis*, 842 S.W.2d 588, at [109]. See also Robertson 1990, 413.

52   *In re F (in utero)* [1988] Fam 122; and *In re MB (Medical Treatment)* [1997] 2 FLR 426. For an alternative approach to the 'right-holding capacity' of an embryo, see Smith 2008.

53   See: *Paton v UK* (1980) 3 EHRR 408; and *Vo v France* (2004) (App. No. 53924/00), [2004] 2 FCR 577. For a general commentary on the European Court's indecisive approach

The European Court's position is neatly summarized in *Vo v France*: either the unborn child is not a 'person' directly protected by Article 2 or, if it is so protected, its rights are implicitly limited by the mother's rights and interests.[54] Evans's claim under Article 2 of the European Convention was therefore always very weak. It was not however beyond argument. Previous authorities have all dealt with the status of the embryo/foetus *in utero* and have thus all been decided within the highly sensitive context of its implications for the mother's potentially competing rights and interests, in particular its implications for abortion. As it was put in *Paton v UK*:

> The 'life' of the foetus is intimately connected with, and cannot be regarded in isolation from, the life of the pregnant woman. If article 2 were held to cover the foetus and its protection under this article were, in the absence of any express limitation, seen as absolute, an abortion would have to be considered as prohibited even where the continuance of the pregnancy would involve a serious risk to the life of the pregnant woman. This would mean that the 'unborn life' of the foetus would be regarded as being of a higher value than the life of the pregnant woman.[55]

Evans was, however, different because of the separation of the embryo from its physical dependence on the mother. The embryo's 'right to life' was thus being raised in a novel context and, most importantly, one in which the mother's physical integrity was not directly engaged. It was just possible that once the embryo's 'rights' were no longer directly entangled with those of the mother, space could be found for a different approach.

Despite the novel context in which the issue was being raised, it would, however, be extremely difficult to justify attributing a different legal status to the embryo depending on whether it was located inside or outside the woman's body. Either an embryo is capable of holding rights or it is not. If it is so capable and it is found that an *ex utero* embryo can hold an independent right to life under Article 2 of the European Convention, this would logically have to apply equally to embryos *in utero* with potentially far-reaching consequences for English law.[56] It is therefore not surprising that neither the domestic courts nor Strasbourg seriously addressed this question, both simply confirming their previous positions.[57] As Ford points

---

to the rights of embryos and foetuses under Article 2, see Hewson 2005.

54   *Vo v France* (2004) (App. No. 53924/00), [2004] 2 FCR 577, at [80].

55   *Paton v UK* (1980) 3 EHRR 408, 415.

56   Clearly such an approach would raise a strong but not insuperable challenge to the legality of abortion. For an attempt to reconcile attributing personhood and associated personhood rights to an embryos/foetus with the competing rights of a woman, see Smith 2008.

57   *Evans v Amicus Healthcare Ltd and others* [2004] EWCA Civ 727, at [19]; *Evans v UK* [2006] 1 FCR 585, at [45]–[46]; and *Evans v UK* [2007] 2 FCR 5, at [55]–[56].

out, whilst not a surprising outcome, this does at least make it clear in English law that when 'freed from its hopeless role as the powerless half of a conflict between legal person and legal non-person' the result is not the attribution of legal status and rights to an embryo or foetus, but a 'redistribution of control between the woman and others' (Ford 2008, 181).

The embryo's lack of personhood does not, however, mean it has no interests capable of protection under English law. As the European Court pointed out in *Vo*, the embryo's lack of rights under Article 2 does not preclude certain safeguards being extended to the unborn child.[58] Indeed, both the HFE Act 1990 and the Abortion Act 1967 are premised on the principle that the embryo/foetus, as a potential person, has a special status under English law worthy of protection.[59] Once fertilization has occurred and the process towards personhood has begun, interests thus attach to the embryo/foetus with those interests strengthening the closer the foetus comes to achieving independent personhood.[60] When so understood, it is clear that at the early embryonic stage the interests of the embryo will be weak. However, it is somewhat inconsistent with other areas of the law for Schedule 3 to preclude all consideration of the embryo's interests.

Throughout the *Evans* litigation, the courts seemed somewhat uncertain as to what to do with the welfare arguments. As both Wall J and the Court of Appeal recognized, the welfare of the child is core to the regulatory regime enshrined in the HFE Act 1990. Whilst some commentators, such as Emily Jackson, may strongly object to the use of the welfare principle to limit access to fertility treatment (it being argued that such matters should turn solely on the reproductive rights of the adult parties, see Jackson 2002), the relevance of the welfare principle in the context of pre-conception decision-making is firmly entrenched within the statutory framework.[61] Section 13(5) of the HFE Act 1990, at the time of the *Evans* decision, provided:

> A woman shall not be provided with treatment services unless account has been taken of the welfare of any child who may be born as a result of treatment

---

58   *Vo v France* (2004) (App. No. 53924/00), [2004] 2 FCR 577, at [80].

59   This approach is sometimes termed the 'gradualist' approach and was endorsed by the Warnock Committee. See DHSS 1984, [11.17].

60   This is exemplified by the Abortion Act 1967.

61   That said, doubts have been expressed in recent case law about whether welfare considerations such as those expressed in *Evans* can ever carry sufficient weight to override the fundamental right of a potential parent to reproductive liberty. See, for example, the comments of the Grand Chamber of the European Court of Human Rights in *Dickson v UK* (Application No. 44362/04) [2008] 1 FLR 1315, at [76]. See also the views of Charles J as to the relative importance of the welfare issues and the autonomy interests of the gamete providers when determining whether permission should be given for gametes to be stored pending export for treatment abroad: *L v the Human Fertilisation and Embryology Authority; Secretary of State for Health* [2008] EWHC 2149 (Fam), [2008] 2 FLR 1999, at [87].

(including the need of that child for a father), and of any other child who may
be affected by the birth.[62]

However, despite the centrality of the welfare principle to the HFE Act 1990,
Thorpe LJ and Sedley LJ, giving the majority judgement in the Court of Appeal,
failed to address the welfare arguments in any substantive way. To the extent that
Wall J at first instance attempted a welfare analysis, he focused on the welfare
of the future child as if he was conducting the exercise in the pre-conception
context. Having heard argument on the issue, he made only oblique reference to
the future child's welfare and the inability of Mr Johnston to play a full paternal
role.[63] This reflected the argument made on behalf of the Secretary of State who
had suggested it was an undesirable state of affairs for a child to be born against
his or her father's wishes.[64] In light of these comments, some commentators have
criticized the *Evans* decision for entrenching opposition to non-traditional families,
in particular single motherhood, which, as explicitly embodied in section 13(5) at
the time, continues to be targeted as a deviant family form (see, for example,
Scully-Hill 2004). Certainly, the welfare arguments when interpreted in this way
dovetailed neatly with Mr Johnston's position as to why he should not be forced
to become an 'absent' genetic father against his will. However, regardless of one's
views as to the impact on a child's welfare of being raised without a father, the
welfare arguments should not have been reduced to a rudimentary debate on the
desirability or otherwise of single motherhood.

Only Arden LJ attempted to grapple with the real welfare question which was
how these arguments should be resolved now we had moved from the abstract
realm of pre-conception decision-making to a situation in which there were actual
embryos in existence and in which specific interests could therefore vest. Once
we are concerned with actual, as opposed to hypothetical, potential persons,
the welfare arguments are fundamentally different (see generally, Harris-Short
2003). In fact, the answer to the welfare question is very clear. The interests of the
embryo, if they point anywhere, must point to being born. It is clearly nonsensical
to suggest that it would be better for the embryo not to be born than to be born
without a father. Arden LJ attempts to avoid this conclusion by distinguishing
between the *current* interests of the embryo and the *future* hypothetical interests of
the 'child', holding that only the latter falls within the scope of section 13(5).[65] On

---

62   Section 14(2)(b) of the Human Fertilisation and Embryology Act 2008 amends s.
13(5) to provide: 'A woman shall not be provided with treatment services unless account
has been taken of the welfare of any child who may be born as a result of the treatment
(including the need of that child for *supportive parenting*), and of any other child who may
be affected by the birth.'

63   *Evans v Amicus Healthcare Ltd and others* [2003] EWHC 2161 (Fam), at [258]
and [319].

64   *Evans v Amicus Healthcare Ltd and others* [2003] EWHC 2161 (Fam), at [239].

65   *Evans v Amicus Healthcare Ltd and others* [2004] EWCA Civ 727, at [84].

the strict wording of section 13(5), that interpretation is perfectly defensible, albeit it requires some mental gymnastics to focus on the future welfare of an existing embryo once born, to the exclusion of its current interest in being born. However, when combined with Schedule 3, the effect of Arden LJ's approach is to render the very existence of the embryo and its special status under English law entirely irrelevant in the decision-making process. This hardly seems correct – it accords greater respect to the interests of a non-existent hypothetical being than one who currently exists.

The problem, as perceived by Arden LJ, is that to admit of the relevance of the embryo's current interests would lead to a fundamental tension in the Act between the embryo's interest in being born and the reproductive liberty of the gamete providers:

> If the life of a child began before the relative embryo was transferred to a woman, it would always (or very nearly always) be in the interests of the child for the embryo to be so transferred unless the mother had contracted some disease which would deprive the child of any meaningful standard of life when born. If indeed the life of a child began before transfer of the relative embryo to a woman, the genetic father would never have any ability to withdraw his consent after the embryo had been created. Nor could an embryo ever be destroyed.[66]

There are, however, several points of confusion in Arden LJ's analysis. She appears to assume that to give consideration to the current interests of the embryo requires the court to treat the embryo in exactly the same way as it would treat a child enjoying full personhood, even to the extent that a dispute over the disposition of a frozen embryo should be resolved in exactly the same way as a custody dispute over a child, with the child's welfare constituting the sole consideration. As Arden LJ suggests, such an approach would almost always favour implantation whenever one of the genetic progenitors wants to use the embryo in further treatment.[67] Furthermore, should neither party wish to use the embryo for further treatment, a welfare-orientated approach would seem to require donation to another couple regardless of the gamete providers' wishes. However, as discussed above, it is not the case that in order to afford cognizable interests to the embryo it must be accorded the same legal status and the same weighty rights and interests as a 'child' – interests which would have an equivalent and perhaps overriding weight when balanced against those of the adult gamete providers. The embryo can hold distinctive interests of its own, albeit they will be much weaker than those that would be held by a child enjoying full personhood. Furthermore, in balancing the interests of the embryo against the reproductive liberty of the adults, the interests of the embryo (a non-person) would not be strong enough to defeat the united reproductive choices of the gamete providers (persons enjoying full rights

---

66 *Evans v Amicus Healthcare Ltd and others* [2004] EWCA Civ 727, at [84].
67 *Davis v Davis*, 842 S.W.2d 588, at [42].

in English law). Therefore, where there was agreement between the two gamete providers, the embryos could clearly be destroyed. Similarly, there would never be any question of forcing a woman to carry an embryo to term against her wishes as the embryo's interests could never justify such a grave violation of the woman's physical integrity. The independent interests of the embryo could, however, play an important part in the decision-making process where the gamete providers are in dispute and an exception to the statute's absolute requirement of mutual ongoing consent to use and storage is justified. In such a case, the interests of the embryo would clearly stand united with the party seeking to preserve and use the embryos in future treatment.[68] And although it is important not to overstate the interests of the embryo which, at such an early stage in its development would not be strong, they may just be sufficient to tip the balance in favour of the infertile party in a finely balanced case such as *Evans*.

Should the Parties be Able to 'Contract Out' of the Schedule 3 Requirements?

Given the uncertainties surrounding any exercise of discretion by decision-making bodies such as the HFEA, it is finally important to consider whether a more radical reform of the statutory regime enshrined in the HFE Act 1990 is required in order to more securely protect the interests of an adult gamete provider in any embryos resulting from treatment using his/her eggs or sperm. It was, for example, argued on behalf of Natallie Evans in the *Evans* case that a promissory estoppel had arisen to prevent Mr Johnston from withdrawing his consent to the storage and use of the embryos in her future treatment. The promissory estoppel was founded on representations allegedly made to Ms Evans by Mr Johnston about the future use of the embryos at the time of their initial consultation concerning the IVF treatment, such representations having arguably been relied upon by Ms Evans to her detriment making it unconscionable for Mr Johnston to now be permitted to withdraw his consent to the embryos being used.[69] The argument was unanimously dismissed at first instance and in the Court of Appeal, both on its facts (Wall J finding that Mr Johnston had not given Natallie Evans any such clear, unequivocal assurance that the embryos created using his sperm would always be available for her use[70]) and on the law (it being held that a promissory estoppel could not arise in the face of clear contrary terms in the legislation permitting Mr Johnston to withdraw his consent to the continued storage and use of the embryos at any point

---

68   Although there would never be any question of forcing the female gamete provider to carry the child against her wishes, the male gamete provider could seek to use the embryos in future treatment with a new partner or surrogate.

69   *Evans v Amicus Healthcare Ltd and others* [2003] EWHC 2161 (Fam), at [12].

70   *Evans v Amicus Healthcare Ltd and others* [2003] EWHC 2161 (Fam), at [306].

until they were used in treatment).[71] Both Wall J at first instance and the Court of Appeal were absolutely clear that gamete providers were not free to opt out of the statutory scheme and that 'any agreement or understanding between those receiving IVF treatment must be unenforceable unless it complies fully with the scheme'.[72] However, although rejected in the *Evans* case, the arguments surrounding the possibility of invoking promissory estoppel to prevent Mr Johnston withdrawing his consent raise the interesting question of whether it would produce a fairer result, particularly to the more vulnerable infertile party, if all gamete providers were to be permitted to 'contract out' of the statutory requirements of Schedule 3 and, in effect, give an irrevocable consent to the storage and future use of the embryos at the outset of the treatment.[73]

To allow the disposition of frozen embryos to be determined by way of private agreement between the parties is the approach which has tended to be adopted in the United States where few states have statutory regulation in place.[74] In *Davis v Davis* and *Kass v Kass*, the Supreme Court of Tennessee and the New York Court of Appeals agreed respectively that where the parties have entered into an agreement over the disposition of the embryos, the agreement should be upheld and the dispute determined in accordance with its terms.[75] There are many advantages to adopting a contractual approach which make it an attractive alternative to exclusive and exhaustive statutory regulation. Many of those advantages were identified by the New York Court of Appeals in *Kass v Kass*:

> Explicit agreements avoid costly litigation in business transactions; they are all the more necessary and desirable in personal matters of reproductive choice, where the intangible costs of any litigation are simply incalculable. Advance directives, subject to mutual change of mind that must be jointly expressed, both minimize misunderstandings and maximize procreative liberty by reserving to the progenitors the authority to make what is in the first instance a quintessentially

---

71   *Evans v Amicus Healthcare Ltd and others* [2003] EWHC 2161 (Fam), at [296].

72   *Evans v Amicus Healthcare Ltd and others* [2003] EWHC 2161 (Fam), at [294]– [295].

73   This ability to contract out of the Schedule 3 consent requirements would be available to all parties entering into IVF. It would thus have a much wider impact than affording a residual discretion to the courts or the HFEA to permit the storage and use of frozen embryos despite the lack of effective consent where the embryos represent the last chance of one of the gamete providers to have their own genetically related child.

74   *Evans v UK* [2007] 2 FCR 5, at [43]. See *Davis v Davis*, 842 S.W.2d 588, 597 (Tenn. 1992); *Kass v Kass*, 91 N.Y.2d 554, 696 N.E.2d 174, 673 N.Y.S.2d 350 (1998); *Litowitz v Litowitz*, 146 Wash. 2d 514, 48 P.3d 261 (2002). A useful summary of the US case law has been published by the National Legal Research Group and is available at <http://www.divorcesource.com/research/dl/children/03mar54.shtml>. This is also the solution suggested by Annett. See Annett 2006, 433.

75   *Davis v Davis*, 842 S.W.2d 588, at [66]–[67].

personal, private decision. Written agreements also provide the certainty needed for effective operation of IVF programs.[76]

To permit private ordering in the sphere of fertility treatment would maximize the autonomy and individual procreative liberty of all patients, allowing the parties themselves, with the safeguard of statutory regulation should they fail to do so, to exercise control over how they wish any surplus stored embryos to be dealt with. As Robertson puts it, 'it gives the parties the opportunity jointly to determine their reproductive futures' (Robertson 1990, 414). Any other approach, even statutory regulation based on the principle of consent, imposes limits on the reproductive liberty of the parties by vesting dispositional authority in others. Although this reform would be of benefit to all patients undertaking fertility treatment, it would be of particular benefit to vulnerable infertile patients, such as Evans, where the embryos represent their last possible opportunity to have a genetically related child. A contractual approach encourages patients to address the difficult question of disposition at the outset of their treatment, ensuring that the particularly vital question of whether the infertile partner will be able to continue to use the embryos for his/her treatment in the event of separation or divorce is openly and transparently discussed and resolved. Provided agreement is reached, this approach allows for 'irrevocable consent' to be given to the use of gametes in any further treatment, thus providing real certainty and reassurance to the more vulnerable infertile party before embarking on the first cycle of IVF. Conversely, lack of agreement would alert the more vulnerable party to the need to explore alternatives.

Allowing the parties to reach prior agreement on the disposition of surplus embryos would not be to enter uncharted territory for the UK. Patients are already required to address the issue of how frozen embryos are to be disposed of in the event of the incapacity or death of one of the gamete providers.[77] What is not currently addressed in an open and transparent way is the disposal of embryos in the event of separation or divorce. The apparent reluctance to address this issue lies in the presumed implications of any suggestion that separation or divorce is in the contemplation of the parties for the welfare assessment carried out under section 13(5). This was clear from the *Evans* case where the evidence from the clinic was that should Ms Evans have wanted to pursue the possibility of egg freezing in case Ms Evans and Mr Johnston should separate it would have raised question marks over the stability of Ms Evans's and Mr Johnston's relationship and necessitated reconsideration of their suitability for treatment together.[78] This

---

76   *Kass v Kass*, 91 N.Y.2d 554, 696 N.E.2d 174, 673 N.Y.S.2d 350 (1998).

77   See, for example, s. 5 of HFEA consent form MT, Consent to the use of sperm and use and storage of embryos in own treatment or research. Available from the HFEA website at: <http://www.hfea.gov.uk/en/1339.html>.

78   *Evans v Amicus Healthcare Ltd and others* [2003] EWHC 2161 (Fam), at [56]. The difficulties caused by the clinic's dual role as health-care provider and welfare 'policeman' are discussed by Sheldon 2004b.

somewhat naïve approach risks prejudicing the ability of a vulnerable patient to make clear, sensible and properly informed decisions about his/her treatment. Given the enormous consequences of the decision for the infertile party, it is eminently sensible for the question of disposal to be openly discussed without the operation of any constraints brought about by fears that it will lead to an adverse judgement as to whether or not treatment should be permitted on the basis of the child's welfare. Moreover, it should be remembered that any agreement over who should exercise control of the embryos in the event of separation or divorce would not preclude reconsideration of the welfare issues by the clinic in light of the changed circumstances before the clinic would be prepared to continue to use the embryos in the treatment of one of the gamete providers either alone or with a new partner.

To allow private ordering to determine the disposition of frozen embryos is not, however, without its difficulties – difficulties which have been evident in the US case law. Problems may arise over the enforceability of the agreement. A fatal ambiguity in the terms of the agreement may mean that it cannot be enforced – although such a problem would be easily avoided by the use of standardized forms.[79] There also remain serious questions as to the basic enforceability of contracts governing reproduction on grounds of public policy. In the US decisions of *A.Z. v B.Z.*[80] and *J.B. v M.B.*,[81] the Supreme Judicial Court of Massachusetts and the Superior Court of New Jersey, respectively, refused to uphold the parties' initial agreements (assuming they had been sufficiently clear) over the disposal of the embryos on grounds of public policy. The Supreme Court of Massachusetts held that, 'it would not enforce an agreement that would compel one donor to become a parent against his or her will' and that as a matter of public policy 'forced procreation is not an area amenable to judicial enforcement'.[82] The Superior Court of New Jersey similarly concluded that 'a contract to procreate is contrary to New Jersey public policy and is unenforceable'.[83] Clearly, to remove any lingering uncertainty, it would be necessary for the enforceability of such agreements in the UK to be put on a clear statutory footing by way of amendment to the HFE Act 1990.

More difficult to resolve is the problem of the passage of time between the agreement being made and the point at which its terms become operative (Robertson 1990, 418). The agreement will have been made in a relative vacuum, with assumptions made on the basis of an uncertain future. Given the length of time that has passed since the agreement was entered into, it may be perceived as grossly unfair or inappropriate to one or both parties to enforce the agreement

---

79   This was just one of the problems leading to the non-enforceability of the initial agreement in *A.Z. v B.Z.*, 431 Mass. 150, 725 N.E.2d 1051 (2000).

80   *A.Z. v B.Z.*, 431 Mass. 150, 725 N.E. 2d 1051 (2000).

81   2001 WL 909294.

82   Cited in *J.B. v M.B.*, 2001 WL 909294, at [44].

83   *J.B. v M.B.*, 2001 WL 909294, at [54].

in light of their changed circumstances. In the intervening period, for example, the female partner may have had to have her ovaries removed, fundamentally changing the importance of the embryos to her reproductive future. Whilst it can be argued, as Robertson does, that in such circumstances it would be just as unfair to the male partner to deprive him of the protection of his contract (Robertson 1990, 414, 420), the impact of these unknowns is just one reason why the law has traditionally been reluctant to allow the regulation of intimate relationships and decisions made within those relationships to be governed by the uncompromising principles of contract law. Interestingly, the New York Court of Appeals agreed with Robertson, holding that uncertainty over future events made reaching an agreement before disputes developed, although 'extraordinarily difficult', even more important:

> Divorce; death, disappearance or incapacity of one or both partners; aging; the birth of other children are but a sampling of obvious changes in individual circumstances that might take place over time. These factors make it particularly important that courts seek to honor the parties' expressions of choice, made before disputes erupt, with the parties' overall direction always uppermost in the analysis. Knowing that advance agreements will be enforced underscores the seriousness and integrity of the consent process; advance arguments as to disposition would have little purpose if they were enforceable only in the event the parties continued to agree. To the extent possible, it should be the progenitors not the State and not the courts who by their prior directive make this deeply personal life choice.[84]

English law has, however, generally demonstrated a much stronger reluctance to preclude its discretionary oversight of agreements reached in the family context – although in this particular case the current alternative is similarly proscriptive. Whilst preserving to the greatest extent possible the advantages of allowing private ordering in the sphere of fertility treatment, it would thus be consistent with the general approach of English law to private ordering in the sphere of intimate relationships to reserve a limited degree of discretion to the courts or the HFEA to reconsider private agreements over the disposition of frozen embryos where intervening events have fundamentally changed the original basis on which the agreement was reached.

Conclusion

The UK's detailed statutory regulation of fertility treatment involving the creation, storage and use of embryos *ex utero* is widely regarded as a model of good practice. However, the inflexibility created by strict statutory regulation can

---

84   *Kass v Kass*, 91 N.Y. 2d 554, 696 N.E. 2d 174, 673 N.Y.S.2d 350 (1998).

also have significant disadvantages and is particularly concerning where it can be shown to impact disproportionately on the position of women. As dramatically demonstrated by the *Evans* case, certainty can come at an unacceptable price. The bright-line approach as enshrined in Schedule 3 of the HFE Act 1990 is too rigid, rendering infertile women intensely vulnerable to the changing will of the male gamete provider. In order to confer much greater protection on women such as Natallie Evans it is thus recommended that two amendments are introduced to the HFE Act 1990 to permit 'individualized justice' to be done in these difficult cases. The first amendment would be to permit *all* parties entering into IVF treatment to reach their own agreement at the outset of treatment as to the disposition of any surplus frozen embryos in the event of their separation or divorce. This would have the major advantage of giving the fullest possible respect to the autonomy of the parties to determine for themselves how any future dispute should be determined, as well as providing vital protection to individuals such as Natallie Evans who will be able to make a truly informed decision as to whether or not they should embark upon IVF with their current partner or explore the possibility of treatment with a donor. In the event of a dispute the terms of the agreement will be determinative unless it can be shown that some supervening event, such as one of the gamete providers unexpectedly being rendered incapable of producing further eggs or sperm, has fundamentally undermined the premises on which the agreement was originally made. In such very rare cases, referral to the court or HFEA should be possible for the respective interests of the parties to be considered afresh. The second amendment would deal with cases where no agreement was entered into between the parties before embarking upon treatment and the statutory regime as currently enshrined in Schedule 3 of the HFE Act 1990 would therefore apply. In such cases, the default position would be that both gamete providers would, at any point, be able to withdraw their consent to the continued storage and use of the embryos until they were actually used in treatment. This approach would achieve the correct balance between the respective rights of the gamete providers in the majority of cases. However, in order to ensure infertile women are not unfairly disadvantaged by the terms of the legislation (although any statutory exceptions would of course apply equally to men and women), Schedule 3 must permit of exceptions to allow a genuine balancing of interests and the consent of a gamete provider to be overridden where the circumstances are sufficiently compelling. Because the core interest at stake is the right to become a genetic parent, this exception should be limited to cases where the embryos genuinely represent the last chance for one of the gamete providers (whether male or female) to have their own genetically related child. However, in such circumstances, the reason why no agreement as to the disposition of the embryos was entered into at the outset of treatment would clearly be an important consideration for the court or the HFEA when balancing the respective interests of the parties.

This approach to the storage and use of frozen embryos is clearly much more complex than the current statutory regime. However, given the huge importance of the interests at stake, the need for certainty, whilst important, should not be the overriding consideration. In this most deeply personal and sensitive area, where individual circumstances can change dramatically, individuals must be allowed the legal space to secure their own interests as they consider best, with the law retaining its discretionary power to protect what for many will be the most important defining factor in their lives: the chance to become a genetic parent. Given the gendered nature of fertility treatment, reproduction and parenting in our society, the impact of denying that chance to someone in the position of Evans needs to be properly provided for in the law. And although there is a very real danger that this approach will reinforce problematic societal assumptions about the centrality of (genetic) motherhood to women's lives, the need for the law to respond effectively to the experiences of ordinary women, and within this particular context the very deep and debilitating pain of infertility, should remain at the heart of the feminist agenda.

References

Annett, T. (2006), Balancing Competing Interests over Frozen Embryos: The Judgment of Solomon?, *Medical Law Review* 14, 425.

Boulton, A. (1996), Britain Poised to extend Storage of Frozen Embryos, *British Medical Journal* 312, 10.

Collier, R. (2003), In Search of the 'Good Father': Law, Family Practices and the Normative Reconstruction of Parenthood, in Dewar, J. and Parker, S. (eds), *Family Law Processes: Practices and Pressures*, (Hart).

Deech, R. (2006), Head to Head – Frozen Embryos, BBC news online, Tuesday 7 March 2006. Available at <http://news.bbc.co.uk/2/hi/health/4781536.stm>.

Department of Health and Social Security (1984), *Report of the Committee of Inquiry into Human Fertilisation and Embryology*, July 1984, Cm. 9314.

Fineman, M. (1995), *The Neutered Mother, the Sexual Family and Other Twentieth Century Tragedies*, (Routledge).

Ford, M. (2008), *Evans v United Kingdom*: What Implications for the Jurisprudence of Pregnancy?, *Human Rights Law Review* 8, 171.

Hewson, B. (2005), Dancing on the head of a pin? Foetal life and the European Convention, *Feminist Legal Studies* 13, 363.

Harris-Short, S. (2003), An 'Identity Crisis' in the International Law of Human Rights? The Challenge of Reproductive Cloning, *International Journal of Children's Rights* 11, 333.

Human Fertilisation and Embryology Act (2007), *A long term analysis of the Human Fertilisation and Embryology Authority Register data (2001–2006)*.

Jackson, E. (2002), Conception and the Irrelevance of the Welfare Principle, *Modern Law Review* 65, 176.

Lind, C. (2006), *Evans v United Kingdom* – Judgments of Solomon: Power, Gender and Procreation, *Child and Family Law Quarterly* 18, 576.

McGlynn, C. (2001), European Union Family Values: Ideologies of 'Family' and 'Motherhood' in European Union Law, *Social Politics* 8, 325.

Morris, C. (2007), *Evans v United Kingdom*: Paradigms of Parenting, *Modern Law Review* 70, 979.

Okin, S. (1989), *Justice, Gender and the Family*, (Basic Books).

Robertson, J.A. (1990), Prior Agreements for Disposition of Frozen Embryos, *Ohio State Law Journal* 51, 407.

Scully-Hill, A. (2004), Consent, Frozen Embryos, Procreative Choice and the Ideal Family, *Cambridge Law Journal* 47.

Sheldon, S. (2004a), Gender equality and reproductive decision-making, *Feminist Legal Studies* 12, 303.

Sheldon, S. (2004b), 'Case commentary: Revealing Cracks in the 'twin pillars'?, *Child and Family Law Quarterly* 16, 437.

Smart, C. and Neale, B. (1999), *Family Fragments*, (Polity Press).

Smith, S. (2008), Precautionary Reasoning in Determining Moral Worth, in Freeman (ed.), *Law and Bioethics, Current Legal Issues*, vol. 11 (Oxford University Press).

Chapter 4

Persons and Their Parts: New Reproductive Technologies and Risks of Commodification[1]

Heather Widdows

Introduction

Over the last few decades the means of family creation have increased dramatically, as have the possible relationships within such 'new' families. For example, it is possible for a child created using, New Reproductive Technologies (NRTs) to have five 'parents': the sperm donor, the egg donor, the gestational mother, and the social mother and father who raise the child. However, despite such seemingly dramatic changes comparatively little attention has been paid to the social implications including the possible impact of such technologies on understandings of family structures and our expectations of children. This paper is going to explore this issue and ask, in particular, whether the possibilities afforded by such technologies result in more contractual and commodified understandings of children.[2] It will argue that there is a *prima facie* connection between body parts and persons and thus, although needing to be balanced with other ethically relevant factors, commodification remains an issue of ethical concern. Accordingly we should only be supporting potentially commodifying practices when there are ethically pressing reasons to do so (such as in organ transplantation). Moreover, given this link between body parts and persons we should attempt to lessen commodifying attitudes and thus should resist the increasing use of practices which regard children as having choose-able parts. In order to do this, first, the possibilities afforded by NRTs and their potential for commodification will be outlined; second, the commodification debate will be explored using the somewhat parallel example of commodification of organs; and third, in light of these debates the link between the commodification of body parts and persons will be addressed.

---

1 The chapter is a reprint of an article that first appeared in (2009) *Health Care Analsysis* 17, 36–46 and is reprinted by permission.

2 Other social consequences could also be explored. For example whether or not genetic-relatedness should be given such high priority in a society where most children do not live with two genetically related parents (Widdows 2006).

NRTs and their Commodificatory Potential

NRTs, particularly IVF, tends to be perceived (by both users of the technology and the wider public) in a benign manner and the risks and burdens of IVF are somewhat neglected even though they are not insubstantial: there are physical risks to the mother, coupled with psychological difficulties for the mother and the father, as well as ongoing financial pressures.[3] There are a number of reasons for this easy acceptance of such technologies – perhaps key among these are the 'cute factor' (the opposite of the often discussed 'yuk' factor) and the willingness of those involved to accept the risks. To caricature these positions for the sake of brevity: first, IVF results in a baby and a 'happy family', both regarded as positive goods and thus deemed acceptable: the 'cute factor'. By contrast, embryo research, for example, has no 'cute' outcome and is viewed by the public as far more problematic despite an overlap in ethical issues, such as the discarding of spare embryos: the yuk factor.[4] In addition, couples who engage in IVF accept the risks willingly regarding them as being of little importance. If we combine the willingness of the couple with the general positive attitude towards NRTs it

---

3   Physically the process of IVF is traumatic and demanding. Women undergo, at best, uncomfortable and, at worst, potentially dangerous processes of hormone therapy, follicle stimulation and egg harvesting. Moreover, the psychological stress that both women and partners are subject to in the process of ongoing IVF treatments is considerable; stress that is added to with every failed cycle of treatment (Ryan 2001). The physical and psychological pressures are compounded by a significant financial burden: a cycle of IVF costs around £3,000 to £4,000. For many couples, meeting the cost of the treatment means a severe reduction in quality of life. For example, one couple in a UK study spent £60,000 on consecutive IVF treatments which meant that, for the duration of the treatment, they were unable to go on holiday, make repairs and improvements to their home and move house, all of which they report they would have done if they had not had to pay for treatment (MacCallum 2004). In addition to the risks to the woman there are also risks to the child, risks derived from the likelihood of multiple gestations. As Mary Mahowald notes 'with each order of multiples, risks to both the fetus and pregnant women escalate' (Mahowald 2002). The risks for the child include not only increased risks in pregnancy and birth (such as respiratory distress and haemorrhage), but also long-term risks and disadvantages associated with premature births (Vayena & Rowe 2002; Olivennes et al. 2002). However the physical risks to the child are reduced as the possibility of multiple births is reduced – something which is increasingly legislated for (it is best practice in the UK is to implant one embryo).

4   The yuk factor is used in bioethics to refer to an emotional rather than reasoned rejection of certain scientific advances. Rather than providing reasons, a practice or procedure is rejected out of hand as 'revolting', 'repugnant', 'repulsive' and 'grotesque'. The term was used particularly with regard to the cloning debate – procedures which were initially uniformly rejected as unethical, and even inhuman – despite the obvious naturally occurring instances of clones in the form of identical twins. This is the classic example of the 'yuk' factor at work – and it is something that bioethicists tend to take seriously as they attempt to unearth moral significance behind such rejection (Midgely 2000).

is unsurprising that whether or not to undergo treatment tends to be viewed as a personal decision and not as an issue of public controversy and social concern.

As a result of this easy acceptance, broader cultural and social consequences are under-theorized and under-researched; including whether or not the use of repo-tech changes our expectations of children created through these technologies (and potentially affects our expectations of all children). For, although the technology might be welcomed in many, even all, individual cases, it might still have damaging social effects; for example, the cumulative effect of these individual cases might be to shift social attitudes towards reproduction in an undesirable way. It is not hard to imagine that the increasing use of such technologies gradually normalizes them to the point where the 'technical fix', and all the options and choices this offers parents pre-birth, becomes regarded as a standard conception option. Such uses of the technologies as valid options for all in order to choose traits, characteristics or parts of the resulting child is a very different scenario from using the technology in order to have 'one's own' child. In such a scenario, technologies of reproduction do not mimic natural conception and merely replicate the 'normal' conception process, but offer new reproductive possibilities and thus potentially change the ethos of reproduction. In particular, they potentially transform our expectations of the parenting relationship from one of 'gift' to one of 'contract' and thus potentially encourage a more commodified view of children.

If we consider IVF when used straightforwardly by couples simply wishing to have 'their own' child then such a shift seems unlikely. Couples are seeking a means of conceiving, giving birth to and raising a child, they are not looking for a particular type of child or a child with certain characteristics. The intention of these couples is essentially no different from couples who wish to have a child without assistance. Thus, in these instances the expectations of the child and the parenting relationship are unlikely to be vastly different from those who conceive naturally. Indeed the experience of infertility and the attendant struggles may enhance the unconditional elements of the relationship. However, if IVF is used for other reasons, for example in conjunction with pre-implantation genetic diagnosis (PGD) (to ensure the implanted embryo is healthy) or sex selection (for X-linked disorders, again in order to have a healthy child), it is possible that we are moving away from the notion of child as a 'gift' and beginning to set conditions. In such cases when the aim is to have a healthy child rather than a particular type of child or a child with certain parts or traits then there does not seem to be any dramatic move to commodity. Although there is a general risk that the increased use of such technologies normalizes intervention per se, however as long as that intervention is only to have a healthy child then the risk of commodity is small.

The issue becomes more complex when we turn to the now familiar debate regarding the legitimacy of deaf couples choosing to select 'deaf embryos' for social and cultural reasons, not for medical reasons. Parents argue that 'deafness is not a disability but a culture which they should be permitted to pass on' (Häyry 2004, 510) with 'distinct language, activities, and institutions of that culture' (Anstey 2002, 287). In such instances how would such parents respond if the deaf embryo they chose turned out to be a hearing child? Would their expectations be unmet and the potential relationship which they were able to have with the child impaired in a way which could not have happened without the possibility given by the technology of being able to choose a deaf child? Likewise, if sex selection is used not for medical reasons but to fulfil a parental preference, for example for a child of a certain sex for reasons of family balancing or social status, if the resulting child is not of the desired and expected sex will the parents be disappointed in a way that pre-NRTs they would not be? In other words, does the ability to choose – to technologically fix – particular parts of children or types of children, in this case to choose deafness or sex, change our expectations of children and commodify them?[5]

At this point other social and ethical issues come to the fore as well as issues of commodification, for example, concerns about eugenics as well as concerns about race and gender discrimination. These related issues also speak to concerns about the selection of certain types of children – for instance beautiful girls and clever boys. For example, it is now possible to purchase eggs from supermodels if one is seeking a beautiful girl, and sperm and eggs from intellectually successful donors if one is seeking a clever boy (the up-take suggests that it is clever boys and beautiful girls that are sought).[6] Alternatively one can choose a child of a different ethnicity and the fact that 'an Asian couple ... chose an egg from a blue-eyed blonde Scandinavian woman' is recorded (Rons' Angels). Thus, while not mainstream, NRTs are already being used not to ensure a healthy child or a genetically related child but a particular type of child or a child with particular characteristics.

If I pay money to have a beautiful, blonde-haired, blue-eyed girl or a clever tall boy and end up with a dark, ugly girl or a small stupid boy, has the contract been broken? Has the child already failed to live up to the expectations I was promised and paid for? Of course before the advent of NRTs, parents had expectations of their children and there are many instances of children being considered 'disappointments'. However, pre-NRTs, expectations regarding sex, deafness or eye colour were outside the control of parents. At least one could not be certain of having a child of a particular sex even if one did have intercourse at prescribed times and in prescribed ways, ate the recommended diet for the desired sex, prayed, used magic charms or any of the many long-standing practices which

---

5   Questions of commodification are also raised in the parallel debate about 'saviour siblings' in which a second child is created as a 'match' for the first (Sheldon and Wilkinson 2004).

6   The website suggests that you should use their services to have a 'better child' or, in the vocabulary of Rons' Angels, 'a better version of you' (Rons' Angels). It suggests that to do so is to give the best to your child as '[b]eauty is its own reward. This is the first society to truly comprehend how important beautiful genes are to our evolution ... Any gift such as beauty, intelligence or social skills will help your children in their quest for happiness and success' (Rons' Angels).

are said to influence the unborn child. Thus even if parents did all they could to influence the sex of their child they had none of the certainty that comes with the use of NRTs and they recognized that such choices were essentially out of their hands: they could not actually choose parts or types of children. However, when parts, traits and types of children become actually choose-able the terminology of commodification becomes applicable, and thus we must consider what commodification means in this context.

Commodification of Body Parts

A narrow understanding of commodification, defined by Radin as the '*actual buying and selling (or legally permitted buying and selling)* of something' (Radin 1987, 1859), clearly is not applicable to children. However, broader definitions which define commodification as a '*social practice* for treating things as commodities, i.e. as properties that can be bought, sold, or rented' (Resnik 1998, 388) – in this instance types or parts of children – might work well. A broad social definition succeeds in capturing this change in thinking and expectations and in the type of relationship invoked. For example Radin's broad definition which 'includes *not only actual buying and selling, but also market rhetoric, the practice of thinking about interactions as if they were sale transactions*' (Radin 1987, 1859) encompasses much of what is relevant here. In particular, the language of commodification is meant to capture elements of objectification – the transformation of persons into things onto which desires can be projected – as well as the contractual nature of the process brought about by the technological and financial elements. Commodification terminology is preferable to the discourse of objectification as it includes these financial and contractual factors, for while children are not bought and sold as such, commerce is an issue and all of these technologies from IVF to the purchasing of gametes are expensive. Commodification appropriately covers these aspects and the resulting expectations created by the financial transaction and the sense of entitlement to what has been purchased.[7] Thus the language of commodification indicates both a more objectified understanding of children and a more mechanical and contractual construction of the parenting relationship.

Commodification is an increasingly important issue in ethics where the debate has primarily focused the buying and selling of body parts. While clearly the debates about commodification of children and organs are different, there are some relevant similarities; most notably, for our purposes, questions about how body parts relate to persons. One of the claims made by those in favour of organ selling is that commodifying body parts does not lead to the commodification of persons. If this is true, then worries about parents selecting body parts or characteristics of their children – such as deafness, sex or blue eyes – prior to birth as being

---

7   There is a parallel debate about 'baby selling' and surrogacy which is also relevant to this discussion (Wilkinson 2003).

commodificatory are lessened. Whereas, if body parts are connected to persons then similar concerns arise, as commodification of parts of bodies may in fact be connected to the commodification of persons.

In addition to claiming that commodification of parts of bodies does not, in fact, lead to the commodification of persons, those in favour of the buying and selling of organs make two additional arguments for their position. However, neither of them is relevant to the commodification of persons debate as the first – that buying and selling of organs is a choice like any other – simply reduces all ethical issues to merely those of individual choice.[8] If one accepts this framework then commodification is a non-issue – as everything is permitted as long as it is chosen. The second argument – that organs are equally commodities whether they are donated or sold[9] – sidesteps commodification concerns by claiming that organs (often kidneys in the debate) are commodities in donation as much as they are in sale. Consequently either commodification is acceptable if donation is acceptable or commodifying body parts does not lead to the commodification of persons. Thus the argument we are left with and the one which directly parallels the concerns about children is the third argument – that commodification of parts of a body does not lead to the commodification of the person. Defenders of this view argue that:

---

8   For example, such an argument is put forward by Julian Savulescu, who argues that 'If we should be allowed to sell our labour, why not sell the means to that labour? If we should be allowed to risk damaging our body for pleasure (by smoking or skiing), why not for money which we will use to realise other goods in life? To ban a market in organs is, paradoxically to constrain what people can do with their own lives' (Savulescu 2003, 138–139). For Savulescu, seemingly the only, ethical issue is that of autonomous choice; thus he argues '[t]hink about a couple with two young children who are contemplating buying a house. They find one for £150,000, but in a heavily polluted and unsafe area. They could spend another £50,000 and live in a cleaner safer area. But they decide to save the money and expose their children to a greater risk in order to pay for private education … People take risks for money. They judge that the benefits for their own lives or their family's outweigh the risks. To prevent them making these decisions is to judge that they are unable to make a decision about what is best for their own lives' (Savulescu 2003, 139). In this framework, ethics is simply about choice and the avoidance of the curtailing of choice; thus commodification and all other issues are irrelevant.

9   This argument addresses what constitutes a commodity, namely its lack of subjectivity, its instrumentality and its fungibility (Wilkinson 2000). First, a kidney is not conscious nor does it have feelings; second, it has instrumental value only, in the sense that it is merely a means in the transplant process; and third, it is replaceable with any other kidney or money. However, even on these terms it is not clear that this is the end of the argument; for example, although in one sense it is true that for the recipient one kidney is replaceable by any other kidney, in the current landscape of scare resources the kidney is in some senses 'priceless' and thus not obviously or easily replaced by money.

> I might buy an organ from a friend for a 'generous' fee (because she needs the money and I need the organ), fully commodify *her organ*, but nevertheless not commodify *her*: i.e. I could continue throughout to regard her (*qua* person) as (a) having morally important subjective preferences etc. (b) non-instrumentally valuable, and (c) a unique and incommensurably valuable individual. Indeed, one could imagine such a mutually beneficial transaction taking place within the context of a loving personal relationship which was in no way commodificatory (as far as attitudes of one *person* to the other *person* are concerned). (Wilkinson, 2000, 196–197)

The claim then is that commodifying the organ does not result in the commodification of the person. However even if one was to grant that in this example commodifying the organ does not necessarily lead to the commodification of the person it is not clear that this is because there is no link between body parts and persons. More ethically pertinent in this instance are the background conditions, the context in which the sale takes place, namely, a 'loving personal relationship'. Because of the loving context the 'seller' is not seen primarily as a kidney-source, but rather as a whole person, with preferences, needs, character and moral significance – in short, as a 'friend'. This attitude of friendship is non-commodified and hence this sale is too. However, even if in this instance the sale of a body-part does not appear to lead to the commodification of the person, does it mean that there is no link between the commodification of body parts and the commodification of persons in all instances? Or rather, that other ethically significant factors are also in play which reduce and perhaps even nullify the commodificatory elements? If it is the second, then commodification is not a non-issue, but needs to be addressed as a *prima facie* concern.

Commodifying the Body Part and Commodifying the Person?

In order to assess whether it is other ethically relevant factors (such as the loving context) which make this instance of organ sale non-commodifying of the person or whether, as the friend example claims, there is no link between the commodifying of body parts and persons we will consider other examples of organ sale. If we consider kidney-selling in the third world, where the context is far from loving, commodification comes to the fore as the most important ethical concern. In such instances those who sell their kidneys – unlike the friend in the previous example – do connect their sense of self to their sale of the body parts and do consider themselves to have been treated as sources of commodities and thus commodified. For example, one seller said: 'we are worse than prostitutes because we have sold something we can never get back' (Scheper-Hughes 2003, 1647). Moreover, the effect on such kidney sellers is long term and substantial and kidney sellers experience '(for complicated medical, social, economic, and psychological reasons) chronic pain, ill health, unemployment, reduced incomes, serious depression and sense of worthlessness, family problems, and social isolation (related to the sale)' (Scheper-Hughes 2003, 1646).[10] Such examples suggest that, in at least some circumstances, there is indeed a link between commodifying body parts and regarding persons as commodities. If this is the case, it would suggest that it is the loving relationship which makes the sale of the organ non-commodifying, thus the context rather than the practice or act itself. In these instances, then, it is the context in which such acts take place that commodifies or does not commodify the person.

This link between body parts and persons is also evident in other instances, for example in the Alder Hey retention of organs scandal when large numbers body parts of children were retained without the knowledge of the parents, including over 2,000 hearts and 1,500 viable foetuses and still births. Here, the parents' main concern was not the lack of consent – the standard ethical concern of bioethicists – but rather the strong need parents felt to trace the body parts of their children. Indeed this wish to find the lost organs of their children was not about knowledge, but about the need to appropriately respect and put to rest the 'missing' parts of their children. Accordingly, there were many instances of parents having additional burial and cremation ceremonies for recovered organs and not only second but third funerals as organs were retrieved over time. Again, such behaviour indicates at least a default assumption that body parts are connected to persons, even if as only one ethically significant factor in any given situation and one which can be overridden by other concerns.

If we conclude then that there is some connection between body parts and persons, even if this is only one ethical concern among others, commodification merits consideration. This is as true for reproductive technologies when parents select parts or traits of their future children as for organ sale. It would also seem that there are levels of connection – all parts are not the same – with perhaps non-depletable parts such as hair and semen being regarded as less connected and thus less problematic than depletable parts and non-reversible practices such as organ sale or the pre-birth selection of characteristics. There are differences between the practices, for example in the case of repo-tech where parents choose body parts and characteristics no existing children are changed and no actual body parts are removed or rejected. However, if there is a relation between the commodification of body parts and persons which is of default ethical significance then simply viewing children as having choose-able parts and characteristics which can be purchased before birth may lead to more commodificatory attitudes. However, even if one accepts this line of argument and agrees that body parts are connected to persons and thus that commodification is a *prima facie* ethical issue, one might still counter that it is likely to be a relatively minor ethical issue in the context of the parenting relationship. Thus it is not likely to have a particularly harmful

---

10   Third world kidney sellers have been studied in India, Iran, the Philippines, and Moldova and all suffer these experiences (Scheper-Hughes 2003, 1646).

outcome or adverse effect on the child, especially if done merely for parental preference.

For example, one could imagine a situation where a mother chose that her child should have, say, green eyes on the ground that all the other family members including older siblings also have green eyes and around which various family myths and stories have developed. In this instance the mother's motives are loving; she wants to ensure that this child has the 'family trait' for greater family identification and to encourage feelings of security and love between the siblings and the wider family group.

What would be so very wrong with such a preference if it is done from concern for the child and for loving reasons of wanting to ensure an outward expression of the family bond – a physical manifestation of family connection and love? In such an instance – even if there is some ethical concern, (for example one might wonder about the strength of a family bond which needs such physical manifestation, just as one might wonder at what kind of a friendship requires payment for a life-saving gift) – one might be tempted to say that it is perhaps undesirable but relatively unimportant. However, such choices are only unimportant if individual cases are viewed as having no connection to, or impact on, wider attitudes regarding what is acceptable and general expectations of children. But if it is the case that the background conditions and the context are key to determining the extent to which commodification occurs, then social and cultural attitudes to such practices, which impact upon the underlying assumptions and evaluation of such practices, are crucial. Therefore practices cannot be merely considered on a case-by-case basis at the individual level.

Conclusion

Given this, at a societal level we should resist the gradual normalizing of practices which make commodification more likely – for example, allowing sex selection for purposes of family balancing as some ethicists argue for (Savulescu 1999; Robertson 2001) – even if we regard it as relatively unimportant on a case-by-case level.[11] The increased use and acceptance of such practices serves to normalize them and expand the range of choices which parents consider they are entitled to. Accordingly, we should resist practices which encourage a view of children as having choose-able parts or which allow certain types of children to be chosen, except when there are strong medical grounds which override these societal concerns. For even if at first glance it appears that there is no reason to interfere with parental preference at the individual case-by-case level for eye colour or sex,

---

11   Such views are controversial and have been rejected not only on the grounds discussed here, but also on feminist grounds (Dickens 2002) and by rejecting the pre-eminence of procreative beneficence (Parker 2007).

this is to disregard the wider social consequences and to risk encouraging and strengthening commodificatory presumptions.

Indeed, if we return to the organ donation or sale debate perhaps it is this wider societal logic which is at work. Thus the reason why organ donation is more acceptable than organ sale is not because the organ is less of a commodity when one considers the status of, say, a kidney *qua* kidney, but because the background conditions and the context are less commodifying in donation than they are in sale. Accordingly, even if it is possible to show that there are individual instances where organ sale is non-commodifying – as arguably in the example of the loving friendship – this is not in itself an argument for allowing organ sale if organ sale in general is likely to lead to more commodficatory assumptions. Furthermore, kidney donors are not regarded by themselves or others as commodities or sources of commodities – unlike the third world kidney sellers – thus they do not suffer the loss of esteem which accompanies kidney selling in the third world, but are proud of their 'gift'. If this is the case, then in instances where commodification is a danger we should attempt to establish social practices and relationships which are as little commodifying as possible. The hope is, then, in instances when we do need to separate parts from persons – and the need for organs is such an instance – we should attempt to nullify the commodificatory tendency by establishing as non-commodificatory practices as possible and thus make commodification of the body part less likely to become commodification of the person. In instances where such separation of parts and persons is unnecessary – for example when choosing parts or traits of children – concerns about commodification at a social level should take precedence over parental preference. In short, we should beware of increased parental selection of parts or types of children on the ground that encouraging commodificatory attitudes may ultimately result in a collectively more commodified attitude not only to particular children but to all children.

References

Anstey, K.W. (2002), Are Attempts to have Impaired Children Justifiable?, *Journal of Medical Ethics* 28, 286–288.

Dickens, B.M. (2002), Can Sex Selection be Ethically Tolerated?, *Journal of Medical Ethics* 28, 335–336.

Häyry, M. (2004), There is a Difference Between Selecting a Deaf Embryo and Deafening a Hearing Child, *Journal of Medical Ethics* 30, 510–512.

MacCallum, F. (2004), Families with a Child Conceived by Embryo Donation: Parenting and Child Development,unpublished PhD thesis, City University, London.

Mahowald, M.B. (2002), The Fewer the Better? Ethical Issues in Multiple Gestation, in Dickenson, D. (ed.), *Ethical Issues in Maternal-Fetal Medicine* (Cambridge University Press).

Midgley, M. (2000), Biotechnology and Monstrosity: Why We Should Pay Attention to the 'Yuk Factor', *The Hastings Center Report* 30:5, 7–15.

Olivennes F., Fanchin, R., Ledee, N., Righini, C., Kadoch, I. and Frydman, R. (2002), Perinatal Outcome and Development Studies on Children Born after IVF', *Human Reproduction Update* 8, 117–128.

Parker, M. (2007), The Best Possible Child, *Journal of Medical Ethics* 33, 279–283.

Price, F. (1999), 'Solutions for life and growth'? Collaborative Conceptions in Reproductive Medicine', in Edwards, J., Franklin, S., Hirsch, E., Price, F., and Strathern, M. (eds), *Technologies of Procreation: Kinship in the Age of Assisted Conception* (Routledge).

Radin, M. (1987), Market-Inalienability, *Harvard Law Review* 100, 1849–1937.

Resnik, D. (1998), The Commodification of Human Reproductive Materials, *Journal of Medical Ethics* 24, 388–393.

Ryan, M.A. (2001), *The Ethics and Economics of Assisted Reproduction: The Cost of Longing* (Georgetown University Press).

Robertson, J.A. (2001), Preconception Gender Selection, *The American Journal of Bioethics* 1:1, 1–9.

Rons' Angels website selling eggs and sperm. Available at: <http://www.ronsangels.com/index2.html> (accessed 5 September 2008).

Savulescu, J. (1999), Sex Selection: The Case For, *The Medical Journal of Australia* 171, 373–375.

Savulescu, J. (2003), Is the Sale of Body Parts Wrong?, *Journal of Medical* 29, 138–139.

Scheper-Hughes, N. (2003), Keeping an Eye on the Global Traffic in Human Organs, *The Lancet* 361, 1645–48.

Sheldon, S. and Wilkinson S. (2004), Should Selecting Saviour Siblings be Banned?, *Journal of Medical Ethics* 30, 533–537.

Vayena, E. and Rowe P. (2002), Current Practices and Controversies in Assisted Reproduction, *Report of WHO Meeting* (World Health Organization).

Widdows, H. (2006), The Impact of New Reproductive Technologies on Concepts of Genetic Relatedness and Non-relatedness, in Widdows, H., Idiakez, I.A. and Cirión, A.E. (eds), *Women's Reproductive Rights* (Palgrave).

Wilkinson, S. (2000), Commodification Arguments for the Legal Prohibition of Organ Sale, *Health Care Analysis* 8: 2, 189–201.

Wilkinson, S. (2003), *Bodies for Sale: Ethics and Exploitation in the Human Body Trade* (Routledge).

PART II
INTERSPECIES EMBRYOS

Chapter 5
Introduction to Part II

Stephen W. Smith

Introduction

One of the important components, we can probably assume, of the concepts of transformation and transgression is a blurring of the lines in important categories. Transformation, after all, is the changing of one thing into something else; transgression is where something is beyond or outside the normal categories and situations. In both of these cases, we have some notion that a particular entity either moves from one category to another or is not part of the normal categories to begin with. It seems quite evident, then, why the issue of interspecies embryos was included in this collection. The creation of what the Human Fertilisation and Embryology Act 2008 (HFEA 2008) refers to as 'human admixed embryos' would seem to be an obvious case of transgressing the normal species boundaries we have traditionally adhered to.

Of course, those species boundaries may no longer be as definitive as we have always believed them to be. At one point, we thought that humans were clearly separate from other animals. We had a number of attributes which we did not attribute to animals and this meant we were distinct from them. We reason, remember our history, have language and are self-aware. Attributes and abilities such as these were used to show how different (and superior) we were from other animals. Research, however, has not necessarily confirmed these beliefs about our differences from non-human animals. Certain kinds of crows, for example, use a process of reasoning to get food and have the ability to use different tools. Great apes, elephants and dolphins all show evidence of being self-aware. Dolphins are known to have language. Elephants mourn their dead. Orang-utans, as shown in a recent BBC documentary series, even seem to share some of our psychological problems. These new discoveries, along with Charles Darwin's theory of evolution and natural selection, have gone a significant way to blurring the boundaries between species that were once thought to be clear and distinct.

Just because lines have been blurred between certain categories, however, does not mean necessarily that we have transgressed those boundaries. The mixing of human and non-human animal gametes to create a human admixed embryo, on the other hand, would seem to have moved us far beyond a simple blurring of lines and into a full fledged transgression of those normal species categories which we used to believe were inviolate. It is that further transgression which is the subject of the two chapters in this section. The two chapters – one by Robert Song, a theologian from the University of Durham, and the other from Marie Fox, a lawyer from the University of Keele – both begin by referencing the HFEA 2008. This Act, for the first time, will make it legal in the UK to create animal–human hybrids past the two-cell stage, provided the appropriate license has been secured. The resulting embryo can only be used for research and cannot be placed in a woman, but the simple fact that the creation of these interspecies hybrids will be legal under the Act has not been without controversy. The chapters here do not attempt to resolve those controversies, but to comprehend aspects of the overarching issues and the ways in which they relate to how we see ourselves as human beings and the sorts of ethical and legal dilemmas that we face. In doing so, the chapters take two very different approaches to helping us achieve a greater understanding.

Robert Song's piece, at first sight, is not concerned primarily with interspecies embryos at all. Instead, his focus is on the nature of hybrids more generally and what this means for our ability to engage with the world. More specifically, his concern is to explore the 'received story' of modernism and postmodernism and how it relates to our notions of hybridity. He argues, following Bruno Latour, that modernity is interested in creating categories to pursue a notion of purity. This purification process, however, results in a proliferation of various hybrids because modernity cannot create sufficient categories to encompass the reality of the world. Our reaction to this proliferation of hybrids, though, should not be postmodernism or even conservative anti-modernism, but should be 'non-modernism' which 'see[s] change as incremental, continuity as real and relations with non-Western others as potentially fraternal in trajectory.'

Song's analysis is not simply a critique of modernity and our possible responses to it. He wants us to further consider Latour's notion of the 'crossed-out God of metaphysics' and how it relates to two of the 'pure types of modernity' which are Nature and Society. Despite modernity's creation of Nature and Society as pure types, the very fact of their existence means they must relate to each other, creating hybrids in the process. Adding divinity to these pure types only creates further hybrids. It is these hybrids with divinity to which Song wants us to pay particular attention. Where this leads is to the notion of 'maker's knowledge' which concerns the ability to create and the idea that it is only in the creation of something that we can truly know and understand it. While this was, at one time, the province only of God, it has now been 'brought down from heaven and placed in the hands of mortals' by our modern way of thinking. To this, we can add the notion of the desire to formulate health, life and well-being as consumable goods – again something explored in greater detail in other chapters of this collection. In other words, we see illness, pain and disfigurement (even ugliness?) as things we can change by remaking ourselves in a different way. Song is not keen to just criticize this developed view, but to understand this as religious or quasi-religious aspirations.

What this does, at least on one reading of Song's hypothesis, is to create further transgressions when we consider animal–human hybrids. In addition to the transgression of species boundaries that occurs with the creation of these embryos, we have the transgression of the line between humans and God. The power of the creation of not only individual entities but entire species no longer resides only in God (whomever or whatever God might be), but also resides in the human species. Collectively, then, we have transgressed the limits of our own species in other ways. For Song, there is something to be said for utilizing the concept of species integrity, although he is keen to stress this does not necessarily extend to species exceptionalism.

The transgressive and transformative elements of interspecies hybridity do not end there. To understand that, we then need to consider Marie Fox's chapter. Fox's chapter is an exploration of the regulatory challenges of the HFEA 2008. In that way, then, it begins as a straightforward legal analysis of the progression from the Warnock report which led to the first HFEA in 1990 which barely considered the question of interspecies hybrids through the changes which have led to the HFEA 2008. But it does more than that. Fox further presents to us an analysis of the arguments presented by the sides in addition to the legislative reasons for the change to allow these hybrid entities. Of particular interest is the way that the scientific community and the various governmental bodies addressed the concerns of others who opposed the creation of animal–human hybrids. The impact of these concerns was minimized by portraying these oppositional voices as essentially irrational, uneducated and anti-science. In other words, the odds were stacked against those who had concerns with the creation of these hybrid entities. They not only had to prove the various points of their arguments; they also had to prove that their arguments were ones that were worthy of consideration in the first place.

We thus have a completely different type of transgression. This is not a transgression of species boundaries which results from a fluidity of genetics. This is, contrariwise, an attempt to create categories of what counts as sufficiently important factors for consideration of argument. If, as was done with those opposing the new provisions for the creation of interspecies hybrids, the arguments that are used are considered to be outside of the acceptable category of reasons, then the entire argument is in some sense a transgression. The arguments themselves may then become deeply flawed as these transgressive arguments play (or are seen to play) on the unsuitability of other transgressions as a base. They thus become inherently unstable.

Fox's concern is not simply to criticize this viewpoint and expose the approach used by these scientific and governmental agencies. Indeed, neither she nor Song is interested in specifically asserting that the animal–human hybrids capable of being created under the HFEA 2008 are inherently wrong. What they seek to do is to show us the back story of the regulation, either in general (for Song) or specifically (for Fox). For both Fox and Song, then, it not only how these particular embryos may be a transgression of species boundaries that is important, it is also in how that transgression (if it is one) relates to the other transgressions which may form a significant part of how we see the world.

Chapter 6

Legislating Interspecies Embryos

Marie Fox

Introduction

In this chapter I aim to explore the regulatory challenges posed by recent developments in embryo research, which have opened up the possibility of creating interspecies animal–human embryos,[1] and to examine how debates about these embryos played out in the lead up to reform of the Human Fertilisation and Embryology Act 2008. My particular focus is two crucial shifts which I argue have occurred in legal debates about embryology since the Warnock Report first examined how law should regulate embryology research in the 1980s. First, I suggest that the main focus of concern is no longer the human embryo itself, and that it has become less visible in legal debates. Secondly, I argue that when the original Human Fertilisation and Embryology Act was passed in 1990 little serious attention was devoted to the creation of interspecies embryos generated by mixing human and animal gametes or cells. However, biotechnological developments since 1990 have placed interspecies embryos at the heart of stem cell and cloning technologies, and, as they have become more prominent, anxieties which formerly attached to the creation of human embryos for research purposes have been displaced by concerns about human–animal hybridity. As I shall show, legislators charged with framing a regulatory response to a bewildering array of possible interspecies embryos are faced with complex definitional questions since popular understandings, scientific terminology and legal meanings do not always cohere. Furthermore, the hybrid nature of animal–human embryos also raises jurisdictional questions regarding whether regulatory regimes focused on human or animal research most appropriately have jurisdiction. An even more formidable challenge requires legislators to balance the putative benefits of this research against the widespread concerns which it evokes, particularly when an

---

1   It is difficult to settle on appropriate terminology in this context as so many of the terms are freighted with popular and scientific meaning or are becoming legal terms of art. I use the term 'interspecies embryo' to mean an embryo created by mixing the cells or gametes of human and non-human animals, with the aim of avoiding the terms 'hybrid' or 'chimera' which are variously used in debates. This was also the term favoured by the Academy of Medical Sciences (2007), and the term used in the original Human Tissue and Embryos Bill.

often unspoken backdrop appears to be a desire to maintain the UK's position as a research leader and pioneer in the field of embryology.

I argue that, as in the case of other UK health care legislation – most notably the Human Tissue Act 2004 – regulation in this field has been driven by a research imperative that underpins both the 1990 legislation and 2008 amendments. In examining debates which surrounded reform of the UK legislation, my argument is that in order to make the permissive approach adopted in the UK palatable, advocates of interspecies embryo research relied upon a number of discursive strategies which sought to promote scientific research and contain the transgressive potential of hybrid technologies. These were to prove influential in policy documents, the media and, ultimately, in Parliament. In particular, proponents of research involving interspecies embryos sought to contest a widespread popular view that this form of research represented 'a step too far', an unjustifiable 'meddling with nature' or an illegitimate attempt to transgress species boundaries. In seeking to interrogate these arguments, this chapter is an attempt to engage with Isabel Karpin's suggestion that we need to 'examine the kind of legislative and cultural work that takes place around the definition and management of embryos' and 'marks some of them for exclusion from the human before they even exist' (Karpin 2006, 617).

The Question of Embryo Status

The question of the ethico-legal status of the human embryo is notoriously vexed. However, since the time of the Warnock Report it has generally been accepted that embryos have a special status – an issue on which all members of the committee were agreed – and should be afforded protection in law (Warnock 1984, para. 1.17). This principle forms a cornerstone of UK law. Thus, for instance, one of the key regulatory principles underpinning the 8th Code of Practice of the Human Fertilisation and Embryology Authority (HFEA) provides that staff in clinics licensed by the HFEA should 'have proper respect for the special status of the embryo when conducting licensed activities' (HFEA 2009, 9; Regulatory Principle 3). Of course, what this special status might mean is open to interpretation – bioethics and law have yet to engage seriously with the meaning and status of the human body (Diprose 1995; Hyde 1997; Fletcher, Fox and McCandless 2008), let alone that of the embryonic body. Debates have tended to revolve around whether the human embryo is more appropriately characterized as person or property (Dyson and Harris 1991; Fox 2000; House of Lords Select Committee 2002, Chapter 4) and what it means to argue that they are worthy of respect (Steinbock 1987; Brazier 1988; Hennette-Vauchez 2009). As embryos have become increasingly visible due to technologies such as ultrasound (Hartouni 1997; Mitchell and Georges 1998), the issue of embryo status and the appropriate level of legal protection to be accorded them has been heavily contested (Mulkay 1997; Steinberg 1997). Throughout the 1980s and 1990s the human embryo emerged as an important political actor, depicted as an endangered body and disputed territory (Fox 2000), while media and parliamentary debates in this period were characterized by 'political wrangling' over the status of embryos (Brown and Webster 2004, 55). As noted above, however, lately the figure of the human embryo seems to have receded somewhat in political and popular debate (Hennette-Vauchez 2009).

Yet, the concerns to which embryo research gave rise simply resurface in new contexts, such as human embryonic stem cell research (Holland et al. 2000; House of Lords Select Committee 2002) or pre-implantation genetic diagnosis (Scott 2007). As Donna Dickenson points out, in these newer contexts it is difficult for both supporters and opponents of stem cell technologies 'to escape the charge of obsession with the status of the embryo' (Dickenson 2007, 63), notwithstanding attempts by proponents of stem cell technologies to construct what Stephanie Hennette-Vachez terms 'a conceptual severance between the "embryo" and "embryonic stem cells"' (Hennette-Vachez 2009, 59). Furthermore, whereas debates pre-1990 tended to revolve around fairly essentialist understandings of the human embryo, in more recent years it has become apparent that how we view embryos is crucially dependent on what type of embryo we are dealing with, and its relation to us. Thus, Charis Thompson notes the huge variability in embryo status within IVF laboratories, where those embryos linked to future pregnancies receive a high standard of care and protection compared to those that do not form part of a pregnancy trail. The latter are consigned to a category of waste embryos that includes embryos destined for research (Thompson 2005, 198). Both Isabel Karpin and I have suggested previously that in UK and Australian legal contexts the human embryo 'hovers closer to legal personhood than property' (Karpin 2006, 603; Fox 2000). However, this observation applies only to those embryos which have some hope of being gestated. Even while suspended in a liquid nitrogen tent they are regarded as our 'biological relative[s]' (Franklin 2005, 313). Yet, as Karpin points out, for other technologically created embryos 'gestation … is not a real trajectory and … they cannot continue to occupy the same symbolical range as the embryo that is destined for gestation' (Karpin 2006, 603). Rather, as Thompson has illustrated, a bifurcation occurs. On the one hand the 'sacred' human embryo is embraced within the reproductive family and 'treated as sacred in the sense of holding intrinsic inviolable worth to the intended parents until or unless the embryo exits by defined paths of viability' (Thompson 2005, 259). On the other hand, 'profane' human embryos are designated as material objects, and, through a process of informed consent, 'enter the politics of what kinds of research are allowed, by whom and with what funding and oversight' (Thompson 2006, 263).

Yet, even research embryos are morally and culturally significant, as Cynthia Waldby and Robert Mitchell note:

> Embryos are particularly problematic forms of human tissue, because they are heavily charged with local ontological significance yet form the starting point

for complex global flows through for-profit biotechnology circuits, with highly
uncertain therapeutic outcomes and destinations. (Waldby and Mitchell 2006, 28)

In the following sections I want to engage with a particular manifestation of the
profane embryo – the interspecies embryo. As we shall see, it not only plays a
key role in 'for-profit biotechnology circuits', but also troubles legislators by
forcing law to confront the kinds of questions it would prefer to avoid. Contrasting
the parliamentary and media debates accompanying the 1990 legislation with
those occurring at the time of the 2008 amendments, it is clear that scientific,
social and legal landscapes have shifted significantly. Although certain core
preoccupations with the meaning of parenthood and what it is to be human recur,
the emphases have altered. Thus, in the run up to the 1990 Act, attention tended
to focus explicitly on the status of the human embryo, and on concerns about
problematic forms of motherhood – specifically so-called virgin mothers[2] and
surrogate mothers.[3] However, by 2008 the focus of media and political interest
was lesbian mothers,[4] while in the case of embryos, the relevant concern was not
the creation of human embryos *per se*, but the legitimacy of creating and using
interspecies embryos, and of using human ones in more novel ways, such as the
creation of 'saviour siblings' through PGD (pre-implantation genetic diagnosis).[5]
Many of the concerns the original HFE legislation had generated had receded by
the time it came to be revised. As noted above, IVF embryos have effectively been
normalized through being incorporated into the reproductive family unit, while the
ethics of human embryo research has been downplayed. Throughout the reform
process the government has consistently been clear that it would not re-visit the
question of whether embryo research was legitimate,[6] and, in any event, embryo
research has to some extent been superseded by more novel forms of research,
including the use of embryonic stem cells and interspecies embryos. Dislodging
the human embryo from its central and problematic role in reprotechnologies has
thus created the space for other, less familiar, embryos to emerge and become the
repositories of our hopes and fears.

---

2   The specific concern here was that women could reproduce autonomously without
being in a relationship with a man (Steinberg 1997).

3   So great was the concern, that this was the first type of assisted reproduction to be
regulated in the Surrogacy Arrangements Act 1985 (Foxcroft 1997).

4   The focus on lesbian mothers was prompted by the proposal to remove the need
for clinics to consider the need of a potential child for a father in assessing its welfare
(Henderson 2008b).

5   See Wright 2008.

6   For instance, the Department of Health's public consultation document was explicit
that: 'The Government does not intend that review of the HFE Act will open up those
fundamental aspects of the legislation which are widely accepted in our society and which
have been recently debated and conclusively resolved in Parliament. These include the
creation and use of embryos for research, the prohibition on human reproductive cloning
and the removal of donor anonymity' (Department of Health 2005, para 1.13).

In contrast to contemporary debates, a striking feature of the post-Warnock debates in the 1980s is the lack of concern with animal–human hybridity. Notwithstanding the controversy over embryo research and use, the 1990 Act resulted in a broadly liberal and permissive framework – allowing embryo research up to a 14 day limit for a number of 'permissible purposes', provided that research was licensed by the HFEA. Sections 3 and 4 of the 1990 legislation purported to outlaw three practices which seemed at the time to inhabit the outer reaches of scientific fiction: human reproductive cloning, the mixing of human and animal gametes to create a hybrid embryo and the implantation of human gametes or embryos in an animal uterus or vice versa. Little reasoning was evident for the express ruling out of such trans-species mixing in the 1990 legislation. The Warnock report simply noted that placing a human embryo in an animal would be a cause for concern and (somewhat bizarrely) that it constituted a criminal offence (Warnock 1984.) Some secondary sources at the time did canvass the issue of what was morally wrong with using camels as surrogate mothers to incubate human foetuses or creating a subclass of monkey-men to act as human slaves (Lee 1986), but there was limited discussion of this issue in either Warnock or the parliamentary debates which preceded the legislation. Subsequently, the provisions governing human reproductive cloning attracted considerable ethico-legal comment (Herring 2003; Morgan and Ford 2004) prompting litigation and statutory amendment.[7] However, until recently, much less attention had been devoted to the possibilities of trans-species bodily mixing which such technologies also harbour.

Monstrous Hybridity: Understanding Interspecies Embryos

In the lead up to the 2008 legislation a number of developments conspired to put interspecies embryo research on the policy and legislative agenda. Following the passage of the 1990 law, scientific research on animal–human hybrids had continued in a number of jurisdictions, and it is now clear that various techniques can produce interspecies embryos in the laboratory. Although the core idea of a hybrid or chimera is relatively straightforward – as Henry Greely notes, it may be broadly defined 'as a single biological entity that is composed of a mixing of material from two or more different organisms' (Greely 2003, 17) – the myriad forms these entities take, coupled with the fact that terms such as 'hybrid' and 'chimera' are used loosely, and often interchangeably, is one issue that poses difficulties for legal regulation. For the sake of simplicity,[8] in this chapter I follow

---

7   The Human Reproductive Cloning Act 2001 was passed when the SCNT (somatic cell nuclear transfer) technique used to create Dolly the sheep appeared to expose a loophole in the legislative ban on reproductive cloning.

8   For a good account of the science behind these practices see Kopinski (2003–4, 622–628) and for an interesting range of case studies in chimeric research see Munzer (2007-8, 129–132.)

Beyleveld et al. in largely sidestepping debate about how chimeras and hybrids are to be defined and distinguished (Beyleveld, Finnegan and Pattinson 2006), beyond offering the following typology of interspecies embryos:

1. Biologically a 'true hybrid' is produced through sexual reproduction between different species (for example, a mule is a naturally occurring hybrid of a donkey and horse). True hybrids contain an equal amount DNA from each species, and its cells are all comprised of the same genetic formation as a result of genetically combining two different species. According to the HFEA, scientific evidence indicates that, although such embryos could be created in laboratory conditions, where gametes from two distinct species are mixed, resultant embryos would be unlikely to develop beyond fertilization, and in any event '[n]one of the scientists that we consulted could see a purpose for carrying out such research using human gametes' (HFEA 2007a, para. 2.13).[9]

2. A 'chimera' may be defined as 'an organism comprised of at least two genetically distinct populations of cells' (Kopinksi 2004, 624–5; Bennett 2006, 347-8). As the HFEA points out, anyone who has undergone a transplant or blood transfusion is therefore technically a chimera (HFEA 2007a, para. 2.15). However, as Greely notes, such chimeras are less controversial because 'a kidney transplant in an adult seems likely to have a narrowed and more defined effect on the recipient' (Greely 2003, 18). By contrast, in 1984 a technique which involved mixing the very early embryos of a goat and a sheep produced a 'geep' – a goat-sheep chimera which possessed the physical traits of both species (Bennett 2006, 351–2). Another highly publicized interspecies animal experiment involved the insertion of quail cells into the developing brains of chickens, resulting in the creation of chickens exhibiting the vocal traits and head bobs unique to quails (Balaban et al. 1988; Ballard 2008). Chimeric embryos are typically formed where cells from one species are inserted into the embryo of another during the early stages of cell division or at the balstocyst stage. The introduced cells then become part of the developing blastocyst until a complete organism is formed with the cells from different species creating a mosaic pattern (Ballard 2008, 303). This research is already extremely common amongst different non-human animal species and is regulated under the Animals (Scientific Procedures) Act 1986 (Fox 2006). Certainly the technology could be used to insert animal cells into a human embryo, although, once again, scientific evidence to the HFEA suggested that this

---

9   Until this point the HFEA had granted licences (under Sch. 2(1)(f) of the 1990 Act) only for human and hamster gametes to be mixed for purposes of testing human sperm, conditional upon this 'hybrid' being destroyed no later than the two-cell stage. Given the poor prognosis generally for hybrid entitles it was unlikely that such a hybrid could actually develop much further beyond the two-cell stage.

was unlikely to have scientific value (HFEA 2007a, para. 2.19; for further detail see Academy of Medical Sciences 2007).

3. Cytoplasmic hybrid embryos (cybrids) are created using somatic cell nuclear transfer (SCNT). Replicating the cloning technology employed to produce Dolly the sheep (Franklin 2007), the nucleus of a human adult cell, such as a skin cell is inserted into a denucleated animal egg which is then activated so that it begins to divide, and allows stem cells to be derived from it. The cybrid which results from this process will be more than 99 per cent human; however, because a small amount of animal DNA will be left behind in the mitochondrial structure outside the nucleus it will not be fully human (HFEA 2007a, 8).

In the lead up to the 2008 legislation, most attention was focused on cybrids, in the wake of publicity regarding the severe shortage of human eggs available for cloning and stem cell research. So-called 'therapeutic cloning' technology, which aims ultimately to generate replacement human tissue and organs for use in therapeutic procedures, has been severely hampered by this egg shortage (Jackson 2008). Scientists have advocated the use of animal eggs to overcome the shortage, as well as ethical problems associated with acquiring eggs from human donors. Hence, the interspecies embryo produced through SCNT using animal eggs was to become the main focus of regulatory debate preceding the 2008 reforms. In turn, this interspecies embryo will be the focus of my discussion here, although the conclusion will turn to some of the broader issues thrown up by the various forms of hybrid research, given the extremely permissive approach ultimately adopted in the 2008 Act, which sanctioned the creation of a variety of interspecies embryos.

Putting Hybridity on the Map

In this section I suggest that, over a period commencing with the new millennium, when the use of interspecies embryos and concerns about hybridity first surfaced as a policy issue, it is possible to trace a shift in the government's thinking on the permissibility of using interspecies embryos in research. At first, and echoing widespread popular distaste for the notion of interspecies embryos, the government adopted a stanch of implacable opposition to their creation. However, in subsequent years, this opposition gradually softened to the point where permitting the creation and use of interspecies embryos became a significant feature of the 2008 reforms. I argue that this U-turn was sparked by the successful tactics of a strong research lobby which ultimately appealed to the government's desire to maintain Britain's position as a leader in biotechnology.

Concerns about the use of SCNT techniques to create interspecies embryos initially emerged as a policy concern in a 2000 report on stem cell research by the Nuffield Council on Bioethics, which flagged up legal uncertainty about the legality of this technology. It suggested that, since the Act had not directly addressed techniques which combined animal gametes with human somatic cells, it 'would be a matter for the courts to decide whether the embryo developing from such a hybrid cell was "human" and thus subject to the Act' (Nuffield Council 2000, 14). In the same year, the Donaldson Report on Stem Cell Research concluded that '[t]he 1990 Act does not control the mixing of animal eggs with other human cells' (Expert Medical Group on Human Cloning 2000, 47), and recommended the enactment of legislation to prohibit the 'mixing of human adult (somatic) cells with the live eggs of any animal species' (Expert Medical Group on Human Cloning 2000, Recommendation 6). Subsequently, the government signalled its acceptance of this proposal, pledging that 'primary legislation to give effect to this recommendation will be brought forward when the Parliamentary time table allows' (Department of Health 2000, 5). It also endorsed the Donaldson Report's view that, in the meantime, 'bodies funding research may wish to make a declaration that they would not fund or support research involving the creation of such hybrids' (Expert Medical Group on Human Cloning 2000, 47).

The first signs of a greater receptivity to hybrid technologies were apparent four years later in the publication of a report by the House of Commons Select Committee on Science and Technology, which reviewed the operation of the 1990 Act. The Committee took the view that, if it were possible to mix human and animal gametes to form hybrid embryos, such embryos could serve as a valuable research tool or model to test the ability of stem cell cultures to form in all types of tissue. It concluded that:

> [T]he ethical status of hybrids and chimeras is complex. While there is revulsion in some quarters that such creations appear to blur the distinction between animals and humans, it could be argued that they are less human than, and therefore pose fewer ethical problems for research than fully human embryos. (House of Commons Select Committee on Science and Technology 2004–5)

The Committee recommended that legislation should 'define the nature of these creations', and argued that (contrary to the position then held by the government) it should be permissible to create interspecies embryos for research purposes only up to a 14-day limit. Utilizing an increasingly familiar reasoning technique, it sought to distinguish this form of interspecies mixing from less desirable forms which, in its view, should remain taboo. Thus, addressing the existing prohibition on placing human embryos in animals or vice versa, the Committee suggested that, while conceivably such research could yield valuable insights into the causes of infertility and miscarriage, nevertheless:

> In this instance ... we have heard no evidence which would lead us to conclude that there is any merit in relaxing the HFE Act's prohibition on placing human embryos in an animal for research purposes. Should the government receive expert advice to the contrary, given the ethical issues involved, any such change

would be a matter for Parliament and primary legislation. (House of Commons Select Committee on Science and Technology 2004–5, para. 62)

As I have suggested elsewhere (Fox 2004, 482) this is a classic regulatory strategy – when boundaries are disrupted by events such as the birth of Dolly the sheep, or, in this instance, the creation of interspecies embryos, law responds by attempting to resettle disrupted boundaries through distinguishing 'good' forms of animal-human mixing from 'bad'.

In the wake of the Select Committee report, the government launched a public consultation in August 2005. One question addressed the ethics of interspecies embryo research, querying whether the law should permit the creation of human–animal hybrid or chimera embryos for research purposes only, subject to the limit of 14 days culture *in vitro*, after which the embryos would have to be destroyed (Department of Health 2005, Question 61). A total of 535 responses were received, of which a high proportion responded negatively to this question. A subsequent White Paper, which set out the Government's proposals for reform, noted the public concerns about hybridity evidenced in the responses to the Consultation:

> The Government recognises that there is considerable public unease with the possible creation of embryos combining human and animal material, and particularly the prospect that such entities could be brought to term … However the Government is also aware of the potential benefits to, for example, research into various diseases that could accrue from laboratory research in those areas. (Department of Health 2006, para. 2.83)

In this paragraph the polarization of the debate between a scientific emphasis on the pursuit of research and potential therapies versus a popular sentiment of deep unease is evident. However, indications of a softening in the government's position is revealed in its conclusion, which stresses once again the undesirable lack of clarity in the law, thus requiring that:

> [R]evised legislation will clarify the extent to which the law and regulation applies to embryos combining human and animal material. The Government will propose that the creation of hybrid and chimera embryos *in vitro* should not be allowed. However, the Government also proposes that the law will contain a power enabling regulations to set out circumstances in which the creation of hybrid and chimera embryos *in vitro* may in future be allowed under licence, for research purposes only. (Department of Health 2006, para. 2.85)

This proposal marks a significant watering down of its earlier pledge to ban such research and discourage funding of it; although clearly at this point the government is still swayed by the significant public opposition to this research.

At precisely this juncture, the issue of animal–human mixing was placed firmly on the political and regulatory agenda, with reports in January 2006 that scientists from three separate research centres planned to submit simultaneous proposals to the HFEA seeking licences to create interspecies embryos (Henderson 2006; Nicholl 2006). In each case, the application built on work which had been reported in China, where a team led by Hui Zhen Dheng of the Shanghai Second Medical University had produced more than 100 embryos and several lines of stem cells in this way (Chen et al. 2003). Each UK research team proposed to use animal eggs to create cybrids, which could ultimately be used for the isolation of embryonic stem cells. A research team at the North East England Stem Cell Institute, led by Lyle Armstrong of Newcastle University, applied for a licence to insert skin cell nuclei into denucleated cow eggs in order to study gene change in early development; while the other research teams led by Stephen Minger at Kings College, London, and Ian Wilmut at Edinburgh[10] sought permission to use eggs from a range of species, but mainly rabbits, to generate stem cells for use in research into neuorodegenerative disorders. Given the legal uncertainty surrounding the status of embryos created via SCNT, coupled with the public unease identified in responses to the Department of Health consultation, it is unsurprising that the licence applications prompted a flurry of media articles. The applications signaled that animal–human hybrids were becoming a scientific reality, rather than a fantasy derived from science fiction. They confronted regulators with a struggle over the legitimacy of creating new types of embryos, which, on Karpin's analysis, law itself it had helped to birth. She observes that, attempts in legislation like the 1990 Act to prohibit certain forms of embryos, had in fact ironically served only to conjure them up:

> [T]he idea that law is, through its prohibitions, actually engaged in fictional productions is a radical view, yet it is clearly happening … The stated aim of law to stop the creation of these forms raises the tantalising possibility that the law will not or cannot stop them. (Karpin 2006, 610)

In this respect, law seems to perfectly exemplify Bruno Latour's claim that modernist acts of purification which seek to separate the human from the non-human in fact create the conditions for hybrids to proliferate (Latour 1993, 141–142; see also Squier 2004, 104–105). Thus, by banning the creation of certain types of embryos, law in fact helps to create the conditions in which they become thinkable. As Karpin notes:

> The exact place of the legislative limit marking the difference between that which *is* and that which is *not yet* allowed, will, in time, shift but it is my contention that these original imagined possibilities will be the standard from which review and amendment will take place. (Karpin 2006, 610)

---

10   Subsequently Wilmut withdrew his licence application, citing his belief that the capacity of adult stem cells to be reprogrammed offered a more promising avenue of research (Highfield 2008).

Certainly, in the UK, Karpin's insight that the act of banning gives articulation to entities which don't yet exist (Karpin 2006, 602) seems to be borne out by the manner in which the legislative prohibition of animal–human mixing served only to postpone the inevitability of an application to create some variant of the prohibited embryo, thus exposing law's unwillingness or inability to prevent its creation (Karpin 2006, 611).

The Official Response: The Emerging Pro-Science Agenda

In January 2007 the HFEA announced that it had concluded that it possessed the necessary authority to licence the creation of interspecies embryos, but that it would, nevertheless, defer the granting of licences until it had held a public consultation. In a press release it stated:

> From the evidence considered so far, this issue is far from black and white. There is not clear agreement within the scientific community about the need for and benefits of this science. (cited in Bridge 2007)

In the same month the House of Commons Science and Technology committee held its first evidence session in an inquiry into the technology which was prompted by the conclusion of the government's White Paper. In this section I aim to explore how these events became significant catalysts in changing how interspecies embryos came to be debated, and to examine how arguments around interspecies embryos played out in three influential reports published in the course of 2007, by the House of Commons Science and Technology Committee, the Academy of Medical Sciences, and the HFEA's Response to its public consultation. In tracking these developments I am not adopting an 'anti-science' position, which is how I shall argue opposition tended to be characterized. Rather, I aim simply to chart the emergence of characteristic patterns of reasoning and the success of scientific lobbies in promoting their agenda. I argue that in this process of valorizing science, dissenting voices were marginalized, and as a result of these efforts the official government line shifted decisively in favour of research.

In this process, it is important to note the impact of the HFEA's decision at the beginning of the year that it had jurisdiction to licence interspecies research. On the day of the HFEA announcement *The Times* published a letter signed by leading scientists, ethicists and lawyers (including the President of the Royal Society) which attacked the government's opposition to interspecies embryo research, noting that:

> Britain is rightly proud of its record in ethical and scientifically valid research on stem cells and therapeutic cloning. This reputation is now under threat because in a recent White Paper the Government has proposed, without giving any proper reason or citing any evidence, that much of this proposed research – that

using animal eggs … should be banned … We urge the HFEA to adopt a policy supportive of this research, subject to its own strict licensing requirements and to the usual 14-day limit which applies to human embryos. (Letter to *The Times* 2007)

This was to prove the opening shot in a quite remarkable campaign waged by UK scientists against the government's position. Liberal Democrat MP Evan Harris, a member of the BMA's (British Medical Association) Ethics committee, and a key figure in this campaign, was cited in the media as predicting that, in the wake of the HFEA's decision, a legislative ban on the research was unlikely. He added that '[t]he Government should take a hint from its independent advisory and regulatory body – its policy in this area is wrong and must be changed' (cited in Bridge, 2007). I argue here that, galvanized by the HFEA announcement, the three 2007 reports were to prove instrumental in prompting the change which Harris advocated, and that they did so by mobilizing particular rhetorical strategies and arguments – which featured prominently in all three reports – and by portraying any opposition as anti-science.

The first type of reasoning which underpins each report is an emphasis on the potential clinical uses or applications of interspecies embryos. These were stated to include research into human diseases, study of human anatomy and its systems, and improvement of drug testing and pharmaceutical development. In each case it was suggested that interspecies embryos were preferable to traditional animal models, as they could potentially overcome problems of transferability between species. Most significant, however, was the manner in which all three reports touted the potential of interspecies embryos to generate an unlimited supply of stem cells, thus in the short term overcoming the severe shortage of human gametes, and in the longer term offering a potential solution to the shortfall in human organs available for transplantation. For instance, the HFEA notes:

> Development of these embryos to the blastocyst stage, will in theory, allow the production of embryonic stem (ES) cells which are genetically identical to the donor cell. This technique could result in significant advances in medicine … ES cells produced in this way could also be differentiated into most cell types and in theory used as a source of patient specific cells to replace disease damaged tissue. (HFEA 2007b, Appendix B, paras. 2.1–2.2)

In similar vein the Science and Technology Committee stated that:

> Because of their ability to reproduce themselves, and to differentiate into other cell types, stem cells offer the prospect of developing cell-based therapy to treat a wide range of degenerative diseases, such as Parkinson's disease and muscular dystrophy. Stem cell therapy may also be of use as a mechanism for repair or replacement of damaged tissues, and we heard from Cancer Research UK that future stem cell research could 'uncover ways of improving outcomes

after treatment for cancer, potentially providing us with the ability to regenerate or replace normal tissue following surgical removal of cancerous tissue, or its destruction by chemotherapy or radiotherapy'. (House of Commons Science and Technology Committee 2007, para. 24)

In such accounts a rhetoric and trope of hope in this research figures prominently (Fox and Murphy, forthcoming). Similar claims featured in favourable newspaper coverage, notably in *The Times* where, in a series of articles, the Science editor Mark Henderson gave a platform to eminent scientists to promote the benefits of the research. For instance, in January 2007, in an account of his research into motor neuron disease, Professor Chris Shaw of King's College London was quoted as follows:

There are hundreds of thousands of patients in Britain with degenerative neurological conditions. We can use these cell lines to study them, and to see if drugs are going to be effective. To shut that down is a real affront to patients who are desperate for therapy. Of all these diseases, none are really treatable. This is a very serious turning point in terms of science and medicine. (Henderson 2007a; see also Henderson 2007c; 2007d; 2008a; Henderson and Hurst 2008)

Tabloid newspapers carried similar endorsements of the scientific potential of interspecies embryos (Staff Reporter 2007; White 2008; Moore 2008). These scientific claims were also supported by personal narratives (Oakeshott and Templeton 2008); and significantly both the Prime Minister and the Leader of the Opposition came out personally in favour of the use of interspecies embryos – which was linked in media reports to the fact that each had a disabled son suffering from a disease for which these technologies offered a potential cure (Staff Reporter 2008a; Chapman 2008). Such positive media coverage of potential clinical applications is significant, given that responses to the HFEA consultation reveal that the therapeutic potential of the technologies is the factor most likely to prove persuasive with the public – 'in both the deliberative work and from the opinion poll it emerged that the *potential* benefits of the research had a significant impact on opinion' (HFEA 2007b, para. 5.11). They also dominated parliamentary debates. For instance, introducing the final reading of the HFE Bill in the House of Commons, Dawn Primarolo, the Health Minister, noted that it:

[C]ontains important provisions that ... have a potentially profound impact ... 350,000 people in this country live with Alzheimer's; every week, five children are born with, and three young people die from, cystic fibrosis. All those issues, and the potential for treatments, this Bill addresses. (HC Deb, 22 October 2008, col. 324)

In a related strategy, the use of interspecies embryos was also presented as infinitely preferable to the alternative of using human gametes, with its risks of harming women. Thus, the Academy of Medical Sciences stated that it would be unethical to alter IVF procedures to induce oocyte donation given its deleterious effects on the doctor–patient relationship, while the 'possibility of altruistic third party donation of oocytes from women not undergoing fertility treatment also raises safety and ethical considerations', including the fact 'that the use of fertility drugs may lead to increased risk of hormone dependent cancers' (Academy of Medical Sciences 2007, para. 5.1). Such concerns were also evident in responses to the HFEA consultation, with one respondent noting that, '[g]iven the difficulty and potential risks to women who donate eggs this would be a safer and potentially richer source of eggs' (James King, cited in HFEA 2007b, para. 5.4).

The second main strategy common to the reports is their tendency to normalize the use of animal–human hybrids in research by locating the development of interspecies embryos as part of an established research lineage. For instance, in the HFEA report on the findings of its consultation, it notes:

> The mixing of human and animal genetic material has a long history in science and has been used in a number of different ways to greatly progress medical research. The fusion of human and animal cells (to create somatic cell hybrids) is extensively used in research and was a technique first used in the 1970s/80s in the mapping of the human genome. (HFEA, 2007b, para. 2.1)

It goes on to stress that '[s]cientists have been creating cytoplasmic hybrid embryos, of various animal species, for over a century' (HFEA 2007b, para. 2.5). Similarly, the Science and Technology Committee emphasizes that '[u]se of hybrid and chimera animal models in research is both legal and relatively common practice' (House of Commons Science and Technology Committee 2007, para. 28). The Academy of Medical Sciences report devotes a section to '[t]he history of human-animal constructs' (Academy of Medical Sciences 2007, 19–20) dating the production of 'inter-specific cell hybrids' as research tools back to the 1960s. This narrative helps to allay concerns about the safety of creating interspecies embryos. Risks or potential problems with the research are addressed in the reports; however these are raised only to be ruled out. For instance, the Science and Technology Committee considers scientific dissent regarding the utility and safety of the research (paras. 52–57), but concludes that 'we do not believe that the existence of differing views of whether a methodology is workable before it has been sufficiently tested is reason enough to prohibit such research' (House of Commons Science and Technology Committee 2007, para. 57). Fears about retroviruses were similarly downplayed '[w]hile this scenario is not impossible, on balance we consider it highly unlikely' (para. 8.1).

A third strategy was to downplay the value and potential of possible alternatives, such as adult stem cells or stem cells derived from cord blood. In this regard, the HFEA noted:

> Not all tissues contain stem cells whilst others are inaccessible, such as stem
> cells from the central nervous system. Populations of adult stem cells are also
> highly heterogeneous, making them hard to isolate and purify … At present
> there is only a very limited range of diseases that can be treated using adult stem
> cells. Cord blood stem cells are also limited in the disorders they can treat and
> though there are some claims that these cells have wider potential, these have
> not been substantiated. (HFEA 2007b, para. 5.30)

Discounting the value or potential of alternative sources of embryonic stem cells
serves to position the creation of interspecies embryos as the only viable way to
progress technologies with valuable clinical potential to combat human diseases
and disorders.

Having made the case for the research, each report then sought to alleviate
public concerns about science 'going too far' through emphasizing the highly
regulated environment in which embryology research takes place in the UK. They
thus promoted faith in the efficacy of legal regulation, alongside faith in science.
Consequently, notwithstanding the criticism which it levelled at the HFEA over
what it saw as excessive caution in its readiness to licence this research, the
Science and Technology Committee concluded that 'it is possible to create a legal
framework within which anything which fell into this or a related category [of
embryo] would be capable of being licensed by the HFEA' (House of Commons
Science and Technology Committee 2007, para. 100). Once again, a similar faith
was evidenced by responses to the HFEA's consultation, which noted that:

> [T]hroughout the consultation the current regulatory framework was considered
> to be appropriate, although some felt that those who breached the standards
> imposed should be subject to penalties. (HFEA 2007b, para. 5.38)

Furthermore, the HFEA's emphasis on public consultation (which entailed
soliciting public views through opinion polls and dissemination and education
work in public meetings) was in many respects designed to engage and further
belief in regulatory structures (for details see HFEA 2007b, Appendix E). That it
also tended to sway those who were initially sceptical or undecided is suggested by
the HFEA's conclusion that 'whilst some members of the public initially reacted
with disgust, after hearing more information and discussing the issues with others,
their opinion often shifted significantly' (HFEA 2007b, para. 6.7). Scientists
stressed the stringent regulatory process in media interviews. For instance, in the
course of announcing the creation of the first UK cybrids at Newcastle University,
Professor John Burns was cited by the BBC: 'This is licensed work which has
been carefully evaluated. This is a process in a dish, and we are dealing with a
clump of cells which would never go on to develop. It's a laboratory process and
these embryos would never be implanted into anyone' (BBC News 2008). Again
this was reiterated by pro-research MPs in Parliament:

[The HFEA] has not sanctioned every proposal that has come forward – and I would hope that it would not do so, because it is a tight, tough regulatory agency … Lord Winston in the other place says it is much too tight and regulatory and that it stops too much happening. (Dr Gibson, HC Deb, 19 May 2008, col. 39)

Related to an emphasis on good regulatory structures is the implicit threat that a failure to legislate would generate legal uncertainty which would encourage unscrupulous researchers. For example, in 2005 *The Times* reported that scientists were calling for closure of 'a legal loophole that permits the creation of human-animal hybrid embryos without any regulatory oversight'. It went on to note that:

The restrictive and out of date remit of the embryology watchdog has left it powerless to control controversial experiments … [t]he gap in the law provides no way of blocking experiments such as those conducted abroad by Panayiotis Zavos, the maverick scientist seeking to clone a human being, who has added human DNA to cow eggs to test his technique. (Henderson 2005)

A key part of this strategy to promote faith in regulatory structures, was an emphasis on the restrictions which legislation imposes. In this regard, a legislative prohibition of breeding was a notable condition. Concern about the prospect of hybrid embryos being gestated was something which advocates of interspecies research were particularly concerned to guard against. This anxiety about birthing hybrid creatures can be traced back to the Warnock Report, which recommended that:

[W]here trans-species fertilisation is used as part of a recognised programme for alleviating infertility or in the assessment or diagnosis of subfertility it should be subject to a licence and that a condition of granting any such licence should be that the development of any resultant hybrid should be terminated at the two cell stage. (Warnock 1984, para. 71)

The Science and Technology Committee was also at pains to emphasize the early embryonic nature of the research:

It is important to distinguish between the creation of a human embryo incorporating animal material that will not exist beyond 14 days, from the possibility of bringing such an embryo to term … For good reasons implanting such an embryo into a woman is illegal in the UK, and we don't want to see this changed. (House of Commons Science and Technology Committee 2007, para. 8.3.1)

Pro-science media reports repeatedly assured their readers of the 'no-breeding' limitation: 'It is already illegal to implant human-animal embryos in the womb or bring them to term' (Henderson 2007a). As Susan Squier observes, the adoption of seemingly contradictory positions here is interesting, given the assumptions:

> [F]irst, that interspecies fertilization exists and indeed is sanctioned as a crucial part of contemporary reproductive technology and ... second, that interspecies reproduction is unacceptable and ... it should be against the law to bring interspecies hybrids to term (Squier 2004, 90)

A final key strategy adopted by advocates of interspecies embryo research was to downplay concerns about hybridity by representing the interspecies embryo as essentially human rather than hybrid. Thus, in the HFEA consultation response it was stated that:

> As hybrid embryos develop towards the blastocyst stage the gene products ... will gradually become more human derived. By 14 days the embryo will be entirely human with respect to protein and DNA apart from 13 proteins encoded by the animal mitochondria. (HFEA 2007b, para 5.18)

Media reports stressed that '[t]he hybrid would be *overwhelmingly human* – 99.9 per cent, according to the team led by Lyle Armstrong' (Hawkes 2006, emphasis added). Such arguments were also later echoed in parliamentary debates with Lord Walton emphasizing at the first report stage of the HFE Bill, that, unlike proper chimeras, the admixed embryo was 99.95 per cent human:[11]

> The animal component is simply the capsule in which that nucleus has been implanted. That is a very minor component, so it is properly called a human admixed embryo. (HL Deb, 15 Jan 2008)

Indeed, and highlighting again the political importance of terminology (Hennette-Vauchez 2009), it was claimed that the wording 'admixed embryo' was adopted in the final version of the legislation precisely in order to emphasize the human nature of these embryos (Wright 2008). Thus, in the House of Lords, during the Grand Committee stage, the Health Minister, Lord Darzi, commented:

> It was suggested that an alternative term to 'inter-species embryo' could be helpfully employed to make it clear that the Bill is ... intended to apply ... only to those embryos that are predominantly human. (HL Deb, 15 January 2008, col. 1183)

---

11   Note the slippage that seems to occur in the percentages; in early discussions, such as the quote from Lyle Armstrong in this paragraph, the interspecies embryo was 99.9 per cent human, whereas later, scientists seemed to agree that it was in fact 99.5 per cent.

There is an inescapable irony here in the way that the figure of the once profane or prohibited embryo is now recuperated by being brought within the ambit of the human – thus demonstrating yet again the elasticity of the concept 'human' (Fox 2004).

One account in *The Sun* newspaper is worth quoting at length because it neatly encapsulates these various rhetorical strategies. Two experts were invited to debate the pros and cons of 'hybrid embryos'. Professor Peter Braude, a Consultant in Reproductive Medicine, drew on the full repertoire of tropes which informed the lobbying in favour of this research, when he argued:

> It's important to realise there are no sweeping changes in this Bill. Nothing is proposed that has not already been approved – on a case-by-case-basis – by the Human Fertilisation and Embryology Authority. The Bill just brings existing research under legislation and control … Stem cells have enormous potential to cure chronic diseases like Parkinson's and diabetes. Adult stem cells and stem cells taken from cord blood have been used successfully in treating some blood cancers, but both are limited compared with the potential of embryonic cells … What would you prefer, asking women to donate eggs for research or using the many thousands of cow eggs which are destroyed every day in abattoirs? We're not talking about creating monsters, the animal egg is simply the shell, a carrier for human DNA … Again this is nothing new. Before ICSI [intracytoplasmic sperm injection] – a fertility treatment for men with poor quality sperm – doctors used to test sperm by seeing it if could penetrate specially treated hamster eggs. That was creating a true human-adult hybrid, but we didn't see 'humsters' running around because the law required them to be destroyed after a day. (cited in Staff Reporter 2008b)

Through mobilizing these discourses and arguments I would contend that the reports issued in 2007 combined to present the creation and use of interspecies embryos as the only rational step to take. Upon publication of the reports this message was successfully conveyed in the media. For instance, when the Science and Technology Committee reported in May 2007, media headlines reflected its views in suggesting that the 'Hybrid embryo ban [was] "unnecessary"' (BBC News 2007). When, in the wake of its public consultation exercise, the HFEA finally announced in September 2007 that it would license interspecies embryo research to be carried out at the University of Newcastle and Kings College London (Henderson 2007f) and the following month the government signalled changes to what was then called the Human Tissue and Embryos Bill (Henderson 2007g), media reports presented this as victory for science over Whitehall. In *The Times*, Henderson saw the victory as setting an important precedent:

> The concessions are the culmination of a remarkable campaign that shows how scientists are starting to acquire the political and media savvy that they lacked in the controversies over GM crops and the MMR vaccine. Once reluctant to

speak out, they are now borrowing the tactics of environmentalist and consumer groups to set out their agenda. They patiently explained the case for carrying out the controversial research to the press and the public, while presenting a united front that isolated ministers. (Henderson 2007g)

It is worth noting that reports applauding the government's U-turn stressed, not the benefits for patients, but how permitting the research to go ahead would secure Britain's role as a leader in this research field (Henderson 2007f; 2007g; Wolpert 2007).[12] In *The Times*, Lyle Armstrong welcomed 'a positive outcome not just for our work but for the progress of British science in general'; while Evan Harris noted that '[o]ur top-class researchers can now proceed with their applications to conduct this world-leading research' (cited in Henderson 2007g). Thus a critical factor in allowing scientists to force a U-turn on the issue was the government's fear that otherwise Britain's role as a pioneer in embryo research might be jeopardized,[13] with scientific expertise and investment lost to emerging biotech markets, particularly China (Henderson 2007c).[14]

Discounting Oppositional Voices

Although space precludes a full consideration of arguments opposed to interspecies embryo research, it is worth noting that the pro-research campaign was facilitated by the weakness of arguments marshaled in opposition. First, the government was wrong-footed and left to defend a position which appeared confused and

---

12   See also earlier accounts hailing a victory for science in Editorial 2007; Henderson 2007.

13   In the House of Commission Research paper it was noted, citing the birth of Dolly the sheep, that:

'The Government has actively positioned the UK as a world leader in regenerative medicine. Many scientists come to work here from less permissive environments' (House of Commons 2008, 33).

14   Ian Wilmot, the creator of Dolly the sheep, was cited in *The Times* at the critical turning point in the debate in 2007: 'This is an area in which Britain has had a lead, and if we prohibit using animal oocytes it would become an area in which we would have a serious disadvantage.' (Henderson 2007a).

A few days later he is once again quoted in the press as warning that the epicentre of work into incurable diseases, such as motor neurone disease, will shift from Britain if interspecies embryo research is banned: 'The role of government is to consult, then to take its own informed decision, rather than do what the public wants … In China there are very talented people at work, many of then trained in the West. There is an intense energy in these technologies and that is where they will move to' (cited in Wade 2007).

Since the US President lifted a ban on federal funding of stem cell research, concerns have been voiced that the UK's fragmented system of regulation will prompt scientists to decamp to the US (Henderson 2009).

contradictory. For instance, in the lead up to the HFEA licensing decision, Caroline Flint, the Public Health Minister responsible for the Bill, was quoted as saying that she expected the HFEA to take the government support for a ban into account, while Tony Blair denied that the government was 'dead set' against the research, 'in fact the opposite ... I'm sure that research that's really going to save lives and improve the quality of life will be able to go forward' (cited in Hawkes 2007). Secondly, neither the Minister nor the Chief Medical Officer clearly articulated their objections to the research, beyond citing public unease.

Such unease was evident in the HFEA response, which revealed that a public survey it commissioned with ICM in July 2007 found that half of a sample of 2,073 adults in the UK disagreed with scientists creating an embryo for research purposes which was mostly human, but contained a small amount of animal genetic material (HFEA 2007b, Appendix F para. 11).[15] In articulating their concerns, 47 per cent stated that their opposition was rooted in the idea of 'meddling with nature'; while 49 per cent were worried 'because of what scientists might want to do next in research' (HFEA 2007b, Appendix F para. 15). It is noteworthy that the HFEA sought to downplay such concerns, by suggesting that they could be alleviated through educating the public about the technologies: '[p]eople who know more about the possibility of creating embryos that contain some human and some animal material are more likely to agree [with the technology]' (HFEA 2007b, Appendix F para. 19). This served to effectively disqualify opposition grounded in notions of 'the natural' or concerns about slippery slopes by suggesting that such opposition was essentially irrational and uneducated. Again, this was a common theme throughout the policy reports and much of the media coverage. For instance, in *The Times*, Mark Henderson argued that:

> Caroline Flint, the Public Health Minister, and Patricia Hewitt, the Health Secretary, have convinced themselves of the existence of a groundswell of public concern that is no more than a phantom. They have been spooked by the outcome of an unrepresentative public consultation [i.e. the response to the Department of Health's 2005 Consultation] and by misleading and hysterical reporting of research. Ms Flint's White Paper has pandered to this agenda. (Henderson 2007b)

In fact, although it was true, as he contended, that headlines featuring 'frankenbunnies', 'half-cow, half-human hybrids' and 'moo-tants' had appeared (in *The Times*, as well as the tabloids that he berated), the articles themselves were generally pro- rather than anti-research. And while, as Henderson noted, there were only 535 responses in total to the DOH consultation, considerable investment of time and effort was required to respond to such a long consultation document. Moreover, the public concerns it flagged up were also evident in the HFEA's public consultation held two years later, as well as the public meeting it

---

15   35 per cent approved of this research with 48 per cent disagreeing with it.

convened in June 2007. A year later a smaller poll commissioned by *The Times* found broad public support for the research, with 50 per cent of a sample of 1,502 adults surveyed indicating their support for proposals to permit interspecies embryo research (Henderson 2008).[16]

In addition to unfairly downplaying the extent of the opposition to interspecies research, it is noteworthy that oppositional voices were often treated as synonymous with religion. A striking example of this occurred in *The Times* in early 2007, when an article by Henderson was subtitled '[m]ove hits hopes of Alzheimer's sufferers; Ministers "caving into religious groups"'. In fact, no one cited in the article – which was clearly an attempt to influence the HFEA's thinking – actually claimed that religious groups had exerted such an influence (Henderson 2007a). A later *Times* article in similar vein noted that '[t]he Government [position] appears to have been influenced by a public consultation that attracted 535 responses, many from those with religious objections or ethical objections to embryo research' (Hawkes 2007). Meanwhile, when a House of Commons Research paper outlined the position of critics, it focused on religious opposition to the research, citing only press pronouncements by 'leading Catholics' (House of Commons 2008, 38). The fact that it was often religious clergy who made the case against interspecies research in the media (for instance Rayfield 2008) or in sermons, such as a highly publicized attack by Scottish Cardinal, Keith O'Brien, on the HFE Bill (Gledhill and Lister 2008) fuelled a sense that dissent was confined to a religious fringe,[17] and allowed the battle to be played out as one between enlightened scientists and a backward religious minority. In Parliament too, many critics of the Bill tended to couch their opposition in the language of humanity, dignity and biblical precepts. For instance, in the House of Lords, Baroness Paisley proclaimed:

> I believe that the creation of animal/human embryos for research is not only unnecessary and undesirable but unethical and would undermine our human dignity and alter the very nature of humanity. Further this proposal totally disregards the biblical law on mixing kinds of species as laid down in Holy Scripture, and would be an offence to the Creator Himself, who made man in His own image. (HL Deb, 19 November 2007)

In consequence, oppositional voices tended to be portrayed as emanating from a position that was anti-science and concerned to prevent transgression – whether of nature, species boundaries or appropriate moral limits. Intellectually such claims are hard to sustain, given the difficulties of defending arguments grounded

---

16   According to this poll, which was criticized for being loaded in favour of the research, 30 per cent opposed interspecies embryo research.

17   Other dissenting voices came from prominent activists in the anti-choice movement – thus Josephine Quintavalle featured in a 'for and against' debate in *The Daily Telegraph* (Quintavalle and Lovell-Badge 2008).

in anything so vague as species integrity, or 'the natural'. As Donna Haraway has observed:

> Global technology appears to *denature* everything, to make everything a malleable matter of strategic decisions and mobile production and reproduction processes. (Haraway 2004, 65)

The notion of species integrity is similarly difficult to defend (Bovenkerk, Brom and Van Den Berg 2002; Rollin 2003). Nevertheless, while I am wary of attempts to recuperate arguments rooted in concepts like 'the natural' or integrity of species, which too often serve as a cover for prejudice, I also wonder if the unease underpinning such concerns was dismissed too readily. As the HFEA acknowledged, 'at the outset of the deliberative work, many of the participants expressed an initial repugnance in reaction to the suggestion of mixing human and animal material' (HFEA 2007b, para. 5.8). Leon Kass has argued that such responses signal:

> [R]evolts against the excesses of human wilfulness, warning us not to transgress what is unspeakably profound. Indeed ... repugnance may be the only voice left that speaks up to defend the central core of our humanity. (Kass 1998, 19)

While I have no desire to shore up the 'central core of our humanity' (whatever that may mean), I do think that it may be worth seeking to tease out what lies at the root of the unease about species-mixing. In the debates about the 2008 reforms such voices were narrowly identified with those who are politically and religiously conservative. Thus, in the press, Melanie Phillips employed the language of repugnance to argue that:

> Scientists claim that the protests are irresponsibly scaremongering, since the proposed hybrids would not be grown into 'monsters' but would be used only as primitive cells for research. In their arrogance, such scientists fail to understand the nature of the objection. It is the idea of creating such a hybrid embryo *at all* that is abhorrent. Experimenting on human embryos is bad enough ... But creating an animal/human embryos breaks an even deeper taboo. It negates the acknowledgement of what it is to be human and, by obliterating the difference between animals and humans, destroys the concept of human uniqueness. (Phillips 2008)

In parliamentary debates, as we have seen, these arguments were linked to the notion of overstepping lines and threats to a shared conception of humanity, and were propounded by prominent 'pro-life' MPs, such as Lord Alton, who, at the first report stage in the House of Lords, stated:

If Members of your Lordships' House believe that the reason for prohibiting a true hybrid from being implanted and born is that that crosses the line between human and other species, and if the problem is that this disturbs our sense of what it is to be human ... we should surely, if it is so important to our common humanity and the basis of our ethics, tread very warily before permitting the creation of an animal interspecies embryo in the first place (HL Deb, 15 Jan 2008 1st col 1204).

More extreme pronouncements stoked newspaper fears that the new laws could produce 'humanzees', 'GM babies or cloned adults or minotaurs' (Prince 2008b). While clearly nonsensical, as *The Times* has earlier suggested (Editorial 2007), the sensationalist headlines devoted to such claim served to further undermine opposition to the Bill's proposals.

Yet, Gail Davies argues that naming things in or against nature need not be inherently conservative. She suggests that:

The language of gut reaction is telling, for ... such corporeal discourses perform an important function in thinking through the implications of new biotechnologies for the way we conceptualise human corporeality and our relationships to the natural world ... [Furthermore], the force of argumentative strategies in different contexts is ultimately linked to a wider context of power, which discounts these as legitimate forms of ethical reasoning. (Davies 2006, 429)

Certainly her contention about the power to suppress dissent seems borne out by how these arguments were downplayed in the course of the 2008 reforms. Davies suggests that the cause of negative popular responses may lie in the potential of certain biotechnologies to dismantle ontological certainties and moral principles. For instance, in the context of xenotransplantation, she notes that:

A new ontological order is ... proposed ... which troubles the application of established ethical principles to new forms of life that are seen as different from existing human or animal bodies ... xenotransplantation is disordering on several fronts ... (Davies 2006, 434)

In similar vein, Scott and Baylis point to the confusion that interspecies mixing can promote:

[T]he engineering of creatures that are part human and part nonhuman animals is objectionable because the existence of such beings would introduce inexorable moral confusion into our existing relationships with nonhuman animals and in our future relationship with part human hybrids and chimeras. (Scott and Baylis 2003, 9)

Biotechnologies, such as genetic engineering, xenotransplantation and the creation of interspecies embryos certainly have the potential to unsettle due to their tendency to fragment, transform and conjoin both animal and human bodies. As Kopinksi points out, scientists may increase the human composition of chimeras dramatically, thus dismantling traditional concepts of personhood as well as species (Kopinski 2003–4 622). Of course, in the parliamentary and media debates leading up to the reformed legislation, we have seen that scientists and other advocates of the research sought to limit this transgressive potential by emphasizing that the interspecies embryo was overwhelmingly human in composition and, moreover, that it was emphatically not destined for gestation. Yet, the first claim is somewhat undercut by the wide definition of interspecies embryos adopted in the revised legislation. Section 4(6) of the 2008 Act (ultimately passed by a decisive majority of 160 votes) provided for the creation of 'human admixed embryos', defined as follows:

a. an embryo created by replacing the nucleus of an animal egg or of an animal egg or of an animal cell, or two animal pronuclei, with –
    (i) two human pronuclei,
    (ii) one nucleus of a human gamete or of any human cell, or
    (iii) one human gamete or other human cell,
b. any other embryo created by using –
    (i) human gametes and animal gametes, or
    (ii) one human pro nucleus and one animal pro nucleus
c. a human embryo that has been altered by the introduction of any sequence of nuclear or mitochondrial DNA of an animal into one or more cells of the embryo,
d. a human embryo that has been altered by the introduction of one or more animal cells, or
e. any embryo not falling within paragraphs (a) to (d) which contains both nuclear or mitochondrial DNA of a human and nuclear or mitochondrial DNA of an animal ('animal DNA') but in which the animal DNA is not predominant.

Notably this definition goes far beyond the much narrower focus on cybrid embryos which had featured so prominently in the 2007 reports, media coverage and parliamentary debates. In explaining the broad category of permissible interspecies embryos in section 4, the Health Minister Dawn Primarolo was forced to concede that:

> [I]n searching around to put the argument on an ethical basis that drew the lines in ethics and science the Government has to admit that we were simply wrong in our original position [that true hybrids were distinguishable and should be prohibited]. (HC Deb, 19 May 2008, col. 58)

The breadth of this definition returns us to the points that Latour and Karpin make about the unruliness of embryos, which seem to frustrate attempts to contain or stop their creation. However, this feature was lost amongst media reports which continued to focus on the potential of cybrid embryos as they proclaimed that:

> Britain is now set to become a world leader in stem cell research ... scientists have been hampered by a lack of human eggs available for research, but will now be able to boost stocks by creating embryos using animal matter, mainly from cows and rabbits. (Prince 2008b; see also Sinclair 2008)

Conclusion

As I outlined in the introduction, the aim of this chapter is not to posit arguments for or against the creation and use of hybrid embryos for human ends, but rather to track how dominant pro-science arguments played out in the course of the debates which reforms to the Human, Fertilisation and Embryology Act have sparked. I have argued that, by downplaying the concerns of opponents of such research, space for dissent about these forms of research was effectively closed off and opponents were marginalized. To express objections entailed being depicted in a largely homogenous way as anti-science, probably influenced by irrational religious beliefs and mired in historical debates that had already been decisively lost. Through the deployment of a range of rhetorical strategies – the promotion of faith in science and the law, the representation of 'human admixed embryos' as effectively human, their creation as a small incremental step in research procedures which have a long and accepted lineage, and a prohibition on their gestation and birth – space for oppositional arguments was minimised. Moreover, the government's concern to secure British pre-eminence in embryology research and regenerative medicine was enough to overcome its undoubted misgivings about the ethics and efficacy of the research.

A number of questions, however, remain. Since the passage of the legislation it has emerged that those projects which secured licences have nevertheless failed to secure funding (Sample 2009; Shaikh 2009) while fresh doubts have been cast on the clinical feasibility of interspecies embryo research (Alleyne 2009). Scientists may have secured a victory, in the sense that this research has been deemed legitimate, but at the considerable cost for many scientists that it has been brought under a regulatory regime overseen by the HFEA, which has been criticized as inappropriate (Hammond 2008). Certainly the 2008 legislation has singularly failed to grapple with the rather *ad hoc* and extremely complex way in which research on humans, animals and, currently, interspecies hybrids is now regulated as biotechnologies have become normalized (Brown and Michael 2004; Williamson, Fox and McLean 2007). The fact that the legislation now sanctions the creation of such a broad range of hybrids also serves to question the extent to which the remaining prohibitions can hold, and whether the spectre of birth and gestation which so many commentators raised has truly been banished.

All of these issues merit further consideration, as does the power dynamic which operated to close off and marginalize opposition. In particular, what I find interesting is the way in which feminist arguments, which were mobilized in relation to other reforms proposed in the 2008 Act were conspicuously absent in the research context. This raises issues about what it would mean to inject feminist vales into the framing of the legislation, and what an appropriately feminist response might be to the creation of those transgressive others which UK law now seems to countenance (Karpin 2006). In the case of interspecies embryos many questions remain to be posed and answered about 'what are the borders that secure their identities and what else are they telling us?' (Franklin 2006, 170). Not least they raise compelling questions about the ways in which we define the human (Giffney and Hird 2008).

Acknowledgement

I would like to thank Margot Brazier, Ronan Deazley and Stephen Smith for their patience with this chapter and for shaping my thoughts on it; for additional feedback and conversations on this issue I am very grateful to Marie-Andrée Jacob, Emily Jackson, Thérèse Murphy, Andrew Sharpe, Mitch Travis and Stephen Wilkinson.

References

Academy of Medical Sciences (2007), *Inter-species Embryos*, (London).

Alleyne, R. (2009), Controversial Hybrid Embryos 'are no Use to Science' new Research Suggests, *Daily Telegraph* (3 February).

Balaban, E. et al. (1988), Application of the Quail-Chick Chimera System to the Study of Brain Development and Behavior, *Science* 241, 1339.

Ballard, R.A. (2008), Animal/Human Hybrids and Chimeras: What Are They? Why Are They Being Created? And What Attempts Have Been Made to Regulate Them?, *Michigan State University Journal of Medicine and Law* 12, 297–319.

BBC News (2007), Hybrid Embryo Ban 'Unnecessary' (4 May).

BBC News (2008), UK's First Hybrid Embryos Created' (4 June).

Bennett, D.S. (2006), Chimera and the Continuum of Humanity: Erasing the Line of Constitutional Personhood, *Emory Law Journal* 55, 347–388.

Beyleveld, D., Finnegan, T. and Pattinson, S.D. (2006), The Regulation of Hybrids and Chimera in the UK, Report produced for CHIMBRIDS (Chimera and Hybrids in Comparative European and International Research), a coordinated project run by the University of Mannheim, funded by the EC Sixth framework, (on file with author).

Bovenkerk, B., Brom, F.W.A. and Van Den Berg, D.J. (2002), Brave New Birds: The Use of Animal Integrity in Animal Ethics', *Hastings Center Report* 32:1, 16–22.

Brazier, M. (1988), Embryo's 'Rights': Abortion and Research, in Freeman, M. (ed.), *Medicine, Ethics and Law*, (Stevens and Son).

Bridge, S. (2007), Hybrid Embryo Research is Legal, Regulator Says', *The Guardian* (11 January).

Brown, N. and Michael, M. (2004), Risky Creatures: Institutional Species Boundary Change in Biotechnology Regulation', *Health, Risk and Society* 6, 207–22.

Brown, N. and Webster, A. (2004), *Reordering Life: New Medical Technologies and Society*, (Wiley-Blackwell).

Chapman, J. (2008), Hybrid Embryos are a Hope for my Son, says David Cameron, *Daily Mail* (21 May).

Chen, Y. at al. (2003), Embryonic Stem Cells Generated by Nuclear Transfer of Human Somatic Nuclei into Rabbit Oocytes, *Cell Research* 13, 251.

Davies, G. (2006), The Sacred and the Profane: Biotechnology, Rationality and Public Debate, *Environment and Planning* 38, 423–444.

Davis-Floyd, R. and Dumit, J. (eds) (1998), *Cyborg Babies: From Techno-Sex to Techno-Tots*, (Routledge).

Dawkins, R. (1993), Gaps in the Mind, in Singer, P. and Cavalieri, P. (eds), *The Great Ape Project: Equality Beyond Humanity*, (St. Martin' Press).

Dickenson, D. (2007), *Property in the Body: Feminist Perspectives*, (Cambridge University Press).

Department of Health, (2000), *Government Response to the Recommendations Made in the Chief Medical Officer's Expert Group Report*, (Department of Health).

Department of Health (2005), *Review of the Human Fertilisation and Embryology Act 1990: A Public Consultation*, (opened 16 August 2005).

Department of Health (2006), *Review of the Human Fertilisation and Embryology Act: Proposals for revised legislation (including establishment of the Regulatory Authority for Tissue and Embryos)* (Cm. 6989).

Diprose, R. (1995), The Body Biomedical Ethics Forgets, in Komesaroff, P. (ed.), *Troubled Bodies: Critical Perspectives on Postmodernism, Medical Ethics and the Body*, (Duke University Press).

Dyson, A. and Harris, J. (1991), *Experiments on Embryos*, (Routledge).

Editorial (2007), The Chimera Question: A Sensible Decision Amid much Nonsense, *The Times* (12 January).

Expert Medical Group on Human Cloning (2000), *Stem Cell Research: Medical Progress with Responsibility*, (Department of Health).

Fletcher, R., Fox, M. and McCandless, J. (2008), Legal Embodiment: Analysing the Body of Healthcare Law, *Medical Law Review* 16:3, 321–345.

Fox, M. (2000), Pre-Persons, Commodities or Cyborgs: The Legal Construction and Representation of the Embryo, *Health Care Analysis* 8:2, 171–188.

Fox, M. (2004), Re-thinking Kinship: Law's Construction of the Animal Body, *Current Legal Problems* 57, 469–493.

Fox, M. (2006), Exposing Harm: The Erasure of Animal Bodies in Health Care Law, in McLean, S. (ed.), *First Do No Harm: Law, Ethics and Healthcare* (Ashgate).

Fox, M. and Murphy, T. (forthcoming), Embryonic Hopes, *Social and Legal Studies*.

Foxcroft, L. (1997), Surrogacy- Warnock and After, *Medical Law International* 2, 337.

Franklin, S, and McKinnon, S. (eds) (2001), *Relative Values: Reconfiguring Kinship Studies*, (Duke University Press).

Franklin, S. (2001), Bioloigization Revisited: Kinship Theory in the Context of the New Biologies, in Franklin, S. and McKinnon, S. (eds), *Relative Values: Reconfiguring Kinship Studies*, (Duke University Press).

Franklin, S. (2006), The Cyborg Embryo: Our Path to Transbiology, *Theory, Culture and Society* 23, 167–187.

Franklin, S. (2007), *Dolly Mixtures: The Remaking of Genealogy*, (Duke University Press).

Freeman, M. (ed.) (1988), *Medicine, Ethics and the Law*, (Stevens and Son).

Freeman, M. (ed.) (2008), *Law and Bioethics*, (Oxford University Press).

Giffney, N. and Hird, M.J. (eds) (2008), *Queering the Non/Human*, (Ashgate Publishing).

Gledhill, R. and Lister, D. (2008), Cardinal Keith O'Brien Attacks 'monstrous' Human Embryo Bill', *The Times* (22 March).

Greely, H.T. (2003), Defining Chimeras … and Chimeric Concerns, *American Journal of Bioethics* 3:3, 17–18.

Hammond, N. (2008), Regulating Hybrid Embryo Research in the UK, *Bionews* (7 April).

Haraway, D. (2004), The Promises of Monsters: A Regenerative Politics for Inappropriate/d Others, in Haraway, D., *The Haraway Reader*, (Routledge).

Hartouni, V. (1997), *Cultural Conceptions: On Reproductive Technologies and the Remaking of Life*, (University of Minnesota Press).

Hawkes, N. (2006), Nobel Scientists urge Fertility Watchdog to back Hybrid Embryos', *The Times* (10 January).

Hawkes, N. (2007), Human-cow Embryo Planned', *The Times* (7 November).

Henderson, M. (2005), Fear over Human-Animal Embryos, *The Times* (16 August).

Henderson, M. (2006), 'British Scientists plan Work on Human-Rabbit Embryos', *The Times* (13 January).

Henderson, M. (2007a), Medicine faces Ban on Rabbit-Human Embryos', *The Times* (5 January).

Henderson, M. (2007b), Ministers have been Spooked by 'Frankenbuny' Headlines', *The Times* (5 January).

Henderson, M. (2007c), The Wild East is now Tamed', *The Times* (10 February).

Henderson, M. (2007d), Scientists Triumph in Battle over Ban on Hybrid Embryos', *The Times* (27 February).

Henderson, M. (2007e), Watchdog should Approve 'Cybrid' Embryos', *The Times* (3 September).

Henderson, M. (2007f), British Scientists given Go-ahead to Create Human–Animal Embryos', *The Times* (6 September).

Henderson, M. (2007g), White Coats Defeat the Grey Suits in a Clash between Science and Whitehall, *The Times* (13 October).

Henderson, M. (2008a), Embryo Research Bill could Block Life-saving Stem Cell Treatments', *The Times* (15 March).

Henderson, M. (2008b), Does every Child Need a Father? How the Nation is Divided', *The Times* (10 April).

Henderson, M. (2009), Brain Drain Fears as Barack Obama lifts Ban on Stem-cell Funding', *The Times* (9 March).

Henderson, M. and Hurst, G. (2008), Scientists Win Public Support on Embryo Research', *The Times* (10 April).

Hennette-Vauchez, S. (2009), Words Count: How Interest in Stem Cells has made the Embryo Available – a Look at the French Law of Bioethics', *Medical Law Review* 17, 52–75.

Herring, J. (2003), Cloning in the House of Lords, *Family Law* 33, 63.

Highfield, R. (2008), Dolly Creator Prof Ian Wilmut shuns Cloning, *Daily Telegraph* (10 November).

Holland, S. et al. (eds) (2001), *The Human Embryonic Stem Cell Debate: Science, Ethics and Public Policy*, (MIT Press).

House of Commons (2008), *Research Paper 08/43: Human Fertilisation and Embryology Bill*, (House of Commons Library).

House of Commons Select Committee on Science and Technology (2004–5), Fifth Report of Session 2004–5, *Human Reproductive Technologies and the Law*, HC 7, (House of Commons Library).

House of Commons Select Committee on Science and Technology (2007), *Government proposals for the regulation of hybrid and chimera embryos*, Fifth Report of Session 2006–7.

House of Lords Select Committee (2002), *Report on Stem Cell Research*, HL Paper 83(i).

Human Fertilisation and Embryology Authority (2007a), *Hybrids and Chimeras: A consultation on the ethical and social implications of creating human/animal embryos in research*, (Human Fertilisation and Embryology Authority).

Human Fertilisation and Embryology Authority (2007b), *Hybrids and Chimeras: A report on the findings of the consultation*, (Human Fertilisation and Embryology Authority).

Human Fertilisation and Embryology Authority (2009), *Code of Practice*, 8th Edition.

Hyde, A. (1997), *Bodies of Law*, (Princeton University Press).

Jackson, E. (2008), The Donation of Eggs for Research and the Rise of Neopaternalism, in Freeman, M. (ed.), *Law and Bioethics*, (Oxford University Press).

Karpin, I. (2006), The Uncanny Embryos: Legal Limits to the Human and Reproduction without Women, *Sydney Law Review* 28, 599–623.

Kass, L.R. (1998), The Wisdom of Repugnance, in Kass, L.R. and Wilson, J.Q. (eds), *The Ethics of Human Cloning*, (AEI Press).

Kass, L.R. and Wilson, J.Q. (1998), *The Ethics of Human Cloning*, (AEI Press).

Komesaroff, P. (ed.) (2004), *Troubled Bodies: Critical Perspectives on Postmodernism, Medical Ethics and the Body*, (Duke University Press).

Kopinski, N.E. (2003-4), Human-Nonhuman Chimera: A Regulatory Proposal on the Blurring of Species Lines, *Boston College Law Review* 619–666.

Latour, B. (1993), *We Have Never Been Modern*, (Harvard University Press).

Lee, S. (1986), *Law and Morals*, (Oxford University Press).

Letter to *The Times* (2007), Stemming Studies, *The Times* (10 January).

McLean, S. (ed.) (2006), *First Do No Harm: Law, Ethics and Healthcare*, (Ashgate).

Mitchell, L.M. and Georges, E. (1998), Baby's First Picture: The Cyborg Fetus of Ultrasound Imaging, in Davis-Floyd, R. and Dumit, J. (eds) (1998), *Cyborg Babies: From Techno-Sex to Techno-Tots*, (Routledge).

Moore, J. (2008), What's Monstrous about Saving Lives? *The Sun* (27 May).

Morgan, D. and Ford, M. (2004), Cell Phoney: Human Cloning after *Quintavalle*, *Journal of Medical Ethics* 30, 524–526.

Mulkay, M. (1997), *The Embryo Research Debate: Science and the Politics of Reproduction*, (Cambridge University Press).

Munzer, S.R. (2007–08), Human-Nonhuman Chimeras in Embryonic Stem Cell Research, *Harvard Journal of Law and Technology* 21:1, 123–178.

Nicholl, H. (2006), British Stem Cell Scientists seek Licence to Create Chimeras, *Bionews* (9 October).

Nuffield Council on Bioethics (2000), *Stem Cell Research Therapy: The Ethical Issues*, (Nuffield Council).

Oakeshott, I. and Templeton S. (2008), An Embryonic Disaster, *The Sunday Times* (16 March).

Phillips, M. (2008), If this Monstrous Bill is not a Matter for MPs, then What is?', *Daily Mail* (23 March).

Prince, R. (2008a), MPs vote against Human-animal Hybrid Embryo Ban, *Daily Telegraph* (19 May).

Prince, R. (2008b), MPs vote to allow Human-animal Hybrids, *Daily Telegraph* (23 October).

Quintavalle, J. and Lovell-Badge, R. (2008), For and against Human-animal Embryos for Research, *Daily Telegraph* (8 April).

Rayfield, L. (2008), We must Pause at this Amber Light, *The Times* (31 March).

Rollin, B.E. (2003), Ethics and Species Integrity, *American Journal of Bioethics* 3:3, 15–17.

Sample, I. (2009), Rival Stem Cell Technique takes the Heat out of Hybrid Embryo Debate, *The Guardian* (13 January).

Scott, J.R. and Baylis, F. (2003), Crossing Species Boundaries, *American Journal of Bioethics* 3:3, 1–9.

Scott, R. (2007), *Choosing Between Possible Lives: Law and Ethics of Prenatal and Preimplantation Genetic Diagnosis*, (Hart Publishing).

Shaikh, N. (2009), Lack of Funding Threatens Progress in Admixed Embryo Research, *Bionews* (19 January).

Sinclair, K. (2008), UK MPs Vote to allow 'Admixed' Embryo Research, *Bionews* (27 May).

Staff Reporter (2007), Ban on Hybrid Embryos is Harmful, *Daily Mail* (5 April).

Staff Reporter (2008a), Embryos could Save Millions, *The Sun* (18 May).

Staff Reporter (2008b), Science behind Stem Cell Debate, *The Sun* (18 May).

Squier, S. (2004), *Liminal Lives: Imagining the Human at the Frontiers of Biomedicine*, (Duke University Press).

Steinberg, D.L. (1997), A Most Selective Practice: The Eugenic Logics of IVF', *Women's Studies International Forum* 2, 33–48.

Steinbock, B. (1987), *Life Before Birth: The Moral and Legal Status of Embryos and Fetuses*, (Oxford University Press).

Thompson, C. (2005), *Making Parents: the Ontological Choreography of Reproductive Technologies*, (MIT Press).

Wade, M. (2007), Cloning Pioneer fears Britain will lose out, *The Sunday Times* (7 January).

Walby, C. (2002), Stem Cells, Tissue Cultures and the Production of Biovalue', *Health* 6, 372–384.

Walby, C. and Mitchell, R. (2006), *Tissue Economies: Blood, Organs, and Cell Lines in Late Capitalism*, (Duke University Press).

Warnock, M. et al. (1984), *Report of the Committee of Inquiry into Human Fertilisation and Embryology*, (Cmnd 9214) (HMSO).

White, E. (2008), Stem Cells could Finish Diseases, *The Sun* (22 May).

Wolpert, L. (2007), Maturity at Last in the Genetic Science Debate?, *The Times* (5 September).

Wright, J. (2008), Rift grows as Embryo Laws nudge Ethical Boundaries, *The Times* (May 10).

Williamson, L., Fox, M. and McLean, S. (2007), The Regulation of Xenotransplantation in the United Kingdom After UKXIRA: Legal and Ethical Issues, *Journal of Law and Society* 34:4, 441–464.

Yeoman, F. and Henderson, M. (2007), Doctors' Rebellion forces Embryos Research U-turn, *The Times* (9 October).

Chapter 7
Humanity, Divinity and Interspecies Embryos

Robert Song

Introduction

The Human Fertilisation and Embryology Act 2008 provides, for the first time in UK law, for the creation of human-animal 'admixed' embryos and the mixing of human and animal gametes. Drafted as a series of amendments to the Human Fertilisation and Embryology Act 1990, a new section 4A (Prohibitions in connection with genetic material not of human origin) includes the following clauses, amongst others:

(1) No person shall place in a woman—
    (a) a human admixed embryo,
    (b) any other embryo which is not a human embryo, or
    (c) any gametes other than human gametes.

(2) No person shall—
    (a) mix human gametes with animal gametes,
    (b) bring about the creation of a human admixed embryo, or
    (c) keep or use a human admixed embryo, except in pursuance of a licence.

Introducing the Bill at its Second Reading, Lord Darzi, a Minister in the Department of Health, outlined the exigencies which demanded such a groundbreaking step. These, he explained, had arisen from the practical constraints being placed on embryonic stem cell research: 'scientists now wish to use animal eggs in place of human eggs for the purpose of creating embryos for stem cell research, in part to overcome the shortage of human eggs available for research' (House of Lords 2007, col. 666). But the measure was also justified by the long-term goals of such scientific work, because of their connection with health: the aims of such research 'would be, for example, to explore the potential for treatment of degenerative conditions such as Parkinson's disease' (House of Lords 2007, col. 666). Of course, despite such laudable ambitions, there were bound to be concerns, not least the possibility that Parliament might be paving the way for the implantation and ultimately the birth of animal–human hybrids; and in the ensuing debate a number of peers were anxious to make clear that the Bill clearly set its face against any such monstrous possibility. As Baroness Tonge demanded:

> Probably the most important provisions of the Bill, which cannot be emphasised enough, are that any embryo must not be kept or used after 14 days or when the primitive streak first appears, which is at around 14 days, and that no interspecies embryo … must be implanted in a woman's uterus. It must not happen. (House of Lords 2007, col. 671)

By contrast, sounding a discordant note against what turned out to be firm majorities in both Houses who were evidently insufficiently perturbed by these developments, Baroness O'Cathain quoted Scripture:

> Those who have known me for years know that I also look at issues from a religious perspective. I will not disappoint them today … God created man in His own image and likeness, and, as is written in Genesis 1:28, He ordained that man should have, 'dominion over the fish of the sea, and over the fowl of the air, and over every living thing that moveth upon the earth'. There is a clear definition between the species, which is how it must remain. (House of Lords 2007, col. 713)

At the same time as ignoring one boundary dear to certain strands of liberal political thought about the appropriate uses of religious discourse in public, the noble Baroness reaffirmed another, namely that between human beings and non-human animals. In doing so, she also gave voice to a profound sense of the portentous nature of the decision that was being taken by Parliament, a concern that was understandably likely to be felt more keenly by those troubled by the decision than those championing it.

Inevitably for those who endorsed the principles of the 1990 legislation in relation to the status of the embryo, this unease was likely to be substantially milder. For them two important boundaries were already firmly established in law, relating on the one hand to the fourteen-day watershed, and on the other to the distinction between embryo research and implantation of embryos in the womb. Whether or not they further agreed that the former of these boundaries also defined an ontological frontier between the presence or non-presence of a human individual, there could be no doubt that before that temporal cut-off the embryo was not to be regarded as a human being possessed of dignity. And if the early embryo did not have the standing of a human individual, then the pool of murky questions posed by hybrid embryos concerning threats to the ontological purity of humankind could remain safely undisturbed, at least for the moment.

Yet if the parliamentary debates intimated anything, it was of a more general nature, that some kind of broader societal shift was being worked out, some modulation of cultural practice and perception, some renegotiation of patterns of knowledge and power. That this was felt so lightly by some, and yet so momentously by others, may be an indication not so much of the reactionary conservatism of the latter, as is often facilely claimed, as of the imbricated complexity and opacity of our cultural situation. It may be that what was here felt – whether dimly or clearly – in relation to the hybridization of the early embryo is one moment in a broader reconfiguration, the contours and significance of which are far from readily apparent. In this chapter I want to suggest that recent developments in medicine and the life sciences, of which interspecies embryos are a prominent contemporary example, are characteristically addressed using an interpretive repertoire which fails to note important dimensions of motivation and desire. While understandings of the augmentation of biopower (Michel Foucault), the reflexive nature of modern self-identity (Anthony Giddens), the molecularization of the body (Nikolas Rose), and so on, surely have a place, they need to be complemented by a sense of the aspirations with which biotechnological medicine and science are invested – aspirations which, I will argue, have a profoundly religious dimension. In the nature of things, I can only present an early sketch, but it is intended to gesture towards an alternative way of thinking and living which has become almost entirely unfamiliar.

Bruno Latour, Hybridization and the Crossed-out God

One of the abiding preoccupations of commentators on contemporary developments in biotechnology is the question of locating them against broader historical and intellectual terrains. There has been a kind of received story about how this act of locating is to be done. This starts by noting that the emergence of the new technologies has been widely greeted as the presence of the radically new, at the same time as there has been profound disagreement about whether this is to be marked positively or negatively, as utopia or apocalypse. On the one hand, some of those who enthuse about these technologies maintain that accelerating knowledge in genomics, cell biology and a multitude of related and unrelated disciplines heralds a new era of radical human self-transformation and biomedical power, a new epoch which needs to be matched by an ethic that will be open to the emergence of a new super-humanity. On the other hand there are those who agree about the revolutionary nature of the times, but look on them as much in despair as in expectation. For them the new world is to be feared as representing the transgression of boundaries between human and non-human and a meddling with human life: it is 'playing God', and the only response can be one of caution or else outright refusal.

Onto this epochal sense of novelty the standard story grafts another set of epochal categories, according to which we are witnessing the material instantiation in the bioscientific realm of the vaporous transition from modernity to postmodernity. Modernity on this account represents a commitment to ontological hygiene, with rigorously policed demarcations between nature and culture, human and non-human, mind and body, organism and machine. Medicine under this regime is governed by the ideal of normalization, returning the diseased body or mind to levels and styles of normality which will observe these boundaries. By contrast, postmodernity spells the dissolution of such restrictions in favour of a polymorphous hybridization of categories, in which all that modernity took to be ontologically solid is dissolved into air. And humanity itself is at the same juncture, evolving from the centred subject of modernist humanism which constructs a catalogue of alterities, to a post-human future of contingent identity and indefinite possibility. Medicine in postmodernity loses any prior commitment either to the body or to the goal of normalization, and instead becomes a utility industry servicing human desire.

According to the received story, the modern construction of the subject and its others should be abandoned. While this rejection indicates an embrace of fluidity and a recognition of the inseparability of nature and artifice, it does not necessarily mean an endorsement of all things transhuman: self-proclaimed transhumanists may be too banally optimistic about the possibilities of human technology, too reductive, too individualistic, altogether too male, to model the kind of emancipation which the abandonment of normalization promises. On the other hand, the received story is resolutely opposed to any possibility of a return to an earlier modernist naivety, in which interventions in the body could be unproblematically differentiated into therapeutic and non-therapeutic enhancements, in which restoration to the statistical norm could be distinguished from elevation above it, and so on. The idea that humanity can be separated from its technological creations fails to recognize that the body is always already technologically constituted.

I want to engage with this received story through a consideration of some writings of the French anthropologist of science, Bruno Latour, particularly in his essay *We Have Never Been Modern* (Latour 1993). Latour's work is intriguing not only because of his instructive account of modernity, but also because unlike many theorists he makes explicit the significance of what he calls 'the crossed-out God of metaphysics' (Latour 1993, 33). Although this theological theme remains fairly marginal in this text, I shall argue that a reading of his account of modernity from this perspective provides an entry into an alternative narrative of modern biomedicine.

As we have just noted, there is a customary story according to which modernity designates a stance of purification and the segregation of human from animal and nature from artifice. Part of this same modernist mentality, Latour says, is the drive for totalizing explanations, the reductions of reality to one critical standpoint, whether these be the reductions to matter in naturalistic science, to power in critical social science, or to discourse in the case of deconstruction. However most of his work has revolved around the empirical study of science in practice, and he argues that none of these purifying strategies does justice to the interwoven stories of science which are simultaneously about real objects, social contexts and rhetorical strategies. Thus when he writes a study about Pasteur's bacteria (Latour 1988), he is indeed referring to microbes, but also, and simultaneously, giving an account of changing valences in nineteenth-century French society and the textual effects of

Pasteur's writing. To understand the networks described in science and technology studies properly, he notes, one has to recognize that they are '*simultaneously real, like nature, narrated, like discourse, and collective, like society*' (Latour 1993, 6; italics in original).

The task of relating these different stances is one of constant translation, weaving together a web to tell a better story which none of them – for all their undeniable power – can admit if they are to retain their purity and effectiveness. In other words, the work of purification itself creates hybrid objects which can only be recognized by a process of mediation. Modernity, for all its commitment to epistemological and ontological purity, is also responsible for a proliferation of hybrids which it is incapable of officially recognizing. Indeed hybrids are precisely what they must be, for modernity only acknowledges pure forms, whereas these are half-caste mixtures which to become intelligible must be parsed into their respective components. Characteristically, such analyses have been in terms of the twin poles of nature and society, subject and object, each of these terms being conceived as a pure type unpolluted by contact with its opposite. Thus, for example, human behaviour may be conceived in terms both of the mental operations of a subject and the neurological functionings of the brain; these are both pure forms of explanation, and yet both refer to a single mind-body whole whose unity remains notoriously resistant to conceptual grasp.

Because modernity is incapable of conceptualizing the hybrids which its demands for purification create, Latour argues that we would be better to abandon the primary commitment to strategies of epistemological and ontological hygiene. Essence should be subordinated to event, purification to mediation, pure form to network. The ontological point of departure should be hybrids, entities which are quasi-objects, quasi-subjects, 'simultaneously real, discursive and social' (Latour 1993, 64). The tired periodizations of history, with their totalizing tendencies, should also be abandoned. The response to modernity is not postmodernism, which secretly preserves the modern story of temporal progress and revolutionary break with the past, with the result that retrieval of the past is always self-conscious and ironic, a stance that is only effective when used to shock the moderns. Nor should the response be one of conservative anti-modernism, which also accepts the narrative of modernity, albeit under a negative sign, and can affirm tradition, but only ever as the shadow created by the rupture with the past. Rather the correct stance should be one of 'non-modernism', not given to modernity's conceits of epochization, totalizing critique, and Western exceptionalism, but seeing change as incremental, continuity as real, and relations with non-Western others as potentially fraternal in trajectory. And this has consequences for the narration of technological developments: '[w]hen we see them as networks, Western innovations remain recognizable and important, but they no longer suffice as the stuff of saga, a vast saga of radical rupture, fatal destiny, irreversible good or bad fortune' (Latour 1993, 48).

Much of this to my mind is illuminating and liberating, and corresponds to certain central theological themes about the equidistance from God of all periods of history after Christ. The mood of suspicion towards epochal narratives is also one that has rightly begun to catch on in the social study of contemporary biomedicine. An emphasis on the complexity of small-scale, local changes and the confluence of multiple histories may help us to pay attention to the density and involution of what is actually happening in the new technologies, without needing to interpret them simply as the avatars of grand historical trends. The traditional games according to which moderns and anti-moderns 'frighten each other' (Latour 1993, 123), each of them defining the modern world over against the past in terms of the radical novelty of its technology (be this technological science or bureaucratic rationality) can be laid to rest, or at least cut down to size.

However there is another element in Latour's analysis which I would like to explore, connected with his sparse but tantalizing references to theology. To understand this, let us consider the account he gives of the concepts of Nature and Society under the conditions of modernity. Under the pressure for purification, both Nature and Society are pure types, which nevertheless paradoxically need each other, and each can be argued to have an objective aspect and a subjective aspect. Thus Nature is conceived as transcendent and universal, but also has to be represented through its authoritative scientific interpreters if it is not to be mute: facts may speak for themselves, but only if their spokespersons give them voice. Likewise Society in the Hobbesian vision is regarded as immanent and created by individuals, but it also has to be conceived of as represented by a transcendent 'mortal God' if it is not to collapse under the weight of being immanently constituted: individuals may contract together to create political authority, but the sovereign only has authority if individual consent is sustained. Nature is transcendent, yet we constantly mobilize it. As social beings we are free, yet our freedom is writ through by the laws of society. Thus Society and Nature can both be seen to be simultaneously transcendent and immanent, and the power of modernity's forms of explanation derive from its embrace of both poles at once, together with the hybrids that are incessantly bred as a result. And so Latour concludes:

> If I am right … modernity has nothing to do with the invention of humanism, with the emergence of the sciences, with the secularization of society, or with the mechanization of the world. Its originality and its strength come from the conjoined production of these three pairings of immanence and transcendence. (Latour 1993, 34)

What is this third pairing of immanence and transcendence, beyond those of Nature and Society? This refers to the transcendence and immanence of God under modernity, a God which Latour suggests is removed from any role in the construction of either Nature or Society, and is no longer allowed to interfere either with the laws of Nature or with the laws of the Republic. God becomes wholly transcendent, a hypothesis of which neither natural nor social scientists have any need. But God also returns in another guise, as the wholly immanent guardian of the souls of moderns. 'Spirituality was reinvented: the all-powerful God could descend into men's heart of hearts without intervening in any way in their external affairs' (Latour 1993, 33). Mastering the world and remaking society, moderns could therefore enjoy the freedom from parental interference bought by banishing God to infinite transcendence, without simultaneously suffering the overwhelming desolation of orphanhood.

Latour is clear that this 'crossed-out God' of modernity is not the God of Jews or Christians. As he rightly notes, 'neither Jewish mystics nor Christian theologians have had any inclination whatever for the modern Constitution' (Latour 1993, 71). But this also means that once we have abandoned the categories of modernity and its coda, postmodernity, the parricide of God, whether quasi (in Kant) or overt (in Nietzsche), is a murder scene that needs to be revisited.

> Do we need to add that the crossed-out God ... turns out to be liberated from the unworthy position to which He had been relegated? The question of God is reopened, and the nonmoderns no longer have to try to generalize the improbable metaphysics of the moderns that forced them to believe in belief. (Latour 1993, 142)

Although Latour maintains his silence here on his own answer to the question of God, he has done enough in this brief compass to show that the self-proclaimed murderers of God may have got the wrong victim: the crossed-out God of metaphysics is not the God of Abraham, Isaac or Jacob.

Purification and Aspiration

That the transcendence and immanence of God is the third pairing produced by modernity invites a further question, one which Latour himself never broaches. If the logic of modernity is the generation of hybrids through the purification stances of Society and Nature, would it not also be legitimate to see modernity as productive of hybrids in relation to God – mixtures of divinity and society, divinity and nature? If so, what might this further class of hybrids look like? For example, might we be encouraged by this train of thought to find hybrids of divinity and society in the political messianisms which the modern world seems to have specialized in spawning – nationalism, fascism, communism and (who knows?) perhaps liberal democracy itself?

The answer to this general question is tied up with Latour's description of the God of modernity as 'crossed out'. God, we might say, must to some extent be *disavowed*. God cannot feature in any overt sense as part of the interpretation of the world or any of its aspects. This is not to say that God no longer serves a function in the modern world, but only that uncovering the operations of the God of the moderns may require a different mode of investigation than, say, parsing the relative roles of Society and Nature in human behaviour. The hybridities of divinity may possess a different logic from other hybridities. To begin to address this issue and to see how it relates to the interpretation of contemporary biomedical technologies, we need to ask a different kind of question.

Let us start by asking what the motivation is behind modernity's desire for purification. Why is it so important that ontological hygiene be preserved? (We might observe that already we may be beginning to trespass on sacred ground: the quest for purification and the desire for ontological cleansing is after all one of the characteristic aspirations of much religious belief and practice.) This is of course a question to which there might be a range of legitimate answers. I will attempt to trace out just one of them by reference to the example of René Descartes, a figure as emblematic of modernity as any.[1]

Amongst interpreters of Descartes' philosophy, the proper philosophical concern with epistemic justification tends to render his thought in terms of a quest for certainty, and to relate this to a dualistic separation of the thinking mind from the *res extensa* of the body. However it is arguable that if we attend to Descartes' own musings about the purpose and value of his philosophy, another perspective begins to emerge. At the beginning of Part Six of *Discourse on the Method*, he notes how his discovery of certain 'general notions in physics ... opened my eyes to the possibility of gaining knowledge which would be very useful in life, and of discovering a practical philosophy which might replace the speculative philosophy taught in the schools'. As a result of this knowledge, human beings might make themselves 'as it were, the lords and masters of nature' (Descartes 1985–91a, vol. 1, 142–143).[2] Such an ambition is desirable, he states, 'not only for the invention of innumerable devices which would facilitate our enjoyment of the fruits of the earth and all the goods we find there, but also, and most importantly, for the maintenance of health, which is undoubtedly the chief good and the foundation of all other goods in this life'. The prospects for medicine might allow us to 'free ourselves from innumerable diseases, both of the body and of the mind, and perhaps even from the infirmity of old age, if we had sufficient knowledge of their causes and of all the remedies that nature has provided' (Descartes 1985–91a, 143). The publication of his philosophical writings, he is suggesting, was motivated by the desire to serve the welfare of humankind in freeing it from the blights of disease and old age. His philosophical concerns were finally moral, and not simply epistemic, in nature.

But Descartes' concerns go deeper still. The distinction between bodily and thinking substances is needed not just to resolve certain philosophical problems about the relation of mind and body, but 'to show that the decay of the body does not imply the destruction of the mind' and 'to give mortals the hope of an after-life'. Even if the lability of the body renders it prone to decaying and perishing, arguments for the immortality of the mind sustain a hope for a future

---

1   See further Song (2003). On Descartes, see also Leder (1990, at pp. 138–141), as discussed by McKenny (1997, at pp. 190–192).

2   With the phrase 'as it were' Descartes doffs his cap to the one Lord of nature.

after death (Descartes 1985–91b, 10).[3] The purity of the soul and the absoluteness of its distinction from the body is motivated at least in part by a desire to rid the self of anything that might endanger its claim on immortality. We may without exaggeration regard Descartes' aim in elevating the mind above the contingencies of the body as ultimately soteriological and religious in nature.

If there are hybridities of divinity in the modern world, we might therefore surmise, one form they may take may be a search for immortality, to be secured in this case through the powers of philosophical argument. For another form of hybridity not unconnected with this, we might look at the radical view of what knowledge involves that was widely adopted in the seventeenth century, and take as our example the English statesman and philosopher of science, Francis Bacon. Bacon is traditionally associated with developing the use of inductive reasoning in scientific method, thereby playing a significant role in the emergence of English empiricism. However, scholarship in more recent times has suggested that his epistemology should be understood in terms of the placing in human hands of 'maker's knowledge' (Pérez-Ramos 1988). For mediaeval thought, the notion of maker's knowledge was characteristically predicated of the Creator alone; thus for Aquinas the most complete knowledge of something comes from creating it and holding it in being, a power which in principle could belong to God alone. For human beings, by contrast, knowledge was fundamentally a passive or receptive notion, though this might be conceived variously in terms of illumination, introspection or abstraction from sense impressions. To the extent that maker's knowledge could be attributed to human beings, it was limited to machines and other human artefacts. In Bacon's thought, however, the identity of knowing with making, which previously had been taken pre-eminently to characterize divine knowledge, was now brought down from heaven and placed in the hands of mortals. This radical, active epistemology equates knowledge of an object not just with a speculative understanding of it, but with the capacity both to construct and at once also to reconstruct it; for an object to be known is *ipso facto* for that object to be manipulable. Under the terms of this new form of knowledge, the realm of the actual becomes the realm of potential; to describe a feature of the world as necessary can only mean that the nature of its specific contingency has yet to be discovered.

The extension of maker's knowledge from the world of minor artefacts to human knowledge of the universe as a whole threatened to transgress the ultimate boundary, that between human beings and God. In the words of the intellectual historian Amos Funkenstein, who finds this constructivist epistemology across a range of seventeenth-century thinkers, 'applying knowledge-through-construction to the whole world was as inevitable as it was dangerous'. It was dangerous because

---

3   It is tempting to comment: if only arguments that the soul is immortal could make it so.

it makes mankind be 'like God, knowing good and evil' (Funkenstein 1986, 327).[4] But, while many contemporaries shrank back in view of the implications, the trajectory was set. There is a strong case for finding it in Immanuel Kant a century and a half later, where the notion of maker's knowledge is radicalized to the point that the human subject is the creator of the whole of space and time. While God may be the creator of our noumenal selves, it is we who are the creators of the entire phenomenal realm. In one sense Kant can be legitimately understood as describing an epistemological humility, in which it is acknowledged that human beings can never know things-in-themselves. But, as Christopher Insole argues, seen from another aspect it is equally – and inseparably – a supreme epistemological hubris: 'if we are without remainder constrained by the subjective conditions of knowing, but still we desire an objective world, then we had better say these subjective conditions actually create the objective world'.[5] It is then only a small step to Friedrich Nietzsche who, far from representing the subversion of the dominant tradition, at least in this respect is in fact the fulfilment of it: Kant without the epistemological humility.

Perhaps this is another example of a hybrid of the divine generated by modernity, epistemological in form, in which creatures grasp for themselves access to a kind of knowledge of the universe as a whole which had once been presumed to be the prerogative of God alone. And if we may weave together some of these themes in our own work of translation, we seem to be building up a picture in which there are connections between (i) the attempt to evade existential threats to the self from disease and death, (ii) transcendence above the contingencies of the body, (iii) a radical view of knowledge in which knowing, making and remaking are intermeshed, (iv) the eviction of God from any role in the providential sustenance of the world, and (v) an effort to put human beings in the place of the Creator. The story could be extended, of course. From the point of view of Trinitarian Christian theology it would not be hard to see in this the elements of an entire anti-theology, with its own doctrines of creation, its own soteriology, eschatology, ethics, and so on. But this suggests that even if with Latour we do wish to abandon periodization in favour of a more hospitable attitude to the non-modern, there might still be good theological reasons for recognizing the peculiar constellation of thought which marked this time. The category of the modern, we might say, picks out a particular patterning of human culture in relation to divinity characterized by the eclipse of God, in which God was banished to the sidelines of the official story, but religious aspirations reappeared through subterranean routes.

---

4   This understanding of the human appropriation of divine knowledge is noted by Latour in relation to Boyle and Hobbes (Latour 1993, 14), though he does not bring out the significance of it.

5   I am indebted to Christopher Insole for this reading of Kant, and for discussions on it. See Insole (unpublished paper).

Nikolas Rose and the 'Politics of Life Itself'

What does this imbroglio of quasi-religious aspirations, attitudes to the body, and epistemological ambitions have to do with contemporary biomedicine, let alone with animal–human hybrids? Do the new biotechnologies have any share in such aspirations? I want to begin addressing these questions through engagement with some of the recent work of the sociologist of medicine Nikolas Rose (Rose 2006).

Like Latour, Rose is rightly wary of narratives of rupture, and is keen to ensure that larger interpretive claims about trends in the politics and cultural meanings of medicine and the life sciences are disciplined by attention to empirical detail. Nevertheless he still argues that 'something is happening' (Rose 2006, 84): we are inhabiting 'an emergent form of life' (Rose 2006, 7), marked by continuity with the past but also by change. Amongst these changes he notes, first, the visualization of the body no longer at the 'molar' level of organs, tissues and limbs, but at the molecular level of genomics, proteomics and cell biology; second, the new space of bioeconomics, together with the growth of what he calls 'the biomedical biotechnology complex' (Rose 2006, 36); third, the rise in new somatic expertises, including not only the ancillary medical professions of genetic counselling and therapy, but also the legitimating discipline of bioethics; and fourth, the increasing 'subjectification' of health, in which individuals renegotiate the relations of power with medical professionals and take greater responsibility for their well-being, not least through the development of novel forms of biosociality and genetic citizenship such as medical self-help groups.

Most relevantly for my purposes, Rose also charts a move from normalization to optimization as the object of medical and technological intervention. While illness and the restoration of health remain important categories for medicine, they are becoming subsumed under a wider politics of vitality. The realm of biological necessity is being replaced by the realm of biological responsibility. This is evidenced in the focus on genetic susceptibility and the new medical category of the pre-symptomatic patient who must submit to medical supervision if she is to contain her hidden pathology. But it is also found in the potential of enhancement technologies, which in their molecular version (rather than, say, their robotic-prosthetic or chemical versions) are having the effect of making the human 'not less biological, but *all the more* biological' (Rose 2006, 20; original emphasis) – a process amplified in the somatization of the mind through the increasing use of psychopharmaceuticals. All of these index the shift of focus from the maintenance of health to the optimization of life: such technologies 'do not just seek to cure organic damage or disease, nor to enhance health, as in dietary and fitness regimens, but change what it is to be a biological organism, by making it possible to refigure – or to hope to refigure – vital processes themselves in order to maximize their functioning and enhance their outcomes' (Rose 2006, 17–18). Pervading all this, Rose suggests, is an emerging epistemology, and connected with that, a new ontology. These arise not in efforts at physical and mental enhancement, which human beings have always aimed at: contemporary technological possibilities are simply scientifically more precise and individually more customizable renderings of the prayers, potions and practices of diet and exercise that are found in every human culture. Rather there is appearing an epistemology and ontology of complex and open systems, which are better understood not through metaphors of depth and the appeal to hidden explanations of visible phenomena, but through metaphors of surface – associations, networks, circuits – and the refusal to prioritize single all-embracing explanations.

No doubt Rose's claims about novelty have some validity at one level. However, if what I have argued holds, they are only a small, local inflection in a much longer trajectory. The move from normalization to optimization, from health to life, may certainly feel new to twenty-first century people, but if maker's knowledge is a knowledge of making that is simultaneously a knowledge that can remake, then optimization was in principle intrinsic to technological science from the seventeenth century. Moreover, while in one sense a process of somatization and of greater identity with the body may be occurring, the capacity for transformation of the body suggests also a dissolution of the body – not in the sense of an impossible dephysicalization, but in the sense of the indefinite substitutability of the body and its molecular (and non-molecular) parts. Indeed perhaps the better part of the truth of contemporary biomedicine is not of greater bodiliness, but a greater *disembodiment*. Molecularization may represent a level of scientific knowledge that was unavailable to Descartes, but it bespeaks a remarkably similar ambition, namely the evasion of existential threats of disease and death through detachment of the self from the body. On this view, the 'politics of life itself' is simply the belated outworking of aspirations that were present from the outset, and it is hard not to see these as ultimately religious in nature as they ever were.[6]

We should note another aspect of an ethic which is centred on the ideals of life and health. Every sacred has its profane, and every idol demands its sacrifice. The requirements of vitality and well-being create their own shadows, secretly constructing their opposite as the object of peculiar horror. This need not be debilitating, as Rose argues:

> Of course, an ethic organized around the ideals of health and life produces anxiety, fear, even dread at what one's biological future, or that of those one cares for, might hold. But while this may engender despair or fortitude, it frequently also generates a moral economy in which ignorance, resignation, and hopelessness in the face of the future is deprecated. (Rose 2006, 26–27)

---

6   My emphasis on cultural aspirations indicates why it is inadequate to dismiss those who are concerned about psychopharmaceuticals or designer babies as too influenced by science fiction and insufficiently informed by empirical realities (as does Rose 2006, 77–108). It is precisely the underlying ambitions, regardlesss of the improbability of their being satisfied in the short term, which concern such thinkers.

In the face of illness and the prospect of death there is information to be garnered, fatalism to be countered, straws of hope to be clutched at.

Yet, even if inhabitants of this culture may have the resources to answer the reception of bad news from their oncologist with a frenzy of activity and not just unremitting despair, it is surely also the case that they do not readily have access to a language which can make suffering and the expectation of death meaningful. The idea that suffering might be a means of moral growth or might be integrated into a valuable life is alien: suffering exists only to be eliminated, death as the *nihil* to be staved off for as long as the will to live is stronger. And yet there is a case for thinking that any ruling ideology which is incapable of helping its subjects to face up to the realities of suffering and death has badly betrayed them. This need not imply the theologically and psychologically questionable identification of true humanity with suffering (Rose's use of Thomas Mann's ascription to a Jesuit of such an ideal – 'the more ailing he was, by so much more was he the more man' – is misleading (Rose 2006, 96, quoting Mann 1960, 466)). Nor does it endorse a passive acceptance of one's fate, as if there is nothing that can or should be done to counter it. Rather it involves an unflinching recognition that suffering and death are inescapable features of human life: in all foreseeable futures, everyone will suffer some of the time, and some will suffer much of the time, and any cultural ideals which attempt to deny or repress this are simply likely to invite the return of the repressed. Indeed any ethic with a claim to integrity must see the failure to attend to this as an escapist refusal to face up to reality – ironically the very charge often made against religion.

Conclusion

A society oriented to the ideal of optimizing life and health should be analyzed, I am suggesting, as having aspirations which are religious or quasi-religious in nature, even if they cannot be avowed as such. These features should be brought together with a variety of other, ostensibly unconnected, themes: amongst them, an epistemology which identifies knowing with making; an instrumentalizing dematerialization of the body which is the secret truth of the apparent trend towards somatization; and the lack of a language which would allow moral meaning to emerge from suffering or the prospect of death. As with Latour's hybrids, it is important that these different threads are woven together if the phenomenon is to be understood properly.

What might theology have to say to this? And how might this bear on the question of animal–human hybrids with which we opened? Perhaps the biggest temptation is to assume that it is the task of theology simply to shore up particular categorizations which have become problematic: the natural and the artificial, the human and the non-human, and so on. But theology no more than any other discipline can proceed as if we had not noticed that the natural and the technological are inseparable, that the body is always already technologically constituted – although equally this recognition cannot justify a theological endorsement of unbounded technologies of the self. Instead therefore of a direct approach to answering these questions, I will venture some exceptionally abbreviated pointers.

First, one crucial step in refusing the modernist ontological hygiene of the self that Descartes articulated, but which still pervades much of our philosophical thinking as well as our biopolitics, is to refuse the identification of ourselves as invulnerable and therefore to refuse the temptation to project disability onto others. As Alasdair MacIntyre has instructively mused, when the Aristotelian and Thomist tradition describes human beings as rational animals, this rationality is the rationality of a particular vulnerable animal: human rationality is an animal property, not a property which separates human beings from non-human animals (MacIntyre 1999, 1–9). Human beings are irretrievably bodily and dependent on each other for their well-being: we should fear any transhumanist ideals which seek not to enhance our care for each other, but by eliminating vulnerability aspire to remove the conditions which make care necessary (Waters 2006, 57). This boundary between human and animal is one which must be transgressed.

Second, we must discover how to love what is given without fatalism and without resentment. The voluntarist and emancipatory strands in modernist humanism, echoed and radicalized in post-humanism, imagine that the only fate human beings can genuinely love is one that they have chosen (Waters 2006, 51). Yet this renders questionable the unconditional love for their children that is intrinsic to the vocation of parents, and ultimately and in principle is in danger of excluding those who have severe and irremediable disabilities from the human community. The mantra of the colonization of the natural by the just runs the danger of succumbing to a moral solipsism.

Third, the Christian understanding of nature as creation, sustained in being and intrinsically intelligible because sustained in being by God and known by God, suggests a repristination of the notion of immanent teleologies, problematic though these may be to a mentality which can only see natural teleology in the etiolated terms of evolutionary function. This may ultimately indicate some notion of species integrity, though this should not be identified with species exceptionalism: human beings may have dignity as a species, and all members of the human species may share in that dignity, but that does not as such imply that *only* human beings are worthy of dignity (Spaemann 2006). At all events, if we cannot think of any good reasons for distinguishing human beings from non-human animals, in a technologically-minded world fuelled by the restless energy of biocapitalism our ontology – or rather our lack of one – will ultimately find us out. And then it will not only be those who care about early human embryos who will have to worry about the possibility of animal–human hybrids.

References

Descartes, R. (1985–91a), *Discourse on the Method* [1637], in *The Philosophical Writings of Descartes*, 3 volumes, tr. Cottingham, J., Stoothoff, R. and Murdoch, D., (Cambridge University Press), Volume 1.

Descartes, R. (1985–91b), *Meditations on First Philosophy* [1641], in *The Philosophical Writings of Descartes*, 3 volumes, tr. Cottingham, J. Stoothoff, R. and Murdoch, D., (Cambridge University Press), Volume 2.

Funkenstein, A. (1986), *Theology and the Scientific Imagination from the Middle Ages to the Seventeenth Century*, (Princeton University Press).

House of Lords (2007), *Parliamentary Debates* [Hansard], 19 November.

Insole, C., The Created God: Theological Aspirations in Kant's Critical Philosophy, (Unpublished).

Latour, B. (1988), *The Pasteurization of France*, tr. Sheridan, A. and Law, J., (Harvard University Press).

Latour, B. (1993), *We Have Never Been Modern* [1991], tr. Porter, C., (Harvard University Press).

Leder, D. (1990), *The Absent Body*, (University of Chicago Press).

MacIntyre, A. (1999), *Dependent Rational Animals: Why Human Beings Need the Virtues*, (Duckworth).

McKenny, G. (1997), *To Relieve the Human Condition: Bioethics, Technology and the Body*, (State University of New York Press).

Mann, T. (1960), *The Magic Mountain* [1924], tr. Lowe-Porter, H.T., (Penguin).

Pérez-Ramos, A. (1988), *Francis Bacon's Idea of Science and the Maker's Knowledge Tradition*, (Clarendon Press).

Rose, N. (2006), *The Politics of Life Itself: Biomedicine, Power, and Subjectivity in the Twenty-First Century*, (New Jersey: Princeton University Press).

Song, R. (2003), The Human Genome Project as Soteriological Project, in Deane-Drummond, C. (ed.), *Theology, Ethics and the Human Genome*, (T.&T. Clark), at pp. 164–184.

Spaemann, R. (2006), *Persons: The Difference between 'Someone' and 'Something'*, [1996], tr. O'Donovan, O., (Oxford University Press).

Waters, B. (2006), *From Human to Posthuman: Christian Theology and Technology in a Postmodern World*, (Ashgate).

PART III
TRANSFORMING THE BODY

Chapter 8
Introduction to Part III

Kate Ince

There are an infinite number of possible ways to transform human bodies, and in the two chapters that follow, consideration is given to a range of practices of transformation that includes the newly acceptable as well as a type still unacceptable to many people. Since the boom in elective surgical modifications to appearance began, in the early 1990s, Body Dysmorphic Disorder – intense dissatisfaction experienced about a particular, usually minor, feature of one's appearance – has become a syndrome often discussed in the press and in women's and lifestyle magazines, but Robert Smith insists that the more extreme desires presented by sufferers of Body Integrity Disorder, of which Amputee Identity Disorder (AID) (his own coinage) is one subcategory, represent a distinct condition. As well as detailing the misery often undergone by AID sufferers (self-injury and 'accidents' resulting in an approximation of the desired amputation are not uncommon) and the amputee-related paraphilias acrotomophilia and apotemnophilia (sexual arousal at, respectively, the idea of one's partner being an amputee and the idea of being an amputee oneself), Smith lists the range of psychiatric symptoms with which AID may co-occur, and notes its apparent similarity to Gender Identity Disorder (GID): both begin in childhood and do not respond to psychiatric treatment, though the documented responses to the wished-for surgery (when it can be carried out) are predominantly highly positive. Indeed, for sufferers of AID, amputation is in Smith's view 'the only therapy that has so far seemed to give long term, if not permanent, relief' (he considers that the decreasing mobility of old age may cause some patients currently happy with their amputation to have some second thoughts), and since elective surgery is not currently legitimately available anywhere in the West, prospects are not good, either for AID sufferers or for the medical practitioners concerned to help them, of which Smith is clearly one. Since criteria (the Harry Benjamin criteria) exist with which to proceed to a therapeutic regime for sufferers of GID, why should similar criteria not be devised for AID?

Legal difficulties beset attainment of the wished-for body image when the amputation of a limb is required to achieve it, whereas debate about and resistance to the immense range of appearance-changing cosmetic surgeries now available (usually at a price) in developed societies has tended to focus more on ethical issues. While taking in how these have divided feminists, and addressing its main argument to feminist theorists, Victoria Pitts-Taylor's chapter treats the universal question of the body's relationship with the self, seeing the regulation and potentially infinite improvement this domain offers up as an example of what sociologist-philosopher-historian Michel Foucault termed 'governmentality', as well as the site of practices of 'the care of the self' he treated in the second and third volumes of his *History of Sexuality*. For the many people now inclined to modify their appearance, the body has become a project, making visible 'processes of subjectivation' produced by cosmetic surgery that Pitts-Taylor argues are the result of developments in neoliberal biocapitalism (the increasing investment of capital in bodies and growth of lifestyle options concerning them). In post-millennial developed societies, individualization and agency are embroiled in processes of social and political power in the most complex ways, and, for Pitts-Taylor, 'Foucault shows us that the production of the self as a necessarily agentic one is one of the accomplishments of neoliberalism'. What this implies, though, is that 'a good biomedical citizen is never done engaging with the body-self', which might serve as a warning to those feminists who have tended to make the body a representative of the self, either through enhanced self-esteem or as a site for political consciousness. By offering a framework for interpreting the prevalence of elective surgical procedures that applies just to contemporary developed societies, Pitts-Taylor's chapter also resonates with the far less routine body practices considered by Smith, extending our understanding of what these mean, and how we might deal with them.

Chapter 9

Less is More:
Body Integrity Identity Disorder

R.C. Smith

Introduction

Body Integrity Identity Disorder (BIID) is a condition characterized by an individual's perception that their body's appearance or function does not correspond to their internal body image. The condition may manifest itself as a 'need' to be 'disabled' in a variety of different ways. The commonest appears to be a need to be an amputee, but others desire forms of paralysis, visual impairment, incontinence or to wear a cast. This chapter concerns purely those who wish to be amputees which I have chosen in this chapter to refer to as Amputee Identity Disorder (AID).

Clinical Features

The typical AID sufferer has a feeling of incompleteness with four limbs, but with a knowledge that their body image will be complete following amputation of one or more limbs. The commonest desire is for amputation of one leg above the knee, but some require amputation of an arm or even more than one limb. The condition usually commences in childhood, even as early as age four or five, and affects both men and women. It appears to be stimulated by the sight of, or contact with, someone with the particular disability. It seems to be more common in the more intelligent and educated male population and in Caucasians rather than other races. This could be due to the greater tendency of this group to communicate about personal feelings and desires and because there is less stigma attached to disability in this population. There is a possible association with gender dysphorias, homosexuality, and cross-dressing; however this may be attributable to the fact that one of the index contacts in early studies within this area was himself homosexual (First 2004). AID sufferers have intense feelings of shame about their condition which, in general, prevents them from talking about their feelings even to therapists. The sight of an individual with 'their disability' engenders strong feelings of jealousy. They often indulge in rehearsal activity (pretending) by binding up their leg and using crutches or wheelchairs. They have episodes of profound depression and anxiety which may stimulate thoughts of suicide and, when offered treatment, often withhold information about the AID from their therapists. The condition appears to be a lifelong affliction, but fluctuates in intensity. It seems to be resistant to conventional psychotherapeutic interventions. AID sufferers have a fixed idea of which limb(s) they want removed and may attempt to manipulate surgeons in to providing surgery by a variety of techniques. When the amputation(s) they desire is/are achieved the condition resolves completely (Furth and Smith 2000).

Aetiology

The aetiology at present is unknown but a number of theories have been proposed. They are as follows:

- An attempt to gain attention from cold and unloving parents. Being an amputee is seen as a very positive state likely to gain the attention and love required by the patient.
- The sight of an amputee in childhood imprints on the psyche as an ideal body image.
- The desire is seen as a manifestation of some unresolved internal conflict.
- The condition is a neuropsychological condition with an abnormality of the 'hard wiring' in the brain present since birth. A recent brain-scanning study has suggested there may be some anomalies in AID patients.

Modes of Presentation

Psychiatric Co-morbidity

These patients may present with psychiatric morbidity which is the result of the condition and never inform their therapists about the condition. There does not appear to be any primary identifiable psychiatric condition in the majority of patients. Treatment of the presenting psychiatric complaint is often unsuccessful.

Example   A patient with a long history of psychiatric treatment for depression attempted to commit suicide by lying on the railway tracks. The train amputated both legs below the knee. He rehabilitated quickly and has had no further psychiatric morbidity.

Unusual Symptoms without Objective Evidence

Patients with some medical knowledge may present with symptoms suggestive of a condition that might be treated by amputation but with no objective evidence of the condition.

Example   A medically qualified patient presented with symptoms of complex regional pain syndrome (Reflex Sympathetic Dystrophy) after arthroscopy for a painful knee. He demanded amputation and a compliant surgeon agreed to carry out an above-knee amputation. All his symptoms have resolved and he is happy with his reformatted state.

Self Injury

Self injury is common, but rarely successful due to the pain of damaging a limb severely enough to warrant amputation (Beresford 1980). However there is a technique for using dry ice freely available on the internet.

Example   A patient sat with his legs immersed in dry ice for a period of eight hours. This resulted in irreversible cold injury. After demarcation the legs were amputated above the knee and the patient was discharged happy in a wheelchair.

Unusual Types or Locations of 'Accidents'

Patients may present with severe limb injury after being involved in strange, inexplicable 'accidents', or accidents occurring in unusual places or at unusual times.

Example   The police were passing an ice works early one morning when the works should have been closed. The lights were on and they heard shouts. On investigation they found the ice works manager with his legs trapped and crushed in an Archimedean screw. He happened to have a walking stick with him with which to switch off the machinery. Both legs were amputated and he returned to work in three weeks, in a wheelchair, a happy man.

Refusal to Permit Re-implantation

Patients who present with traumatic amputations may refuse to allow surgical treatment to salvage a damaged limb. This appears logically contrary and surgeons may then operate contrary to the patients wishes.

Example   A patient presented with an almost severed leg after an 'accident' with a shotgun. The leg was still attached by the sciatic nerve and some skin and was reattached against his wishes. He did not cooperate with post-operative therapy and the leg was amputated a year later. He has since had the other leg amputated above the knee electively in the Far East.

With BIID and Requesting Elective Amputation

Patients may present with a request for elective amputation and have the typical features. At present there is no possibility of elective amputation for these people except in third world clinics.

Example   A university lecturer presented with a request for amputation of his left leg above the knee. After widespread discussion and careful psychiatric assessment, elective amputation was performed and the patient reports that his life has been transformed.

Other Conditions which may present with Amputation Requests or Self Injury

There are a number of other conditions which may present with requests for amputation or with attempts to achieve amputation and it is essential that these are recognized and treated appropriately.

Amputee-Related Paraphilias

Paraphilias are a family of persistent intense fantasies, aberrant urges or behaviours involving sexual arousal to non-human objects, to pain or humiliation experienced by oneself or one's partner, to children, non-consenting adults or unsuitable adults (Money Jobaris and Furth 1997; Riddle 1989; Bruno 1997). There are two amputee-related paraphilias:

- Acrotomophilia: Sexual arousal at the concept of one's partner being an amputee.
- Apotemnophilia: Sexual arousal at the concept of oneself being an amputee.

Clearly it is important to eliminate patients who are purely apotemnophiles from the AID group. They are unlikely to be satisfied with amputation as their desire is purely related to sexual activity and not to normal activities of daily life. However some genuine AID patients do have one or both of these paraphilias to a minor degree.

Body Dysmorphic Disorder

Body Dysmorphic Disorder (BDD) is a psychiatric condition in which the person is excessively concerned about and preoccupied by an imagined or minor defect in their physical appearance (Veale et al. 1996). This is quite different from the AID patient for whom the limb looks normal but is surplus to their body image.

The differences between BDD and AID are shown in Table 9.1. Clearly Body Dysmorphism must be excluded, but the Body Dysmorphic rarely requests surgery as mutilating as an amputation. Rarely do they attempt self-injury to achieve their aims.

Schizophrenia

Schizophrenics may present with self-injury usually in response to internal voices.

Depression

Depressed patients on occasions injure themselves in an attempt to atone for perceived transgressions.

The Confused or Demented

These patients may self-injure due to altered perceptions.

Personality Disorder

Those present with self-injury in order to relieve tension or gain some form of advancement.

Factitious Disorder

In this condition the patient wishes to assume the role of the sick person. This usually takes the form of a simulated illness for which surgery may be appropriate.

Somatophrenia and Misoplegia

These are conditions in which a lesion in the parietal lobe of the brain results in the patient regarding their limb (usually left-sided limbs due to a right parietal lobe lesion) as alien and not belonging to them. In Misoplegia the patient will actually verbally and physically abuse the limb and try to damage it (Loetscher Regard and Brugger 2006).

Gender Identity Disorder

On rare occasions the patient with Gender Identity Disorder (GID) will attempt amputation of their genitalia to achieve their ideal (Cohen-Kettenis and Gooren 1999; Green and Fleming 1990). GID is defined as a condition in which the individual has been assigned a gender, usually on the basis of their sex at birth, but identifies as belonging to another gender and feels significant discomfort or the inability to deal with this situation. The aetiology of GID is obscure but some recent brain-scanning has shown some female features in male to female GID patients (Zhou et al. 1995).

The GID is the only group in which surgery can be currently justified and there are considerable similarities between this group and the AID patients (Lawrence 2006). These similarities are shown in Table 9.2.

Table 9.1   Comparison of the features of Body Dysmorphic Disorder and Amputee Identity Disorder

BDD	AID
Starts in adolescence	Starts in childhood
Part is seen as ugly or deformed	Part is seen as normal but surplus to body image
Significant underlying psychiatric disorder	No significant underlying psychiatric disorder
Responds poorly to psychiatric treatment	Does not respond to psychiatric treatment
Poor results from surgery	Good results from surgery

Table 9.2   Comparison of the features of Gender Identity Disorder and Amputee Identity Disorder

GID	AID
Starts in childhood	Starts in childhood
Causes great emotional distress	Causes great emotional distress
Significant effect on working life	Significant effect on working life
Unresponsive to psychiatric treatment	Unresponsive to psychiatric treatment
Responds well to surgery	Responds well to surgery

Current Therapeutic Options

Currently, patients are being treated in a large number of different ways, often by psychiatrists who are unaware of the condition and to whom the patient may not even disclose the underlying symptoms because of their embarrassment.

Interventions that have been tried include psychotherapy, cognitive behavioural therapy, psychoanalysis, pharmacological therapy, caloric vestibular stimulation (Ramachandran and McGeoch 2006; Braam et al. 2006) and amputation. The only therapy that has so far seemed to give long-term, if not permanent, relief is amputation. The use of a serotonin reuptake inhibitor (SSRI) seems to provide some relief and helps the patient to live with the condition. Some patients use 'distractional therapy' by which they keep themselves busy and active to keep their mind off the condition.

Concerns Regarding Surgical Treatment

Ethics

The first concern of a doctor is to do no harm to the patient and the general reaction of most doctors to the concept of amputating a healthy limb is that this is totally contrary to this tenet. Most members of the medical profession imagine that amputation is a mutilating and disabling procedure, and consider that surgeons who accede to the patient's demands are harming their patients and are therefore acting unethically. Clearly, if the patient is mentally incompetent it is the duty of the doctor to protect that patient from his actions. I have shown however that there does not seem to be any identifiable recognizable psychiatric condition in these patients.

If we look at the four principles of bioethics there is considerable support for surgical therapy:

- Autonomy: Amputation is the treatment which the patient knows they need and denial of this treatment infringes this principle.
- Beneficence: Although the concept of amputation is alien to non-sufferers, the achievement of amputation for the AID patient is the answer to their problem and transforms their lives for the better. It also prevents them from embarking on hazardous and potentially fatal strategies for self-injury. This is a harm avoidance strategy.
- Non-malificence: Amputation seems to inflict serious harm on patients, but to the AID patient this is not harm but benefit. This is a problem of perception which differs dramatically between sufferers and their therapists.
- Justice: Justice for the patient seems to be clear, but justice for the community is a more difficult issue. Amputation will result in add-on costs, such as disability benefits, costs of amputation and prosthetic replacement. Many AID patients however do not use prostheses as they wish to be seen as an amputee and not as someone who has been cosmetically restored by a prosthesis. The cost of surgery may in fact be offset by the reduction in consumption of other medical services such as psychiatric care. The individuals pursue happier and more fruitful lives after surgery and are often more productive.

Public Health

A concern about the acceptance of the condition by the medical community and society at large and its treatment by surgery is that with widespread publicity it might become a 'fashionable' condition and result in a large number of patients requesting surgery. It can be compared to the 'Fugue States' which used to be fashionable in the past wherein people were found to have disappeared from their normal environment only to reappear in some distant place (Elliot 2000). However, unlike the Fugue States which were temporary, amputation is a major and permanent physical change and is unlikely to become a 'fashion'.

Legality

By carrying out an amputation can the surgeon be liable for a charge of grievous bodily harm? Provided that the patient has been properly consented and correctly diagnosed it is unlikely that he will initiate any legal action against the surgeon; however, the Crown Prosecution Service have been known to prosecute in a case of bodily harm when the injured person in question has not in fact complained. It is difficult to understand what the prosecution services are likely to achieve by prosecuting the surgeon, but if society determines that AID patients should not have surgery the threat of prosecution may be an effective way of preventing surgeons from operating.

Consent

In any event, can a patient really give consent for a procedure that will convert them into a disabled state, the problems and difficulties of which cannot be anticipated? Is the patient sane, or should a request for mutilation be construed as a form of mental illness? Although the patient may be satisfied with an amputation when young and fit, will they still be happy if mobility becomes even more difficult in later life?

The AID patients have been extensively assessed by psychiatrists and psychologists and no specific diagnosis has been applied to them other than for the illnesses, usually depression, that develop as a result of their condition. Most AID patients are in the higher intellectual and educational groups and are very well informed about the consequences of amputation, having researched it extensively. Many have actually pretended to be amputees in private and in public. However, one concern remains the effect of ageing as this will have a disproportionate effect on the amputee. Walking with an above knee prosthesis or on crutches uses much more energy than walking with two normal legs. Deteriorating cardio-respiratory reserve may make independent mobility impossible. I doubt if many AID patients can appreciate this.

Public and Media Opinion

The concept of amputation of a healthy limb is so alien to the general public and to the media that it creates sensationalist reporting, 'knee jerk' opinionating and little in the way of constructive discussion. The average man in the street is unable to understand the concept of the severe mental torment involved with a condition that regards amputation as a blessing rather than a curse.

I operated on two patients in the late 1990s who both requested unilateral above knee amputations. Both were successfully completed with no controversy and with the full knowledge of the Medical Director and Chief Executive of the hospital. However, in 2000 I was involved in the production of a Horizon documentary on the subject ('Complete Obsession') which included a third patient referred for amputation. At this point someone released information about the first two patients to the Scottish press and this resulted in an initial massive and ill-informed publicity. I was supported by some individuals, but was criticized heavily by others, including the local MSP who called for me to be dismissed. There was much sensationalist reporting and considerable intrusion into my professional and private life. This made all the relevant organizations dissociate themselves from further involvement. The Hospital Board in Falkirk decided that no further amputations for BIID would be carried out in Falkirk unless the patient lived locally and the procedure was cleared through the local ethical committee. I received a letter at this time from a lady of 76, who had had a through knee amputation at the age of 23. She wrote that 'living with an amputation is nothing compared to a lifetime of mental torment'.

Sexual Aspects

Is AID simply a sexual fetish? As described above, there are two recognized paraphilias associated with amputation: Apotemnophilia and Acrotomophilia. Some AID patients do have some paraphilic tendencies, but the main thrust of their desire is to change permanently their physical appearance. Paraphilics only wish the change as part of sexual arousal and are therefore unlikely to be satisfied with a permanent change in body format. Paraphilics rehearse (pretend) only during sexual activity, whilst AID patients pretend during activities of daily life as well as during sexual activity. The sexual component seems only to be part of the normal sexuality in relation to body image.

Current Therapeutic Situation

In terms of the current therapeutic situation, a number of points can be made:

- No elective surgery is available legitimately in the Western World.
- There is little prospect of controlled trials as any AID patient is unlikely to want to enter a control arm. Moreover, there is little surgical interest in becoming involved in such controversial activity.
- Psychiatric therapy seems to be of little value except in helping patients to live with the condition.
- There is the possibility of temporary relief by physical therapy such as caloric vestibular stimulation and in future some pharmacological therapy might be able to mimic this.

- Overseas clinics continue to offer 'black market' surgery of variable quality, at a cost, and with no proper selection process, audit or quality control.
- Patients continue to self-injure and some die in the attempt.

Conclusion: Requirements for Progress

To make further progress in the management of these patients we need to have some clarification of the legal situation and this must involve a calm and unemotive discussion of the ethical concerns. It is important to obtain some information on the long-term outcome of amputation in these patients and I doubt if controlled trials will be feasible. Finally, it would be useful to establish specific criteria with which to proceed to therapeutic regime for the patient with BIID (cf. Harry Benjamin Criteria for GID).

References

Braam, A.W., Visser, S., Danielle, C.C. and Hoogendijk, W.J.G. (2006), Investigation of the Syndrome of Apotemnophilia and Course of Cognitive Behavioural Therapy, *Psychopathology* 39, 32–37.

Bruno, R.L. (1997), Devotees, Pretenders and Wannabes, *Journal of Sexuality and Disability* 15, 243–260.

Beresford, T.P. (1980), The Dynamics of Aggression in an Amputee. A Case Report, *General Hospital Psychiatry* 3, 219–225.

Cohen-Kettenis, P. and Gooren, L. (1999), Transsexualism: A Review of Etiology, Diagnosis and Treatment, *Journal of Psychosomatic Research* 46, 315–333.

Elliott, C. (2000), 'A New Way to be Mad', *Atlantic Monthly*, December,72–84.

First, M.B. (2004), Desire for Amputation of a Limb: Paraphilia, Psychosis or a New Type of Identity Disorder, *Psychological Medicine* 34, 1–10.

Furth, G. and Smith, R.C. (2000), *Amputee Identity Disorder. Information, questions, answers and recommendations about self-demand amputations* (Authorhouse).

Green, R. and Fleming, D. (1990), Transsexual Surgery Follow-up: Status in the 1990s, *Annual Review of Sex Research* I, 163–S174.

Lawrence, A.A. (2006), Clinical and Theoretical Parallels between Desire for Limb Amputation and Gender Identity Disorder, *Archives of Sexual Behaviour* 35, 263–278.

Loetscher, T., Regard, M. and Brugger, P. (2006), Misoplegia: A Review of the Literature and a Case without Hemiplegia, *Journal of Neurol. Neurosurg. Psychiatry* 77, 1099–1100.

Money, J., Jobaris, R. and Furth, G. (1977), Apotemnophilia: Two Cases of Self-demand Amputation as a Sexual Preference, *Journal of Sexual Research* 13, 115–124.

Ramachandran, V.S. and McGeoch, P. (2006), Can Vestibular Caloric Stimulation be used to Treat Apotemnophilia?, *Medical Hypotheses* 69, 250–252.

Riddle, G.C. (1989), *Amputees and Devotees* (Irvington Publishers Inc.).

Veale, D., Boocock, A., Gournay, K., Dryden, W., Shah, F., Willson, R. and Walburn, J. (1996), Body Dysmorphic Disorder: A Survey of 50 Cases, *British Journal of Psychiatry* 169, 196–201.

Zhou, J., Hofman, M.A., Gooren, L.J.G. and Swaab, D.F. (1995), A Sex Difference in the Human Brain and its Relation to Transsexuality, *Nature* 378, 68–70.

Chapter 10

Medicine, Governmentality and Biopower in Cosmetic Surgery

Victoria Pitts-Taylor

The body is a space of intense cultural investment. Indeed, scholars have argued that the treatment of the body as a 'project' is dominant in post-millennial culture, giving rise to a whole range of practices from low-tech matters of adornment to the high-tech genetic, surgical and biochemical transformations of the body escalating in various nations across the globe.[1] Through these, the body is increasingly understood as plastic; further, the body's flexibility or plasticity is weighted with a heavy investment in the significance of the body for the meanings of the self. Body practices are increasingly positioned in various ways as expressing, reflecting or revealing various aspects of the self, and in myriad ways bodies are seen to make the inner self visible, render it public, manage it, or establish or even affirm its 'authenticity'. As the plethora of social and cultural investigations of various academic disciplines into the body attests, the body-self relation is, among other things, political. While the body's plasticity seems to defy any natural, and even cultural, determinism in relation to its appearance, comportment, functioning or meaning, the circulation of technologies of the body is not a free market, in the sense that it does not flow unimpeded by constraints, material or cultural. Rather the circulation of techno-bodies is implicated in the circulation of power itself.

The politics of body projects have been debated by numerous feminist scholars in particular for several decades, with the primary focus on the subjectivities of women who undertake various body practices. In what have been come to be known as the 'structure and agency' debates, which have dominated much of the Western feminist scholarship on the body, feminists have wrangled over fashion, body art, sex, dieting and cosmetic surgery, among other body practices. With regard to cosmetic surgery, the debate has largely been dominated by critics who view women who undergo cosmetic surgery as enacting bodily self-hatred. Critics of cosmetic surgery have also argued that the practices render the female body whitened (anglicized) and homogenized; they have pointed out that in addition to patriarchy, racist beauty ideals inform cosmetic surgery practices.[2] Cosmetic

---

1 This term 'body project' is generally attributed to Shilling, C. (1993), *The Body and Social Theory*, (Sage).

2 See Kaw, E. (2003), The Medicalization of Racial Features, in Weitz, R. (ed.), *The Politics of Women's Bodies*, (Oxford University Press).

surgery is seen by some as a particularly heinous form of self-harm, and has been equated with Delicate Self-Harm Syndrome (cutting), anorexia and other eating disorders.[3] For these reasons, to varying degrees women who undergo cosmetic surgery are positioned in much of this literature as dupes, as victims or, at the furthest end of the spectrum, as mentally ill.

On the other side are the so-called 'agency' feminists like Kathy Davis, who defend the rationality of women who get cosmetic surgery, hearing women's own explanations for undergoing cosmetic surgery more sympathetically.[4] They have argued that women's decisions to get cosmetic surgery are reasonable given the pressures women face regarding their appearance. Even for Davis, though, women's cosmetic surgeries take place in the context of enormous psychic suffering. In this sense, while Davis' defence of the rationality of cosmetic surgery patients has irritated some feminists, it is hardly a resounding embrace of the mental health of female cosmetic surgery patients. Women are not cultural dupes, according to Davis. Rather, she sees cosmetic surgery as a rational practice motivated by suffering.

The most recent feminist scholarship has decided that this debate is a 'dead-end' and numerous writers have been thinking of ways to reconsider the politics of cosmetic surgery in ways that do not depend upon diagnosing women and determining the status of their consciousness as the primary methods of exploring what cosmetic surgery means.[5] Following Suzanne Fraser and others, in my own work I have called for a 'decentering' of the subject of cosmetic surgery in order to see processes of subjectivation as part of what cosmetic surgery produces.[6] To do this we need new frameworks to move beyond the agency–structure debate. Here, instead of debating the character of the self, I reconsider the very relation between the body and self as an outcome of broader developments in neoliberal biocapitalism. Like other practices in contemporary neoliberal societies, I highlight how cosmetic surgery foregrounds the relation between the body and the self and promotes the body as a site of self-management, self-care and wellness; I describe how it is also positioned to reveal, in contrast, the body-self's potential pathology. Through the expert knowledges of psychology and psychiatry, cosmetic surgery is linked to both empowerment and risk, key features of what Foucault has called governmentality. Through using the governmentality framework, I position

---

3   See Blum, V. (2003), *Flesh Wounds: The Culture of Cosmetic Surgery*, (University of California Press); Jeffreys, S. (2005), *Beauty and Misogyny: Harmful Beauty Practices in the West*, (Psychology Press).

4   Davis, K. (1995), *Reshaping the Female Body*, (Routledge).

5   Ancheta, R.W. (2002), Discourse of Rules: Women Talk about Cosmetic Surgery, in Ratcliff, R. (ed.), *Women's Health: Power, Technology, Inequality and Conflict in a Gendered World*, (Allyn and Bacon).

6   Fraser, S. (2003), *Cosmetic Surgery, Gender, and Culture*, (Palgrave); Pitts-Taylor, V. (2007), *Surgery Junkies: Wellness and Pathology in Cosmetic Culture*, (Rutgers University Press).

cosmetic surgery in a wide range of practices that 'care for' the body-self, and attempt to reveal ethico-political implications to cosmetic surgery that are not accounted for in prior feminist debates on the subject. I begin with exploring first the agentic self and then the optimized body in neoliberalism before returning to governmentality in cosmetic surgery and the implications for feminist and critical thinking.

Technologies of the Self and Governmentality

While Foucault is best known for his work on discipline that imposes categories of subjectivity, usually through scientific knowledges and in institutions, in his later writings he took up problems of the self's relation to itself, specifically the possibility of self-action and 'the care of the self'. Importantly, he identified historical variations in the ways in which people care for and transform their own body-selves; historically different sets of ethics create different modes of relating to and transforming the self.[7] Technologies of the self are intimately related to power. 'Governmentality' is the term Foucault uses to describe the governance of conduct, or the conduct of conduct, which takes place on a continuum, which extends from government at the level of the state to the self-governance of personal life.[8] Thus the notion of governmentality bridges state regulations of populations with the self-regard and action of individuals.

In his lectures at the College de France on neoliberalism and biopolitics, specifically the series *La naissance de la biopolitique*, Foucault outlined the importance of a certain version of the self in market-based, neoliberal societies, describing a subjectivation that links individuals with choices and renders them responsible for themselves. For example, the neoliberal program of the post-war Chicago School viewed the individual as a *homo oeconomicus*, conducting herself through rational choice, but also promoted the cultivation and multiplication of differences among the body politic.[9] As Foucault sees it, neoliberal societies rely upon this kind of cultivation of 'autonomous' selves because they govern primarily through identification and allegiance rather than overt coercion, and because they are divested from collective and social modes of care. Thus, as he describes in his lectures now collected in the volume *Security, Territory, and Population*, governmentality entails a shift from disciplinary practices and overt regulation to 'security', which leads to an open kind of governance, to greater circulations and

---

7   Foucault, M. (2008), *Security, Territory, Population: Lectures at the College de France 1977–78*, (Picador).

8   Lemke, T. (2001), The Birth of Bio-politics: Michel Foucault's Lecture at the College de France on Neo-Liberal Governmentality, *Economy and Society* 30:2, 190–207.

9   Lemke 2001, 200.

diversities, and to proliferations and enablements of individuals and populations.[10] (In regulating less than discipline, security also, we should point out, not only leaves more to contingency, but allows for more of its negative consequences.)

In the history of feminist debates over structure and agency, practices of the self in neoliberalism have been seen on the one hand as instances of false consciousness, and on the other hand as voluntary acts of agency. The outcome of the debate between these two positions, if there is to be one, depends upon one's optimism or pessimism towards the possibility of an independently agentic self in the context of a power-saturated social world. But Foucault's analysis of governmentality renders either position inadequate because he suggests that an agentic self is in fact part of what is produced in power relations. In this framework, individuals are 'conceived not as coerced objects or ideological dupes, but as agents whose [very] subjectivity is formed through active engagement with the powers that govern them and through which they govern themselves'.[11] What Foucault is suggesting is the existence of a kind of power in Western governmental practice which, in Colin Gordon's summary, 'takes freedom itself and the soul of the citizen, the life and life-conduct of the ethically free subject, as in some sense the correlative object of its own suasive capacity'.[12] Or, to put it another way, the very ideals such as freedom, autonomy and choice are, 'bound up with a profoundly ambiguous set of relations between human subjects and political power'.[13] Freedom and power do not cancel each other out here but rather are co-constitutive.

We can explore this further with one of the aspects of the body-self that is at stake in such debates, that of 'body image'. Far from being either a painful outcome of internalizing patriarchy that obliterates an authentic sense of self (as radical feminists portray a 'negative' body image), or an authentic resource for one's own agency in regard to selfhood (as liberal feminists have depicted a 'positive' body image), body image can be considered in the governmentality framework as a key part of the architecture of the modern self, built by certain social vocabularies of self-awareness, that is neither inauthentic nor authentic, neither free of power – part of a 'true' self – nor only an expression of power working against a 'true' self.

---

10   For one summary of the latter see Elden, S. (2007), Rethinking Governmentality, *Political Geography* 26, 29–33.

11   Petersen, A. (2003), Governmentality, Critical Scholarship and Medical Humanities, *Journal of Medical Humanities* 24:3/4, 187–201, at p. 192; Garland, D. (1997), Governentality and the Problem of Crime: Foucault, Criminology, Sociology, *Theoretical Criminology* 1:2, 173–214, at p. 183.

12   Gordon, C. (1991), Governmental Rationality: An Introduction, in Graham Burchell et al. (eds), *The Foucault Effect: Studies in Governmentality*, (University of Chicago Press).

13   Rose, N. (1996), *Inventing Ourselves: Psychology, Power, and Personhood*, (Cambridge University Press), at p. 152.

Of course, in this reading, the truth of the self is undermined altogether; the self is positioned as an accomplishment of the social. In taking up Foucault's argument regarding the care of the self in modernity, Rose has prominently argued that through various processes of subjectivation, our selves are being invented; our various 'individual desires to fulfill ourselves in our everyday lives' are aimed at nurturing, establishing and maintaining our sense of self.[14] Rose argues that the 'psy' knowledges – psychology, psychotherapy, psychoanalysis, psychiatry and so on – have been integral to contemporary ethics of 'governing the self'. The governance of the self has been accomplished not only through overtly coercive mechanisms in relation to institutions and the state, but more subtly through the seemingly innocuous vehicles of concepts like self-esteem that become part of the grammar of the self in modern liberal societies. We can add the concept of 'body image' to 'self-esteem' as one of the vehicles through which we now relate to the self, and through which we are encouraged to relate to the self. Through the vehicles of self-esteem and body image, the self is governed in ways that are seemingly open and linked to self-definition, self-action and self-care, but also in ways that are shaped by socio-historical knowledges. Foucault shows us that the production of the self as a necessarily agentic one is one of the accomplishments of neoliberalism.

To a population of agentic selves who are encouraged to establish their own identities, ensure their own health and promote their own personal wellness and success, elective forms of medicine like cosmetic surgery are particularly compelling practices. This is especially so because, as Patricia Clough points out, we can no longer think that the contemporary biopolitical economy is only producing *subjects* who internalize social norms, because the affective, informational and material capacities of the *body* are also sites of social investment, modification and production.[15] Individualization still matters, but the individual is literally *mattered* in biopolitical relations of the body and the biological. In biomediated capitalism, biology both drives production and is the resource mined, excavated and produced. Contemporary biomedical culture now identifies the body, from the levels of surface flesh all the way to molecule, neuron and gene, as the key site for practices of self-care and the cultivation of 'deserving' biomedical citizenship.

The development of 'enhancement' medicine, the vast expansion of pharmacology and the intensification of commercial interests in the body, self and identity are among the many social transformations related to 'health, reproduction … [and] everyday life itself' that express neoliberalist power relations.[16] In neoliberal societies, those who might have been patients of health care become consumers, health maintenance becomes a responsibility rather than a right, and bodies and selves are targeted for intense personal investment and enhancement.

---

14   Rose 1996, 17.

15   Clough, P. (2008), The Affective Turn: Political Economy, Biomedia, and Bodies, *Theory Culture and Society* 25:1, 1–22.

16   Petersen 2003, 192.

We see the creation of what Deleuze calls 'subjects at risk', which make potential patients out of all of us, and the extension of biomedical technologies even beyond risk, beyond disease and illness, towards enhancement and healthicization.[17] As Petersen puts it, summarizing Rose, the notions of risk and empowerment 'have come to play a crucial role as techniques and technologies of governance, in shaping the conduct of individuals in ways which make them more self-governing'.[18] Notions of empowerment promise that through elective, lifestyle and enhancement practices, people can become 'better than well'. Alternatively, notions of risk provide an impetus for the self's constant engagement with medicine and technology: everyone, whether sick or healthy, is a potential patient, subjecting the body to various forms of self-surveillance. Further, in various computations of bodily risk and value, the individual is 'massified', placed in configurations of populations which are quantified and sorted, and which stimulate investment in (or, on the flip side, point to neglect of) biological capacities.

Nicholas Rose, Brian Maussumi and numerous others have pointed out that contemporary biopolitical power relations are not limited to normative conceptions of health and illness. They are not limited to producing 'normal', 'healthy', docile bodies and subjects, like heterosexual and reproductive subjects available for various kinds of labour. Instead, what is now at stake is also, in Rose's phrasing, 'the optimization of life itself'.[19] This does not elevate a singular ideal or set of ideals for bodies; instead it involves the modulation of and modification of the material body to proliferate possibilities for the body-self. In Brian Mausummi's terms, the normal 'is now free-standing', no longer dependent upon its direct opposition to the identifiably abnormal, dysfunctional or pathological.[20] Instead of aiming for coherent, fixed outcomes that speak only to hegemonic models of normalcy, biomedicine constantly extends the possibilities of bodily and self-transformation. While the dichotomy 'normal'/'pathological' implied an achievable aim and thus an endpoint to the body-as-project, a good biomedical citizen is never done engaging with the body-self.

---

17   As Adele Clarke and her colleagues have summarized, biomedicalization now aims at the 'transformation of new bodies and identities,' customizing bodies and selves via individualizing drugs, devices and technologies. Clarke A., et al. (2003), Biomedicalization: Technoscientific Transformations of Health, Illness and US Biomedicine, *American Sociological Review* 68, 161–194, at p. 169.

18   Petersen 2003, 193; Rose 1996, 348–350.

19   Rose, N. (2007b), *The Politics of Life Itself: Biomedicine, Power and Subjectivity in the Twenty-First Century*, (University Press).

20   Massumi, B. (2008), Requiem for Our Prospective Dead (Toward a Participatory Critique of Capitalist Power), in Kaufman, E. et al. (eds), *Deleuze and Guattari: New Mappings in Politics, Philosophy, and Culture*, (University of Minnesota Press), cited in Clough 2008.

Cosmetic Surgery, Governmentality and the Care of the Self

Biomedical cultures offer technological, pharmacological and surgical transformations as forms of the care and empowerment of the body, and as techniques for understanding, improving and relating to the self. As can be seen in the example of cosmetic surgery, they do so with the aid of psychiatry and psychotherapy – expert knowledges of the self.

Cosmetic surgery's engagement with the languages of the self more broadly, and with psychiatry and psychotherapy specifically, is part of its story of unprecedented expansion. The cosmetic surgery industry sells its procedures based on the languages of body image and self-esteem – cosmetic surgery is framed by both proponents and by patients themselves as a boon to one's sense of self, as a practice of self-care and as a way to treat oneself well.[21] In medical and popular representations of cosmetic surgery we find references to agency and empowerment, to body image and self-esteem, to personal fitness and improvement.[22] On one level this is marketing, but it is more than a simple exercise of manipulation; instead what is happening is the co-construction of selves and needs in and through new ways of living made possible through medicalized practices. Selves are not simply manipulated to use medical products and technologies, but rather the technologies are aimed at the constitution of selves. I quote at length Nick Rose's description of the marketing of depression drugs, in order to appropriate it for cosmetic surgery as well:

> Marketing does not so much invent false needs, as suggested by cultural critics, but rather seeks to understand the desires of potential consumers, to affiliate those with their products, and to link these with the habits needed to use those products. It is this process of mutual construction, the intertwining of products, expectations, ethics and forms of life, that we observe ... This process is not a brute attempt to impose a way of receding miseries, but the creation of delicate affiliations between subjective hopes and dissatisfactions and the alleged capacities of the drug [or, perhaps, the surgery? the injection?]. Such a medicalisation ... can occur only within a political economy of subjectification, a public habitat of images of the good life for identification, a plurality of

21 Cosmetic surgery societies in the United States, made up of cosmetic surgeons, have funded research which suggests that cosmetic surgery is psychologically beneficial to its patients. See a lengthy discussion of 'wellness' in Pitts-Taylor 2007.

22 See, for example, Brooks, A. (2004), Under the Knife and Proud of It: An Analysis of the Normalization of Cosmetic Surgery, *Critical Sociology* 30:2, 207–239; Ancheta 2002; Phillips, K.A. et al., (2002), Does Cosmetic Surgery Improve Psychosocial Well Being?, *Medical Journal of Australia* 176, 601–604; Copeland, M. (2003), *Change Your Looks, Change Your Life*, (Harper Collins); Fraser, S. (2003), The Agent Within: Agency Repertoires in Medical Discourse on Cosmetic Surgery, *Australian Feminist Studies* 18:40, 27–44.

pedagogies of everyday existence, which display, in meticulous if banal detail, the ways of conducting oneself that make possible a life that is personally pleasurable and socially acceptable.[23]

Cosmetic surgery is escalating not simply because it says it is good for us; rather it escalates because it cultivates 'new conceptions' of living embodied lives and being embodied selves. I believe that careful reading of recent ethnographic research on cosmetic surgery tells us that the practices of cosmetic surgery are not passively received, to paraphrase Rose, as a 'brute way of receding miseries', or of stemming self-hatred, as some radical feminists might tell us, but instead indicate complex experiences of active self-body-engagement. To be clear: by this I do not mean that they are simply expressions of individual 'agency'. Rather, I am arguing that they are experienced as ways of relating to the self in the context of individual and collective enmeshment in various notions and measurements of bodily risk and value.

One of the primary reasons that feminist critics have so often described cosmetic surgery patients as cultural victims is because of cosmetic surgery's history of promoting narrow, racialized and gendered beauty ideals. In this light, cosmetic surgery seems classically disciplinary. We might be content to assert that people of colour who get cosmetic surgery are being whitened, that Asians are being Westernized, and so on. But I want to remind us that while cosmetic surgeries do inscribe hierarchies of gender and race onto the body, they do not any longer only, or simplistically, do this. Rather, to borrow Thomas Lemke's phrase, they create a 'new topography of the social domain', including inequalities of gender and race, out of the material of the body and self.[24] Take, for instance, the new fashionability in the United States of 'ethnically-appropriate' cosmetic surgery, which aims to create ethnically specific surgeries to meet a growing consumer demand for non-anglicizing procedures.[25] No longer are bodies entirely whitened; instead, cosmetic surgeries are being planned to 'help' a person express her ethnic identity. We can also look to the diversity of cosmetic surgeries around the globe, such as facial feminization surgeries for men in Asia that have no Western counterpart, and the popularity of breast reduction among elite women in Brazil that reflect, among other things, regional class conflicts. In contrast to the eugenics model of cosmetic surgery often described in feminist critiques, where all diversity is obliterated, we must be prepared to think beyond eugenics and homogenization to biocapital's interest in proliferating new bodies, interests, identities and desires. Twenty-first-century beauty medicine includes, but also now extends beyond, discipline. The global cosmetic surgery industry is giving us a constant stream of new choices, new areas of the body to enhance, new reasons for cosmetic surgery and new technologies to explore. It is part of a new 'politics of vitality' in which the constant technological

---

23   Rose, N. (2007a), Beyond Medicalisation, *The Lancet* 369:9562, 700–703.
24   Lemke 2001, 203.
25   See Pitts-Taylor 2007.

optimization of the body is presented, at the level of the individual, as a key aspect of one's relation to herself, and at another level, is creating population slices out of many millions of patients and potential patients while generating transnational trade in tourists and organic and inorganic body parts.

Meanwhile, in much of the world the psychological and psychiatric discourses which have been appropriated by cosmetic surgery to sell itself are also employed to offer up cosmetic surgery patients for psychic scrutiny. Long understood as both psychologically and morally suspect, the character of the cosmetic surgery patient has been variously understood in the Western medical annals of the past 50 years as psychopathological: in the 1950s she was accused of having higher propensities for sexual neuroses; in the 1960s she had a greater likelihood of having a personality disorder. But since the mid-1990s, the diagnosis of concern is Body Dysmorphic Disorder, defined as a primarily biologically rooted condition involving brain function, expressed by an obsession with flaws in appearance. It is usually treated with the use of serotonin reuptake inhibitor (SSRIs). Once considered a rare disorder, it is now achieving prominence (labelled by the media as an epidemic) because of its perceived applicability to the growing populations of cosmetic surgery enthusiasts. Screening *all* cosmetic surgery patients for Body Dysmorphic Disorder is now being proposed as standard practice for cosmetic surgery in the United States and Britain.[26] The application of psychiatric discourse here accomplishes not only what Foucault has referred to as an 'incitement to speak' placed upon the individual cosmetic surgery patient, but also generates the at-risk self at the level of population. The 'technical frame', to borrow Clough's term, of Body Dysmorphic Disorder invites molecular-level understandings of both psychic wellness and embodiment, positions millions of women and men into new population slices (of various types of prospective cosmetic surgery patients, prospective mental health patients) and advances psychopharmacology and diagnostic screening as technical supports for embodied practices.

Cosmetic surgery subjects are thus semantically unstable and enmeshed in discourses that celebrate their wellness and self-care, as well as those that place them into categories of risk and surveillance. The semantic instability of bodies and selves makes endless and forever 'unfinished' the targeting of the body as a representative of the self. In cosmetic surgery, personal body-self relationships – the relations between one's sense of body and self – are ever opening to analysis, scrutiny, modification, 'expression', enhancement and improvement. One can improve oneself and one's body image through a successful face lift, or one can reveal one's pathology through a bandaged nose. Either way, cosmetic surgery offers the visibility of the self on and through the body, and it creates, to recite Rose's words, 'delicate affiliations between subjective hopes and dissatisfactions' and the capacities of technology.

---

26   See Pitts-Taylor 2007.

Feminism, Governmentality and Cosmetic Surgery

While a further review of feminist literature is beyond the scope of this chapter, elsewhere I have carefully argued that feminist critics of cosmetic surgery have generally positioned the cosmetic surgery patient as a woman who experiences self-hatred or, at the very least, hates her body, and is preyed upon by an imperialist medical industry.[27] Feminist scholarship on cosmetic surgery has often uncritically relied up the language of psychopathology – poor self-esteem, body image and so on – and implied that women who undergo cosmetic surgery experience a false consciousness, or at least cave in to normalizing or disciplinary pressures. The models of subjectivity and embodiment in such arguments are passive, and the model of medicine is eugenic. I want to argue here that in neoliberal biomedical culture, cosmetic surgery might instead be thought as an instance of the care of the self – in the context of neoliberal power relations, a necessarily agentic self – that engages with desires and habits, self-definitions and aptitudes, and affiliations in a way that is consistent with a whole range of other practices and expectations in biomedical, biomediated culture.

Thinking about cosmetic surgery as a technology of the self, and one linked to a hermeneutics of the self provided by the psy- disciplines, shifts the ethico-political critique in a new direction. Critical examinations of twenty-first-century biopolitics highlight points of exposure between biological production, psychic regulation and intervention, and capital. Alongside other regimens of the body, cosmetic surgery is suggestive of the ways the opening of bodies for enhancement and the opening of psyches for biological screening and regulation can be linked in biocapital economies. Thus we may be required to regard more critically the languages of self-hatred, self-esteem and body image as they are variously linked to cosmetic surgery, including within feminism's own debates, and how they may contribute to promoting the self-as/at-risk. Perhaps also the commitments feminists have made to the body as a representative of the self – for example, of her self-esteem or political consciousness – might be reconsidered in light of their worrying compatibility with biocommercial investments in generating the deep significance of body-self relations and with the technical framing of psychic dimensions of embodiment.

References

Ancheta, R.W. (2002), Discourse of Rules: Women Talk about Cosmetic Surgery, in Ratcliff, R. (ed.), *Women's Health: Power, Technology, Inequality and Conflict in a Gendered World*, (Allyn and Bacon).

Blum, V. (2003), *Flesh Wounds: The Culture of Cosmetic Surgery*, (University of California Press).

---

27   See Pitts-Taylor 2007; Davis 1995.

Brooks, A. (2004), Under the Knife and Proud of It: An Analysis of the Normalization of Cosmetic Surgery, *Critical Sociology* 30:2, 207–239.

Clarke A., et al. (2003), Biomedicalization: Technoscientific Transformations of Health, Illness and U.S. Biomedicine, *American Sociological Review* 68, 161–194.

Clough, P. (2008), The Affective Turn: Political Economy, Biomedia, and Bodies, *Theory Culture and Society* 25:1, 1–22.

Copeland, M. (2003), *Change Your Looks, Change Your Life*, (Harper Collins).

Davis, K. (1995), *Reshaping the Female Body*, (Routledge).

Elden, S. (2007), Rethinking Governmentality, *Political Geography* 26, 29–33.

Foucault, M. (2008), *Security, Territory, Population: Lectures at the College de France 1977-78*, (Picador).

Fraser, S. (2003), The Agent Within: Agency Repertoires in Medical Discourse on Cosmetic Surgery, *Australian Feminist Studies* 18:40, 27–44.

Fraser, S. (2003), *Cosmetic Surgery, Gender, and Culture*, (Palgrave).

Garland, D. (1997), Governentality and the Problem of Crime: Foucault, Criminology, Sociology, *Theoretical Criminology* 1:2, 173–214.

Gordon, C. (1991), Governmental Rationality: An Introduction, in Burchell et al. (eds), *The Foucault Effect: Studies in Governmentality*, (University of Chicago Press).

Jeffreys, S. (2005), *Beauty and Misogyny: Harmful Beauty Practices in the West*, (Psychology Press).

Kaw, E. (2003), The Medicalization of Racial Features, in Weitz, R. (ed.), *The Politics of Women's Bodies*, (Oxford University Press).

Lemke, T. (2001), The Birth of Bio-politics: Michel Foucault's Lecture at the College de France on Neo-Liberal Governmentality, *Economy and Society* 30:2, 190–207.

Massumi, B. (2008), Requiem for Our Prospective Dead (Toward a Participatory Critique of Capitalist Power), in Kaufman, E. et al., (eds), *Deleuze and Guattari: New Mappings in Politics, Philosophy, and Culture*, (University of Minnesota Press).

Petersen, A. (2003), Governmentality, Critical Scholarship and Medical Humanities, *Journal of Medical Humanities* 24:3/4, 187–201.

Phillips, K.A. et al. (2002), Does Cosmetic Surgery Improve Psychosocial Well Being?, *Medical Journal of Australia* 176, 601–604.

Pitts-Taylor, V. (2007), *Surgery Junkies: Wellness and Pathology in Cosmetic Culture*, (Rutgers University Press).

Ratcliff, R. (ed.), *Women's Health: Power, Technology, Inequality and Conflict in a Gendered World*, (Allyn and Bacon).

Rose, N. (1996), *Inventing Ourselves: Psychology, Power, and Personhood*, (Cambridge University Press).

Rose, N. (2007a), Beyond Medicalisation, *The Lancet* 369:9562, 700–703.

PART IV
SELF-HARM AND
SELF-DETERMINATION

Somebody – Jonathan Miller, Woody Allen – was asked: 'Are you a Jew?' The answer: 'Jewish'. I suspect that most of us asked, 'are you a liberal?' and inclined to say, 'Yes', really mean 'Liberalish'. Especially, I think that this is true about lawyers, assuming, that is, that the question means anything at all anymore. The idea of a 'liberal' lawyer has become a label to be attached to those who want the State to *do* things, rather than leaving people to their own devices. There is a contrary tendency which equates liberalism with libertarianism, but liberals are not so hostile to government action, are not so suspicious of it and not so doubtful that government can do any good. Nonetheless, the temptation to see the two ideas in the same light is particularly strong when we are considering the justifications for the use of State power to criminalize conduct, because adherents to both philosophies would set high thresholds to justify action. Here, both are concerned about 'negative liberty', about setting the limits of legitimate State action. Libertarian theory would see government action itself as a harm from which the individual should be protected, but the liberal concedes a significant role for the State. Although the metaphor is frequently deprecated, we are used to thinking about the 'balance' which must be struck between individual rights and the public interest, the public interest which includes the power to protect the rights of other people. The application of the ECHR, the European Court of Human Rights (ECtHR) frequently tells us, is a search for the proper balance. The Convention does not work by postulating an area of residual freedom where the individual may make his own choices unencumbered by any preferences of authority backed up by coercive sanctions (save in very particular circumstances such as the right not to be tortured, and so on). The Convention provides a matrix within which these balancing exercises may be carried out but, as Munby points out, this is a jurisdiction limited to those rights identified in the Convention, a list which does not satisfy everyone and, which, of course, will not satisfy the requirements of any general theory, not least because of the leeway left to national decision-makers by the European Court – the margin of appreciation. This criticism seems to me to misunderstand what the Convention is about: it is to provide minimum standards through an international agreement within which States may work out their political arrangements, rather than being the established constitutional settlement for any particular society. These characteristics – the catalogue of rights, the deferential standard of review – are among those which contribute to the conclusion that the Convention is a 'liberalish' document, much like the lawyers who have to work it. However, this is not to tell the whole story because there are other aspects of the ECtHR's jurisprudence which extend the protection beyond what a formal reading of its terms might suggest. The ECtHR has from time to time found that there exist positive obligations on States to take action, a distinct step beyond the idea of negative liberty and, what is more, that there are circumstances when the State must use its capacity to make conduct criminal to impose liability on individuals.

The European Court has not had to take on directly Bob Sullivan's hypotheticals, but its case law in cognate matters displays some theoretical uncertainty. There is a strong line of authority which prohibits the criminalization of private, consensual homosexual activities, but in *Laskey* (*Laskey, Jaggard, and Brown v UK* (1997) 24 EHRR 39), there are hints that the European Court would have taken an even stronger line than the English courts did in *Brown* (*R v Brown and others* [1994] AC 212) about sadomasochistic activity. The cases in Strasbourg and domestically about assisted suicide hardly comport with a liberal inclination, but the rather peculiar nature of the legal claims might be part of the explanation for that. While we may be sure than Alan Clarke's suggestion that a razor blade be placed under every prisoner's pillow will not become public policy, however benighted a Home Secretary is eventually given to us, nor satisfy the ECtHR if it did, how would we square this with the treatment of hunger strikers? So long as his wishes are known and clear, the prison authorities in this country will not forcibly administer sustenance to a hunger-striking prisoner. Most hunger strikers do not act from despair or (as Clarke hoped) to save the State the costs of their maintenance. The fact is that hunger strikers are not suicidists in the ordinary way. Rather, they act for a political purpose, using the ultimate weapon they have against the government. As the commander of Guantanamo said about the suicides on his watch, '[t]his was not an act of desperation but an act of asymmetric warfare committed against us.' So characterized, prison suicide is not the exercise of a protected right, but a grievous assault against authority, such that the most degrading processes of force-feeding can be justified in repelling the attack, the apparently absolute nature of the obligation in Article 3 (the right not be subjected to inhuman treatment) notwithstanding. The Convention case law is not clear on the rights of hunger strikers, but the indications are that the State has a very substantial right to intervene to prevent the suicide of those it has incarcerated. If a State has a right to intervene, it is hard to see how that right is not, in fact, a duty of positive action (as it is to protect (ordinary) potential suicidists). If so, the British prison policy is problematic. A more convincing reading of the Convention would be that a prisoner's right not to be subjected to degrading treatment is unqualified. The State may not invoke reasons of public policy to justify action incompatible with that right. The suggestions in the cases are that the State has a positive obligation to take action to protect its prisoners – indeed it does: it must make food and medical care available; keep the cells warm and clean and so on. But the right to life which engenders these duties is the prisoner's *right* – and as he might have waived his right to a fair trial by pleading guilty, so he might waive his right to take advantage of the facilities to which the State is obliged to give him access. States and the Court seem to be reluctant to acknowledge the fact that this is the prisoner's right – the liberal would say, it his right to exercise or not. The authorities may disapprove, but we can hardly say that the prisoner is misinformed, unwilling, irrational. But the institutions waver. They are, it turns out again, only liberalish.

There is, I think, an overlap but not an identity between the reservations of the courts and Sullivan about the limits, on the one hand, of the liberalism built into the Convention and, on the other, of liberal theory. He preserves his liberal credentials by restricting the circumstances in which the State may criminalize conduct that affects only the potential defendant in the way which liberal theory would demand. However, he can't go all the way – persons may use the rights in ways of which he disapproves, reasons which he concedes provide only a non-liberal ground for intervention, some form of paternalism. He has set out the dangers if this became a broad ground for criminalization. He seeks to meet the objections of the principled liberal by confining the State's right to intervene to civil commitment alongside robust review of the continuing necessity for it. The difficulty I see is not the measure of any intervention, but the circumstances which trigger even this lesser form of interference with the individual's liberal right. He has his doubts about young adult suicidists – should the State intervene to prevent their considered choices on grounds that some of them might think better of it if they were afforded a cooling off period (not, I think, that he would allow them another go if they were still minded to self-destruction after seven days)? Like the European Court, he, too, turns out to be liberalish.

This is not a criticism of either. In the practical world, pure theory will meet strong forces challenging its precepts, often, of course, some of the limiting examples of the kind Sullivan invokes. He has practical suggestions to make as to how some of the discordances he identifies might be reduced, though without more, I should have some doubts about the practical value of the substituting civil commitment for criminal confinement, where paternalism is the ground for intervention, given the easy slide that there has been from the civil to the criminal in recent experiments, such as Anti-Social Behaviour Orders (ASBOs) or for asset confiscation. The value of theory here, even if it yields from time to time to majoritarianism, to short-term political opportunism, to well-meaning paternalism or to an anti-theory prejudice ('do I not like that!'), is that it can make it clear what we are doing, it can preserve a space for rationality and critical assessment, which, we might hope, may avoid such inconsistency of reaction which criminalizes the private conduct in *Brown* but permits the public violence of professional boxing. If we can't, as individuals or as societies, always submit to the demands that theory makes of us, we should know what we are doing, and why, when we depart from the great principles – the danger is not just to the treatment of the person of extraordinary inclinations, but that the exceptional case will be used to justify the infiltration of State power into activities not confined to a few idiosyncratic individuals but to ones of significant minorities or disadvantaged groups who cannot protect themselves against an insensitive legislature or an uncomprehending judge.

The question treated by Sullivan is complex enough. From a liberal perspective, the matter which Munby and McIvor address – the right to medical treatment – is even more taxing. As I asserted earlier, there is for lawyers a liberalish basis for taking on this question and it was the one adopted by Sir James in the instance judgement in *Burke* (*R (On the Application of Oliver Leslie Burke) v. GMC* [2005] 3 WLR 1132). Primarily, he used the ECHR for his analysis. He relied on Article 3 and Article 8 (the right to respect for private life) of the Convention to establish that there were circumstances (including Burke's) where a patient did have a right to continue to be treated, even in the face of a decision by a medical professional that the treatment was no longer in his (Burke's) best interests as understood by the doctor. This certainly looks like a liberal decision and was so taken by many of the academic commentators on the case, commentators who were in the main dismissive of the subsequent Court of Appeal judgement overturning Munby's earlier decision. Those who praised Munby and excoriated the Court of Appeal did so in liberal terms – the earlier judgement had given proper priority to the individual's liberty over the later preferred paternalism of the medics. McIvor is on the side of the judges in the Court of Appeal, whose judgement was later found to be compatible with the ECHR by the European Court. She would not, I imagine, consider herself unliberal, so on what ground does she stand? Burke's claim was not that of the orthodox invocator of liberalism – 'leave me alone' – but that he was entitled to a good from the State, entitled, that is, to its intervention for his self-perceived benefit. By going directly to the Convention, we may put to one side the question of whether or not liberalism has anything to say about positive rights, for the Convention certainly does. The express rights in the Convention are, with the narrowest exceptions, 'civil and political rights', so that the obvious starting point for Burke's complaint – a right to health care – is not protected by the Convention. If it were, the existence of some positive obligations would have been unproblematic, though it would not have necessarily followed that Burke would have had his remedy. Instead, he sought to rely on Articles 2 (the right to life), Article 3 and Article 8 to fashion an obligation for the State to provide the treatment which he sought. Now, one feature of positive obligations is that they have *some* resource implication for the State and, if they are widely drawn or materially demanding, the resource consequences can be substantial and manageable only to the detriment of other goods which the State has chosen to provide. Here, though, Munby and the Court of Appeal considered that the resources consequence of a decision in favour of Burke were not of significance. To the extent that matters of principle were being decided this would not always be the case, but Munby in his judgement and McIvor in her chapter both emphasized the particulars of Burke's claim. Munby was able to satisfy himself that Burke did have a right to (the continuation of) a specific treatment to protect him from the inhuman and degrading consequences of its withdrawal. The positive, substantive content of any Article 3 right so far considered by the ECtHR is pretty derisory as cases like *Limbuela* (*R (Limbuela) v Secretary of State for the Home Department* [2006] 1 AC 396) show and it is not clear that the obligation of the State would have been triggered by the contemplated facts in this (Burke's) case. Article 8, even if it did give Burke his right, is a right subject to interference by a State, so that it would be necessary to assess the exercise of any power the State had when it declined to treat Burke. Nonetheless, Munby makes it clear that (even) a *Bolam*-compliant refusal by the doctor would not be in accordance with Burke's · rights – his right to autonomy would allow him to determine his best interests. McIvor's objection of principle to this is that positive rights do (or do in cases like the present one) implicate the interests of other people. It is one thing to argue that liberalism gives an individual the right to refuse treatment because then only the patient will be affected by his own decision. If Burke were entitled to his treatment, a doctor would be required to administer treatment which he (the doctor) regarded as medically not warranted. The doctor's interest is a powerful one, with which Burke's rights must be accommodated. It is here that the precise normative nature of McIvor's claim comes under scrutiny. I am not convinced that broad liberal theory would support her (though specific medical ethics schemes may very well do so). Of course, according to Court of Appeal, the doctor can rely on the ordinary law and that is fine for him (and for her), so long as they are right that there is no ECHR obligation to make the (or conceivably, a) doctor act, which there is not. The liberal answer is not that we should defer to the doctor's rights, but that the patient does not have from the State a right to treatment which is not medically indicated. The interesting case, not of course the one here, is where the patient's and the doctor's inclinations coincide – that is to say, that the doctor is prepared to give the patient what he wants but there is some obstacle to the doctor doing so – a regulatory or budgetary restriction of prescribing a particular drug, say. Liberal theory, if it were to concede the legitimacy of positive rights, might then require that the means be provided for the doctor to go ahead – but that theory would not necessarily convince the European Court. It might turn out to be only liberalish on this matter, too. Munby's chapter, giving a sharp account of English law, confirms its liberalish qualities also, recognizing that positive obligations to broad social and economic goods would put strains on the legal system with which the courts may not be able to cope very well. They would lower the barrier of non-justicability and hope that decisions from the ECtHR would not make them raise them. McIvor is not saying that she is not a liberal, but that the question of the positive right to treatment cannot get a liberal answer. Indeed, she contrasts the value of dignity (which she sees as pointing towards the solution) to that of autonomy, undoubtedly a liberal value. The question, then, I suppose, is, are positive economic and social rights liberal? – a question for another time.

Chapter 12

A Duty to Treat? – A Legal Analysis

Mr Justice Munby

I am honoured to be asked to contribute to this edited collection and in the short chapter that follows I would like to discuss a topic of vital significance. But my task is limited. I am by training and profession a lawyer, and whatever competence I may have in that regard I certainly have no competence in the many other fields – ethics, morality, philosophy, theology, medicine and public administration – which in this context also have such important roles to play.

I start with what lawyers call public law – the law which regulates relations between private individuals and the State or public bodies such as the National Health Service. This is not of much significance for present purposes. There are, I think, three reasons for this.

First, under the common law – our traditional judge-made law – the State was under few, if any, legally enforceable duties; such duties as it owed the citizen were enforceable only politically through the ballot box. Certainly the State was under no duty to provide medical care or treatment.

Second, while the Acts of Parliament which created and regulate the National Health Service may create all kinds of duties, these obligations barely transmit through to any specific duty enforceable by the individual patient. There are a number of reasons for this. In the first place, the most general and aspirational provisions in the legislation have been held not to be justiciable at all, their enforcement being a matter not for judges but rather through political means. Secondly, and prior to the coming into force of the Human Rights Act 1998, the public law remedies available to a disgruntled patient for alleged breaches of the statutes regulating the NHS were few and usually, at least from the patient's perspective, unsatisfactory. A decision could be successfully challenged only if the patient could establish that it was what the lawyers call *Wednesbury* unreasonable – so unreasonable that no competent and conscientious decision-maker could have arrived at it.[1] That is a very high test to have to satisfy, and it rarely is. Moreover, the courts have tended to hold that even where the relevant legislation does contain justiciable duties which have been breached, they are enforceable by public law remedies only and give no private law remedy. The practical effect of this is that the patient cannot obtain an order requiring the NHS to provide a specific form of treatment for him, nor damages if it fails to do so. The court cannot take the decision itself, for these are

---

1   *Associated Provincial Picture Houses v Wednesbury Corporation* [1947] EWCA Civ 1.

matters which Parliament has left to the relevant decision-makers identified in the legislation. The duty of the judge is merely – though importantly – to ensure that those taking decisions act lawfully and rationally. Thirdly, the courts were – and are – particularly reluctant to intervene to investigate, let alone overturn, decisions having to do with the allocation and prioritization of resources, whether financial or human, which are, almost inevitably, in short supply. There are, I think, two reasons for this judicial reticence: (i) one is that the courts simply lack the relevant expertise and, even more pertinently, lack the relevant information; (ii) the other is that, since there will always be priorities to be assessed and evaluated, and, at the sharp end, excruciatingly difficult decisions to be made, there are powerful arguments for saying that these are, in the final analysis, matters to be decided by public officials who are democratically accountable and not by unelected and in that sense unaccountable judges.

The third reason why public law rarely provides any very effective remedy in this context is that the Human Rights Act, although on one level its impact has been revolutionary – for the first time imposing on the State and on public bodies such as the NHS legally enforceable duties, including in some circumstances legally enforceable duties to take *positive* steps – is, for various reasons, not a panacea for disgruntled patients. In the first place the European Convention on Human Rights and Fundamental Freedoms to which the Act gives effect is focused on *political* and *civil* rather than on *social* or *economic* rights. Secondly, as has been pointed out elsewhere, it is accordingly not concerned with distributive justice, that is with the allocation of social or economic resources. Thirdly, the extent of the positive duties imposed on the State by the Convention is limited. It has been recognized that, although the Convention may protect the pursuit of happiness it does not confer a right to happiness. In all these respects the Convention is to be contrasted with other and more recent constitutional documents, the Constitution of South Africa, for example. So in day-to-day medical practice the Convention and the Act are of rather limited impact.

Let me turn now to what lawyers call private law – the law which regulates relations between private individuals, including for present purposes the patient and the doctor. The starting point is that private law traditionally draws a fundamental distinction between acts and omissions, penalizing or providing financial remedies against those who commit wrongful acts but, generally speaking, providing no remedy for omissions, however wrongful or even immoral. Positive duties to care for someone – duties which give rise to liability for omissions as well as acts – arise only if one has assumed the burden of caring for them. There need be no contract, typically there is not. Parents owe a positive duty of care to their helpless children, just as we do if we take an elderly and helpless relative into our home to look after them. If I allow my baby or my bedridden grandmother to starve to death in my house, then I commit a criminal offence: manslaughter if I was merely feckless or incompetent; murder if I intended death or really serious harm.

Now exactly the same principle applies to doctors. A doctor who has assumed care for someone as his patient thereby assumes, in the eyes of the law, a duty to take positive steps where these are appropriate. So the doctor becomes liable not merely for acts which injure, but also for injurious omissions. *Bland*[2] established that there is no special 'doctor's defence' and the Court of Appeal in *Burke*[3] was clear as to the consequences if a doctor causes a patient's death by unjustifiably withdrawing treatment:

> [W]here a competent patient indicates his or her wish to be kept alive by the provision of ANH [artificial nutrition and hydration] any doctor who deliberately brings that patient's life to an end by discontinuing the supply of ANH will not merely be in breach of duty but guilty of murder. Where life depends upon the continued provision of ANH there can be no question of the supply of ANH not being clinically indicated unless a clinical decision has been taken that the life in question should come to an end. That is not a decision that can lawfully be taken in the case of a competent patient who expresses the wish to remain alive.[4]

That seems clear enough, but just how far can the patient go in telling the doctor what to do? Stark cases like *Burke* apart, the answer probably is not very far.

At this point one turns, at least rhetorically, to the principle of patient autonomy and self-determination, a principle of the very first importance. It is decisive when the question is whether a doctor can impose treatment on a competent and unwilling patient: he cannot, even if the patient's reasons for declining treatment are irrational or even non-existent. But it plays little part where the dispute arises the other way round, where the patient is seeking treatment which the doctor is unwilling to provide. Here the law has tended to limit the right of patient choice.

There are a number of reasons why this is so. In the first place, the predilection of the law – uncontroversial in an earlier age when laymen tended to defer to professional expertise, more controversial today when such deference has in large part gone – is to assume that, because the doctor knows best, he must be left to decide matters by reference to professional skill and, perhaps more controversially, by reference to professional judgement.

Secondly, the law traditionally tests professional performance by reference to the law of negligence. And a doctor is not negligent if he adopts an approach acceptable to a respectable body of medical opinion (even if it is not in accordance with majority medical opinion) and if he exhibits the standard of care and skill to be expected of an averagely competent practitioner (even if it falls short of the standards of the leaders of the profession). This is the principle enshrined, as we all know, in the *Bolam* test.[5]

---

2   *Airedale Hospital Trustees v Bland* [1992] UKHL 5.

3   *Burke, R (On the Application of) v The General Medical Council* [2005] EWCA Civ 1003.

4   At [53].

5   *Bolam v Friern Hospital Management Committee* [1957] 1 WLR 582

Thirdly, the law does not compel doctors to act in a manner contrary to personal conscience. There is, therefore, a gap between what the law permits a doctor to do and what the law requires a doctor to do – performing an abortion is an obvious example – though the gap is, I suspect, quite narrow.

Finally, the law recognizes the reality, that mutual trust and confidence are usually central to any effective relationship between a doctor and his patient. Where there is a breakdown in that mutual trust and confidence, or where conscience properly intervenes, the time has come for the parting of the ways. But does this mean that the doctor can simply abandon his patient, especially where treatment has started and the patient is dependent upon continuing professional care? Surely not. Surely the doctor's obligation then is to do his best to assist his patient in finding another doctor who will be able to work together with the patient.

It is at this point that we confront the fundamental question. Are there circumstances in which the competent adult patient can demand to be treated or to be given a particular form of treatment? Does the principle of patient autonomy and self-determination entitle the patient not merely to refuse consent to treatment X being offered by the doctor or to choose between treatments X and Y, both of which are being offered by the doctor; does it entitle him to demand treatment Z which is not being offered by the doctor? Expressed in these wide terms the answer can only be no. But are there circumstances where the answer might be yes? I suspect there may be, though the circumstances in which the point might arise in theory are probably sufficiently narrow as to make it unlikely that they will in fact arise in practice.

No doubt the doctor is in a better position than the patient to decide what is in the patient's best *medical* interests, but a patient's best interests are not defined by or confined to his *medical* interests. And there are good reasons, I would suggest, why it is the patient, and not the doctor, who is in the best position to decide where the patient's best interests in the widest sense truly lie and to decide what medical treatment is in his best interests. And doctors and judges must have the humility to recognize this and must not seek to impose their own views, however seemingly reasonable, on the competent patient. But it does not follow from this that, as a matter of law, the patient is entitled to demand that he receives the treatment he thinks is best suited to his interests. The fact remains that there will be cases where the patient's wishes, even in the case of seemingly routine treatment, will come into conflict with either the treating doctor's clinical assessment or the administrator's budget. Does the patient in that situation hold the trump card? The answer, almost certainly, is that he does not. His remedy then lies not in a court of law. If the issue is one of clinical assessment, his remedy is to find another doctor who is prepared to give him the treatment he wants. If the issue is one of resources, his remedy, at least in theory, is to fund the treatment himself or find a healthcare provider whose budget will run to it.

Is this desirable? It is not for me to say. The issues engaged are surely such that they cannot be resolved, in the final analysis, by mere lawyers.

Chapter 13

Bursting the Autonomy Bubble: A Defence of the Court of Appeal Decision in *R (On the Application of Oliver Leslie Burke) v GMC*

Claire McIvor

Introduction

In *R (On the Application of Oliver Leslie Burke) v GMC*,[1] a terminally ill man sought judicial review of certain General Medical Council guidance to the medical profession which he argued was unlawful in so far as it failed to recognize the right of patients to insist on the provision of life-sustaining treatment. The application succeeded in the High Court. Delivering a lengthy judgement replete with references to the principles of autonomy and self-determination, Munby J based this hitherto unrecognized legal right to treatment on Articles 3 and 8 of the European Convention on Human Rights (ECHR). For many who had long sought to advance the interests of patients in the face of a historically paternalistic medical law regime, and who lamented the absence in English judicial reasoning of any kind of sustained bioethical discourse, Munby J attained almost hero-like status. In the face of such veneration, it is perhaps not surprising that the reaction to his subsequent censure by the Court of Appeal has been so strong. For not only did the Court of Appeal reverse his decision, they reprimanded him personally for exceeding his remit in the case and accused him of having, at times, 'lost the wood for the trees'.[2]

The Court of Appeal specifically refuted the idea that patients have a right to life-saving medical treatment which they can enforce against doctors who are unwilling to provide it on the basis that it is not clinically indicated. Crucially, however, it made clear that Mr Burke's particular fear that he would be exposed to pain and suffering as a result of basic treatment being taken away from him during the final sentient stages of his disease was entirely unfounded. The Court explained that the existing common law rules already provide him with adequate legal protection against such a fate. Doctors have a common law duty to provide

1 [2004] EWHC 1879 (Admin); [2005] 3 WLR 1132.
2 [2005] 3 WLR 1132, at [38] *per* Lord Phillips MR.

treatment in the best interests of their patients. It is beyond question that it would be in Mr Burke's best interests to avoid unnecessary pain and suffering in the final sentient stages of his disease, thus his doctors would be legally obliged to continue treatment. From Mr Burke's perspective, his ultimate position remains exactly the same under the Court of Appeal approach as under that of Munby J. All that has changed is the legal basis upon which his entitlement to treatment is founded. Rather than it arising from a free-standing legal right to life-sustaining treatment, it stems instead from his doctors' ordinary common law duties to treat.

In managing to provide Mr Burke with his requested legal guarantee without recourse to the language of rights, the Court of Appeal cleverly avoided the pitfalls associated with the use of broad rights-based rationales within medical law contexts. For, as will be demonstrated, the problems with Munby J's approach are clear to see for anyone who cares to look. Regrettably, the majority of legal academics writing in this field appear not to want to look, and as a result they have tarnished the Court of Appeal decision with strident but, for the most part, entirely misconceived and misplaced criticism. They have portrayed the decision as being 'anti-patients' generally and 'anti-dignity interests' in particular, and as signalling a return to old medical paternalism.

This chapter seeks to defend the Court of Appeal decision in *Burke* against its critics. It does so by arguing that much of their criticism stems from a conception of the autonomy principle that is both legally and ethically untenable, as well as being unworkable in practice. While the decision does place limits on the operation of the autonomy principle, and on one of its corollaries, the right to self-determination, these limits must be seen as both necessary and legitimate in the context of a positive, as opposed to negative, legal duty scenario. To demonstrate this, it is necessary to engage in a more substantive discussion of the meaning of the autonomy principle than has typically been undertaken by the critics of *Burke*, and to look in particular at the contextual significance of the act/omission distinction. This chapter will further challenge the apparently widely held belief that there is a necessary correlation between the protection of both autonomy interests and dignity interests, in the sense that any judicial qualification of patient autonomy involves a simultaneous diminution of the legal value attached to patient dignity. On the contrary, it is contended that, notwithstanding their obvious interrelations, the autonomy principle and the dignity principle are to be viewed as separate ethical principles having independent value. It is also contended that while the Court of Appeal in *Burke* may have qualified the autonomy principle, it attached supreme value to the dignity principle and treated it, albeit implicitly, as a primary guiding criterion in the all-important assessment of individual best interests.

The Legal Issues Raised by the *Burke* Litigation

Stated briefly, the facts of Burke are as follows: Oliver Leslie Burke suffered from a congenital degenerative brain condition that results in serious physical disabilities and would eventually make his survival dependent on a life-prolonging treatment known as artificial nutrition and hydration (ANH). He was concerned that a medical assessment could be made at that stage that his life was no longer worth living and that it would be better to hasten his death by withdrawing the ANH. The medical evidence relating to the claimant's condition indicated that he would retain his full cognitive faculties right up until death was imminent; this meant that, were ANH to be withdrawn, he would be fully aware of the pain and discomfort that this would bring. Mr Burke's wish was instead to be fed and provided with appropriate hydration until he died of natural causes. In the hope of obtaining a guarantee that his wish would be respected, Mr Burke sought a clarification of the existing law as to the circumstances in which such life-prolonging treatment could be withdrawn. He did this by claiming judicial review of GMC guidance to the medical profession entitled 'Witholding and Withdrawing of Life-prolonging Treatments: Good Practice in Decision-Making 2002'. Mr Burke's primary contention was that, in purporting to vest sole responsibility for such decision-making in the doctor, this GMC guidance was incompatible with his rights at common law and under Article 2 (the right to life), Article 3 (the right to freedom from inhuman and degrading treatment) and Article 8 (the right to respect for private and family life) of the ECHR and thus unlawful.

To appreciate fully the significance of the *Burke* litigation, it is necessary to understand the precise nature of the legal issues at stake, as it would be easy to make the mistake of thinking that this case relates to the general medical duty to treat. In fact, Mr Burke's claim is very narrowly focused in that it relates specifically to the *positive* medical duty to provide *life-sustaining treatment* to *competent* patients. The significance of both the positive label and the life-sustaining nature of the medical treatment will be elaborated upon in due course. For now, it is important to concentrate on the latter special feature for it is specifically the fact that Mr Burke is a competent patient that makes his case such a novel one in legal terms. For while the courts have in the past been called upon on numerous occasions to determine the nature and extent of the doctor's duty to provide life-sustaining treatment to incompetent patients,[3] this was the first time they had ever been formally required to decide the issue in relation to competent patients.

The distinction between competent and incompetent patients plays a central role in English medical law. Most notably, it is largely determinative of the existence of the right to refuse treatment: competent patients have such a right whereas incompetent patients do not. Thus, in a situation where a competent patient refuses to consent to a medical procedure involving some kind of interference with her bodily integrity, the doctor who persists with the procedure will fall foul of both the civil and criminal rules on assault and battery.[4] Nor does the competent patient

---

3   See, for example, *Arthur* (1981) 12 B Med LR 1; *In re J* [1991] Fam 33; *Airedale NHS Trust v Bland* [1993] AC 789; *Portsmouth NHS Trust v Wyatt* [2004] EWHC 2247.

4   *Re T (Adult: Refusal of Medical Treatment)* [1992] 4 All ER 649.

have to demonstrate that her refusal of the treatment is based on rational grounds.[5] This right of veto extends to all medical treatment, regardless of whether the refusal will result in the avoidable death of the patient and/or even an unborn child.[6] In relation to incompetent patients, however, section 5 of the Mental Capacity Act 2005 allows doctors to override patient objections in order to provide treatment that they reasonably believe is in the best interests of the patient. This provision merely places on a statutory footing the common law rule that had been set out in *F v West Berkshire Area Health Authority*.[7] From section 4 of the 2005 Act, which sets out a checklist of factors to be taken into account in determining the best interests of an incompetent patient, it is clear that the statutory approach to best interests is designed to mirror the broad welfare approach that had developed in the common law.[8]

Thus, where refusals of treatment are concerned, the law governing the doctor's duty to a competent patient such as Mr Burke is very straightforward and generally uncontroversial: the patient's right to self-determination takes priority over the doctor's professional wishes. But of course the *Burke* case is not about a patient wanting to refuse treatment that a doctor wishes to provide. It is instead about a patient wanting to insist on treatment that a doctor does not wish to provide on the basis that it is not clinically indicated. And this legal problem is much more complicated, not least because it has obvious resource implications that the refusal scenario does not and because there are many professional and ethical issues associated with the idea of making a doctor provide treatment that is not clinically indicated. These extra considerations have to be weighed into the balance, and they prevent the scales from tipping so easily down on the side of the autonomy principle. Arguably, Munby J's judgement in *Burke* does not satisfactorily address these crucial differences between the refusal scenario and the demand scenario.

Munby J's Decision

Finding in favour of Mr Burke, Munby J held that the guidance was incompatible with his rights insofar as it: (a) placed emphasis throughout on the right of the competent patient to refuse treatment rather than his right to require treatment; (b) failed sufficiently to acknowledge that it was the duty of a doctor who was unwilling or unable to carry out the wishes of the patient to go on providing treatment until he could find another doctor who would do so; (c) failed sufficiently to acknowledge the heavy presumption in favour of life-prolonging treatment and to recognize that

---

5   See, for example, *Re MB (Caesarean Section)* [1997] 8 Med LR 217.

6   *St George's Healthcare NHS Trust v S* [1998] 3 All ER 673; *B v An NHS Trust* [2002] EWHC 429 (Fam).

7   [1990] 2 AC 1.

8   For a good example of the modern common law approach, see *Re S (Adult Patient: Sterilisation)* [2000] 3 WLR 1288.

the touchstone of best interests was intolerability; and, (d) failed to spell out the legal requirement to obtain prior judicial sanction for the withdrawal of ANH in certain circumstances.

The specific grounds upon which he based his declarations can be summarized as follows:

- A competent patient who believes that ANH is necessary to protect him from what he sees as acute physical and mental suffering is entitled, by virtue of his fundamental rights to personal autonomy and dignity as protected by Articles 3 and 8 of the ECHR, to insist on the provision of ANH until the end stage of his disease when he has lapsed into a coma and death is imminent. This is because the personal autonomy which is protected by Article 8 is to be regarded as embracing such matters as how one chooses to pass the closing days and moments of one's life and how one manages one's death, while the dignity interests protected by Article 3 include the right to die with dignity and the right to be protected from treatment, or from a lack of treatment, which would result in one dying in avoidably distressing circumstances. Article 3 continues to be in play, even when there is no awareness on the part of the patient, if the treatment would have the effect on the right-thinking bystander of humiliating or debasing the victim.

- The right to require the provision of ANH lapses once the patient has entered into the final stage of the illness and slipped into a coma. As long as the patient is otherwise being treated with dignity, the withdrawal of ANH at this point could not be said to constitute a breach of either Article 3 or 8 for at this stage it will be serving no purpose other than the very short prolongation of the life of a dying patient who has slipped into his final coma and lacks all awareness of what is happening.

- The doctor's decision as to what is in the patient's best interests cannot be determinative, for the idea of 'best interests' involves a broad welfare appraisal going well beyond medical considerations to take into account also the ethical, social, moral and emotional implications of treatment. It follows that the *Bolam* test is no longer to be regarded as determinative: the doctor's duty is not merely to act in accordance with a responsible and competent body of relevant professional opinion, it is to act in accordance with the patient's best interests. Where the patient is competent, the decision as to best interests is for the patient to make, whereas if the patient is incompetent, it is the court which must decide.

- While a doctor cannot be compelled to compromise his professional integrity by providing treatment which in his or her own clinical judgement is not in the best interests of the patient, in order to discharge his or her common law duty of care to the patient, he or she will be obliged to find a replacement doctor who is willing to provide the requested treatment. In the interim, the doctor has a continuing duty to provide treatment.

- Where there is any doubt as to capacity or where there is a lack of unanimity amongst the doctors or between the doctors and the patient or members of the immediate family, ANH cannot be withheld or withdrawn without prior judicial sanction.

Although Munby J makes it clear throughout the course of his judgement that the right to require ANH, on the basis of Articles 3 and 8, only arises in this case because of the claimant's *belief* that a lack of such treatment would subject him to severe mental and physical suffering, it is unfortunate that he omits to include this important qualification in his final declaratory order. It is arguably this omission, in conjunction with the inclusion of many general statements about contextually irrelevant legal and ethical issues,[9] which has led to the decision being mistakenly interpreted as bearing on the right to treatment generally.[10] Indeed, if his findings could have been limited to the precise factual context of the *Burke* case, they would have given little cause for concern.[11] The provision of ANH to a terminally-ill patient, in accordance with their wishes, during the final *sentient* stages of their disease is uncontroversial: it is a clinically-indicated, routine and relatively inexpensive treatment which, on any assessment of the test, is undeniably going to be in the best interests of the patient. The only responsible medical decision in such circumstances would be to provide the treatment. But inevitably, the findings could not have remained so limited. It would only have been a matter of time before they would have been, in the words of Lord Phillips MR in the Court of Appeal, 'seized upon and dissected by lawyers seeking supportive material for future cases'.[12] Most obviously, the right could be extended to cover all life-prolonging treatments,[13] not just ANH. It is not hard to imagine a scenario where a desperate patient, refusing to accept medical opinion, wants to insist on a highly expensive

---

9   In particular, those relating to incompetent patients.

10   Such misinterpretations were noted by Lord Phillips MR in the Court of Appeal: [2005] 3 WLR 1132, at [20].

11   That is not to suggest that even then they would be problem free. For instance, Munby J does not address whether this pivotal notion of fear of suffering has to be objectively validated. In Mr Burke's case, it is not clear to what extent his right to ANH was actually dependent on the medical evidence supporting his concern about possible exposure to pain and distress in the event of treatment being removed. In other words, is it the patient's actual and genuine belief in the potential for exposure to mental and physical anguish that triggers the right to treatment, or is the right founded rather on a kind of conceptual understanding of human degradation that requires an objective appraisal of the circumstances and thus makes its enforceability dependent on the reasonableness of the belief that mental and physical suffering is likely to occur? For example, what would be the position in relation to the patient who believes that the amputation of a particular body part is necessary to combat a perceived, but medically unsupported, risk of getting cancer?

12   [2005] 3 WLR 1132, at [24].

13   Indeed, the Court of Appeal appears to have treated the decision as relating to all life-prolonging treatments, although Lord Phillips MR's judgement is admittedly rather

treatment that is clearly not clinically indicated in that it will neither prolong their life nor relieve their pain and suffering, and that will divert resources away from another non-terminal patient requiring urgent life-saving care. Munby J refused to engage with the resource implications of his decision, dismissing the issue out of hand at the outset by stating that the case was not about 'the prioritisation or allocation of resources, whether human, medical or financial'.[14]

Moreover, there is no particular link between the Article 3 and 8 reasoning used by Munby J and the provision of treatment that is specifically life-prolonging, such that it would be difficult to prevent the decision from ultimately being used to establish an entitlement to any form of medical treatment that could be said to alleviate a fear of suffering. Even leaving aside the resources issue, the potential under such a state of affairs for gross interferences with the rights and interests of the medical profession is clear. And therein lies arguably the biggest problem with the rights-based approach to the provision of medical treatment: in focusing solely on the interests of the patient, it ignores the equally valid and legitimate interests of the doctor. It positions the two parties directly against each other, treating the relationship antagonistically as a power struggle in which one side alone must necessarily dominate.[15] The better approach is to conceive of the relationship as a partnership in which both sides work together to achieve the best practical outcome for the patient, and one in which both acknowledge each other's abilities and limitations. Arguably, the law has a role to play in helping to cultivate doctor–patient relationships that are based on mutual trust, and the Court of Appeal decision in *Burke*, if not necessarily representing a clear forward step on this front, at least puts the brakes on any further regression in this regard.

The Decision of the Court of Appeal

Reversing the High Court decision, the Court of Appeal held that the specific guarantee sought by Mr Burke was already provided by the common law and that no change in the law was therefore warranted. Under the common law, a doctor has a positive duty, so long as the treatment is prolonging the life of the patient, to provide ANH in accordance with the patient's expressed wishes. Given that the GMC guidance did not provide otherwise, there were no grounds for declaring it

---

ambiguous in this respect, in that at times he uses the term 'life-prolonging treatment' and at others he refers specifically to ANH.

14   [2004] EWHC 1879, at [27].

15   Note, in this respect, Gurnham's presentation of the central issue of the *Burke* litigation as being 'the patient's opportunity to enforce his convention rights against doctors acting in accordance with the GMC guidelines': Gurnham, D. (2006), Losing the Wood for the Trees: *Burke* and the Court of Appeal, *Medical Law Review* 14, 253 (Losing the Wood for the Trees).

to be unlawful[16]. The source of the duty is not the right of the patient to demand the treatment.[17] Rather the positive medical duty to take reasonable steps to keep a patient alive may be said to stem from a combination of the doctor's assumption of responsibility to care for the patient (which arises as soon as the patient is accepted into the hospital) and the operation in the law of a presumption in favour of life.

It is of crucial importance that the doctor's duty has been made dependent on the condition that the treatment will prolong the life of the patient. Medical evidence before the Court of Appeal indicated that there will be situations in which administration of ANH will not have that effect. Indeed, in the final stages of a terminal disease, such as that suffered by Mr Burke, it would appear that, not only would such treatment fail to sustain life, it could even hasten death. In such cases, there would be no legal duty to provide ANH, even if a patient has previously indicated that they wished to receive ANH until the very end.[18] Thus, if there is medical evidence to suggest that the administration of ANH would not have the effect of prolonging the life of the patient, the doctor would be legally entitled to withhold such treatment against the wishes of the patient. The Court of Appeal did however dismiss such a scenario as being 'extremely unlikely to arise in practice'.[19] It is important to note that, relative to the position afforded to him by Munby J, Mr Burke is no worse off as a result of this aspect of the Court of Appeal decision, for it will be recalled that even Munby J had found that the right to insist treatment would lapse as soon as the patient had entered in the final stages of the disease.

The main advantage of making the duty contingent on the condition that the treatment will provide some benefit to the patient, in the sense that it will either prolong life or provide palliative care, is that it allows room for manoeuvre in dealing with cases that are much less straightforward than Mr Burke's. For instance, this legal formulation would allow a doctor to deny treatment in the example scenario referred to earlier – the desperate patient who refuses to believe that a certain form of expensive and invasive treatment will be both futile and harmful in the sense that it will cause considerable pain and suffering.

Following the Court of Appeal decision, a patient's entitlement to life-prolonging treatment may categorically be said to relate to whatever treatment

---

16   [2005] 3 WLR 1132, at [23].

17   'Where the competent patient makes it plain that he or she wishes to be kept alive by ANH, this will not be the source of the duty to provide it. The patient's wish will merely underscore that duty': *per* Lord Phillips MR, *ibid.*, at [32].

18   In this respect, the Court of Appeal wisely pre-empted the use of advance directives by stating that, while they could be validly used to refuse consent to treatment, the position at common law and under statute was that they did not make the wishes of the patient to be kept alive determinative. The Court pointed out that while s. 26 of the Mental Capacity Act 2005 required compliance with a valid advance directive to refuse treatment, s. 4 did no more than require such a directive to be taken into consideration when determining what was in the best interests of the patient: [2005] 2 WLR 1132, at [57].

19   *Ibid.*, at [55].

is in the patient's best interests. This is because the entitlement stems from the existence of the doctor's duty to act in the patient's best interests. And it is in relation to the method of assessing best interests that the Court of Appeal's approach differs most significantly from Munby J's. While Munby J made the wishes of the patient determinative, the Court of Appeal reverted back to the ordinary common law approach of a broad and objective welfare approach. Despite what some commentators have suggested,[20] this does not signal a return to old medical paternalism where the doctor has almost free rein over decision-making, for under the modern approach to best interests the doctor is obliged to consider non-clinical factors and, crucially, he is no longer shielded by the *Bolam* principle.[21] As made clear by Butler-Sloss P in *Re S (Adult Patient: Sterilisation)*, when best interests have to be assessed for the purposes of deciding on the provision of treatment, the *Bolam* principle is only relevant to the issue of the range of medical options presented by the doctor.[22] In other words, the doctor has to ensure that each of the treatment options presented fall within the range of acceptable opinion among reasonable and competent medical practitioners, otherwise he will automatically expose himself to liability. However, from the range of *Bolam*-compliant options, he must work out which, if any, are in the best interests of the individual patient by taking into account factors such as the patient's ethical and religious beliefs, the patient's social and family circumstances, the reaction of the patient and interested third parties to the options presented, and so on. Thus, a doctor who assessed only the patient's clinical needs, and who on that basis offered only the certain treatment options to the patient, would breach his duty to the patient and would be subject to legal challenge, notwithstanding the fact that the treatment choices he offered would have been approved by a responsible body of professional opinion.

While clinical considerations may no longer provide the sole basis for the best interests assessment in a health care context, they still need to remain an integral part of that assessment. That is, it does not follow that because they are no longer the only relevant factor they are no longer relevant at all. It is contrary to basic common sense to hold that a treatment that not only would not provide any benefit, but would actually prove to be harmful to the patient, could be said to be in the patient's best interests. But in making the patient's wishes determinative of best

---

20   See, for example, Foster, C. (2005), Burke: A Tale of Unhappy Endings, *Journal of Personal Injury Law* 2, 293; Biggs, H. (2007), 'Taking Account of the Views of the Patient', but only if the Clinician (and the Court Agrees): *R (Burke) v GMC, Child and Family Law Quarterly* 19, 225 (Taking Account of the Views of the Patient).

21   The *Bolam* principle, as derived from the judgement of McNair J in *Bolam v Friern Hospital Management Committee* [1957] 1 WLR 582, and subsequently qualified by the House of Lords in *Bolitho v City and Hackney HA* [1998] AC 232, sets out that a doctor is not to be found in breach of his/her duty of care if he/she has acted in accordance with a practice accepted as proper by a responsible body of doctors whose evidence withstands logical analysis.

22   [2000] 3 WLR 1288, at p. 1299.

interests, Munby J allows for exactly this kind of scenario. Rather than promoting the dignity interests of the patient, this kind of blind adherence to the principle of self-determination arguably creates potential for them to be compromised instead.[23] Consider, for example, a situation involving a competent but irrational terminally ill cancer patient who, unable to cope with the prospect of death and despite having been given unanimous medical advice to the contrary, refused to accept that surgery to remove her large intestine would not cure her. On any ethical assessment, can it be regarded as right to allow her to needlessly expose herself to the risk that she will die on the operating table, or to the post-operative pain and suffering that will follow should she survive the surgery, or to the indignity of having an unnecessary stoma? The bottom line is that the best interests assessment has to incorporate clinical considerations, so that the only treatments to which the patient's legal entitlement can be said to extend will be those providing some kind of medical benefit to the patient, be it in prolonging life or in alleviating pain and suffering. It will be up to the doctor to assess the patient's best interests and to decide which treatment options best meet those interests. The doctor will then present the patient with the available options and allow her to choose which, if any, she wishes to receive. From a practical point of view, the doctor is best placed to be the ultimate decision-maker. In an ideal world, it would be desirable to have every best interests assessment carried out by the courts, but as the evidence put before the Court of Appeal in *Burke* indicates, this is just not feasible in practice.[24] Moreover, while there are many instances in which the best interests assessment can become very complicated and controversial because of the sheer range of welfare factors to be taken into account and because of the consequent scope for differences of opinion to arise,[25] the case of the competent terminally ill patient wishing to receive life-saving treatment is happily not one of them. In fact, in this scenario, the only relevant considerations are going to be whether the treatment is capable of providing some clinical benefit and whether the patient agrees to

---

23   Of course, the law already allows competent patients to expose themselves to painful and undignified circumstances through its recognition of an absolute personal right to *refuse* potentially beneficial medical treatment. As already explained, the principle of self-determination is absolute in these refusal circumstances. But this is only because the conferral of the right here does not interfere directly with the protected interests of anyone else. The interests of the patient are really the only ones in the balance and liberal theory dictates that, as long as we do not interfere with the protected rights and interests of others, we should be free to do whatever we want to ourselves. By contrast, in a demand scenario, to compel a doctor to provide clinically inappropriate treatment against his wishes is to interfere with his legitimate professional and ethical rights and interests.

24   The Intensive Care Society, joined as an intervener to the Court of Appeal proceedings in *Burke*, advised that if Munby J's criteria for seeking court authorization in withdrawal scenarios were to be applied then approximately 10 court applications a day would have to be made: [2005] 3 WLR 1132, at [69].

25   Arguably, the most difficult best interests assessments concern the provision of therapeutic treatments to mentally disabled adults.

receive it. If so, the treatment is in the patient's best interests and the doctor must provide it.

On this assessment, the Court of Appeal's decision is eminently preferable to that of Munby J. Unfortunately, as already indicated, not everyone would agree.

Academic Hostility to the Court of Appeal Decision

The harshest critics of the Court of Appeal decision in *Burke* portray it as a clear denunciation of patient interests. Casting the Court in a villainous light, they rebuke it for undoing the good work of the heroic Munby J. Their approach to the legal issues raised by the case is simplistically clear-cut: it is all about the autonomy principle. To endorse the full supremacy of the principle is to fight on the side of the good; to seek to qualify it in any way is to fight on the side of the bad. And those who reject absolute patient autonomy would not only then deny the importance of personal dignity interests, but would actively deprive them of any legal or moral respect.

Gurnham immediately demonizes the Court of Appeal in the introductory paragraph of his critique by describing it as having 'brusquely' swept aside Munby J's 'impassioned defence of the moral value of patient autonomy'.[26] Several pages in, he proceeds to accuse the Court of being dismissive of the importance attached by Munby J to the moral value of patient dignity.[27] This particular accusation is based on the fact that the Court rejected Munby J's Article 3-based reasoning, and would indicate that Gurnham considers that the only way in which the law can protect dignity is by using Article 3 to create specific individual rights. He also misleadingly describes the Court of Appeal as having expressed the view that ANH would only be necessary in Mr Burke's case while he was still competent.[28] Given that, from a legal perspective, Mr Burke would be treated as losing competence as soon as he loses his ability to communicate, this statement could easily be read as meaning that the Court was prepared to countenance the withdrawal of treatment during Mr Burke's final sentient stages when he would be aware of the painful and distressing effects of withdrawal. A close reading of Gurnham's commentary however reveals that, somewhat oddly, he is applying his own personal definition of competence, and that he would label as competent a patient who has lost the ability to communicate his wishes but who nevertheless retains his mental capacity.

In a similar vein, Dupre accuses the Court of Appeal of '[forgetting] a patient's basic humanity and personality by giving priority to medical expertise when it comes to deciding what is best for him or her'[29] and of minimizing the patient's

---

26   Losing the Wood for the Trees, at p. 253.

27   *Ibid.*, at p. 257.

28   *Ibid.*

29   Dupre, C. (2006), Human Dignity and Withdrawal of Medical Treatment: A Missed Opportunity, *European Human Rights Law Review* 6, 678, at p. 693.

involvement.[30] She describes Munby J's decision as having extended the best interests test to include 'the patient's interests and rights',[31] thereby implying that the patient's interests were not previously taken into account. And she goes on to accuse the Court of Appeal of refusing to treat the patient's welfare as the dominant consideration in deciding on treatment.[32] However, her main problem with the decision is what she perceives to be its anti-dignity stance. In her eyes, in rejecting Munby J's reasoning based on Articles 3 and 8, the Court of Appeal dismissed the relevance and importance of the human dignity argument to Mr Burke's situation.[33] The necessary implication is that Mr Burke's dignity interests have been left entirely unprotected by the Court of Appeal's decision. Thus she too would appear to suggest that the only real way to ensure respect for patient dignity is through the creation of an express legal right to the same.

Biggs is even more sweeping in her accusations against the Court of Appeal, describing it, rather puzzlingly, as having rejected the significance of 'best interests' altogether.[34] She would appear to use the term 'best interests' to refer solely to the wishes and views of the patient. Presenting the case as being about 'patient autonomy, decision-making and choice',[35] she contends that the only way to respect the autonomy principle is to take the wishes of the patient into account, by which she would appear to mean allowing these wishes to be determinative of treatment.[36] She goes on to imply that, by failing to treat the patient's wishes as determinative, the Court effectively denied the fundamental importance of the patient's views altogether.[37] Treating the decision as a 'dangerous endorsement of medical paternalism', she accuses the Court of 'endorsing the view that the medical practitioner's assessment of the patient's best interests takes primacy in the determination of which treatments should be available'.[38]

She furthermore puts a highly negative and emotive spin on the practical ramifications of the decision for Mr Burke, implying that he may well be left to end his days in pain and distress, dying of thirst and starvation because his doctors

---

30   *Ibid.*, at p. 681.

31   *Ibid.*

32   *Ibid.*

33   *Ibid.*, in particular see pp. 685, 694.

34   Taking Account of the Views of the Patient', at pp. 227, 230.

35   *Ibid.*, at p. 237.

36   *Ibid.*

37   *Ibid.*, at p. 232. In an attempt to demonstrate the importance of taking account of the views of the patient, Biggs refers to the example used by Munby J (at [97]) of two clinically similar cancer patients being offered chemotherapy. One accepts the treatment and the inevitable debilitating side effects because he wants to survive long enough to attend an important family event. The other refuses the treatment because he wants to complete some project, such as a book, for which he needs a clear mind free of the side effects. However, both Biggs and Munby J fail to recognize that the example is flawed in so far as it relates exclusively to a refusal scenario rather than a demand for treatment.

38   *Ibid.*, at p. 238.

have been granted the freedom to withhold ANH by a cold and uncaring court unprepared to 'reassure [a dying man] that he will be treated with respect and according to his wishes in the final days of his life'.[39] She states that 'in seeking the continuation of ANH until the natural end of his life, and possibly against the wishes of the clinical team, it appears that Leslie Burke is looking for a treatment option that common law and paragraph 81 of the GMC guidance permits the medical team to decide not to make available'.[40] She further suggests that even if the greatest weight were attached to his wishes, he still would not necessarily succeed since he would be seeking a treatment that would perhaps not be offered: 'The clinical team is entitled to exercise therapeutic discretion in making its best interests assessment and may legitimately therefore decide that the continuation of ANH is not in his best interests and so should not be made available.'[41] This is simply untrue. As made abundantly clear by the Court of Appeal, Mr Burke's doctors would be obliged to provide him with ANH during his final sentient stages, on the basis that it would necessarily be in his best interests to avoid the pain and distress associated with ANH withdrawal. He has received from the Court of Appeal the exact reassurance he asked for, the only distinction with the nature of the reassurance provided by Munby J being that it is founded on a different legal theoretical basis.

Contextualizing the Significance of the Autonomy Principle

As set out in Beauchamp and Childress's seminal work,[42] autonomy constitutes one of four general principle of biomedical ethics, the others being non-maleficence, beneficence and justice. However, as noted by Brazier, at the end of the twentieth century, autonomy had somehow become the dominant one, 'a trump card beating all the other principles'.[43] To the extent that it signals a change in judicial attitudes away from deep-seated medical paternalism and attempts to redress the balance of power in the doctor–patient relationship, the rise of autonomy is obviously to be welcomed. And yet, as Brazier comments, it has been allowed to extend so far that it has now arguably over-corrected the balance.[44] The problems associated with medical paternalism are thus simply replaced with a new set of problems.

For present purposes, the problem at the heart of the unwarranted hostility to the *Burke* decision may be said to lie in the superficiality of the mainstream legal academic approach to the significance of the autonomy principle in the health care

---

39 *Ibid.*, at p. 238.

40 *Ibid.*, at p. 232.

41 *Ibid.*, at p. 234.

42 Beauchamp, T.L. and Childress, J.F. (1989), *Principles of Bioethics*, (New York).

43 Brazier, M. (2006), Do no Harm – do Patients have Responsibilities too?', *Cambridge Law Journal* 397, at p. 400 (Do no Harm).

44 *Ibid.*, at p. 398.

context. For not only do legal academics tend to be absolutists on this front, they treat the principle as amounting to a generic and all-encompassing right to choose. They also regard it as a 'free' right, that is, one unconstrained by any concomitant responsibilities. Their promotion of the autonomy principle generally focuses exclusively on the individual interests of the patient, and ignores the existence of other competing, but nevertheless equally valid, third-party interests, such as those of other patients and those of the attending doctors.

A more legally and ethically defensible approach to autonomy is one which not only takes account of competing third-party interests, but also recognizes that the principle manifests itself in different guises in different health care contexts. For instance, in a straightforward battery action, autonomy would be equated with the fundamental right to bodily integrity; in a negligence action on risk disclosure, it would feature as a right to informed consent; and in an access to treatment action it would be invoked as a right to choose. In some guises, the individual autonomy principle involves no real interference with the rights and interests of third parties, in which case it is easy to accord full legal recognition to it; in others, the operation of the principle will interfere substantially with the rights and interests of others, in which case a whole range of difficult legal and ethical issues are engaged with the likely outcome that the principle will be qualified in some fashion. Much will depend on the nature of the interference. The most serious interferences, and consequently those which necessitate the more significant qualifications of individual autonomy, will be those which impact on another's fundamental liberty by compelling them to act against their protected wishes. Wishes or interests can be described as protected where they are unconstrained by pre-existing moral, social, professional or legal obligations. By registering to practise, doctors accept that their professional freedoms will be fettered by relevant professional norms, and family members arguably fall subject to moral duties to render reasonable assistance to each other in times of need.[45] For present purposes, it is very fortunate that the most relevant legal scenarios will generally operate at opposite extremes of the interference spectrum wherein the answers to the question of the degree of legal weight to be applied to the autonomy principle are relatively easy and uncontroversial. A competent patient's refusal of life-saving treatment will not interfere with the protected liberty of the doctor and as such the patient's right to self-determination may be accorded absolute legal weight. By contrast, if respected, a competent patient's request for a treatment that a doctor does not wish to provide on the grounds that it is not clinically indicated would obviously involve a direct interference with the individual liberty of the doctor and would thus require the 'right to choose' manifestation of the autonomy principle to be heavily qualified.

---

45   Thus a patient who requires additional nursing care, either at home or in a hospital, as a result of refusing beneficial medical treatment will not usually interfere with the protected freedoms of medical staff or relatives who are consequently called upon to act.

Therein lies the primary significance of the aforementioned distinction between positive and negative duties. To prohibit a person from acting is to impose on him a negative duty. To compel him to act is, by contrast, is to impose on him a positive (or affirmative) duty. To the extent that positive duties involve much greater interferences with individual liberty that their negative counterparts, the approach of the common law has generally been to refuse to impose such duties unless there are special justifications for doing do. Hence the existence in English law of a general rule against liability for omissions.[46] Obviously, the doctor–patient relationship has long been recognized as one of the classic exceptions to the rule, with the specific justifications for the imposition of exceptional positive duties on the part of the doctor lying in the doctor's assumption of responsibility to improve the situation of patients accepted into his care, taken in conjunction with the patient's vulnerability and her specific reliance on the special skills of the doctor. However, these positive duties are limited in both nature and extent. First and foremost, they are only duties to take reasonable care to improve the plight of the patient, as opposed to absolute duties to effect cures. And secondly, as discussed above, they are governed by the best interests test. The duty only extends to the provision of treatment that will, *at the very least*, promote the clinical interests of the patient.[47] Given that the source of the duty is essentially the existence of the doctor's special skills alongside his agreement to apply those skills to the benefit of others, there is no justification for extending the duty to the provision of treatment that, while desired by the patient, is not clinically indicated. For the doctor's skills lie not just in her ability to perform medical procedures, but also in her knowledge of the appropriate circumstances in which to offer to perform them and to what end.

---

46   This explains the absence in both tort and criminal law of a general duty to rescue.

47   Where a doctor has a conscientious objection to the provision of a treatment that, both from a clinical and a broad welfare perspective, is in the best interests of the patient, GMC guidance (*Good Medical Practice* (2006) – available at <http://www.gmc-uk.org/guidance/good_medical_practice/index.asp>) provides that the doctor must explain her position to the patient and inform the patient of her right to see another doctor. To treat the doctor as remaining under a legal obligation to the patient until another doctor is found is fairly easy to justify. Given that the objection is personal, and that the treatment is clinically indicated, finding a willing replacement doctor should be relatively unproblematic in practice. This is in contrast to the scenario where the doctor objects to the provision of a treatment on the basis that it is not clinically indicated. As long as her objections are *Bolam* compliant, she would be likely to encounter great difficulties in finding a replacement doctor. Hence the reason why Munby's suggestion, that in conferring patient rights to treatment, the law can protect a doctor's professional integrity by enabling her to pass her obligation on to someone else, is simply not feasible in practice. Note that if the doctor's objections are not *Bolam* compliant, she will be in breach of her legal duty to the patient and thereby face possible criminal and civil liability.

If a treatment is not in a patient's best interests on the grounds that it can provide no medical benefit, then the doctor's positive duty lapses. After that point, a doctor's failure to act will not expose her to potential civil or criminal liability because the general no-duty-for-omissions rule will apply.[48]

The Ethical Responsibilities of Patients

Further compelling justifications for qualifying the autonomy principle in demand-for-treatment scenarios may be found in the debate about the ethical responsibilities owed by patients. While the idea that patients have ethical duties and responsibilities is a prevalent one in medical scholarship, it has not yet attracted the general attention of legal academics.[49]

The basic existence of a doctrine of patient responsibility appears to have been more or less taken for granted by medical scholars. The debate tends to focus rather on the substance of the doctrine, and in particular on the identification of specific duties and obligations. Evans, for example, would assert that a competent individual seeking health care from a publicly funded health care system that she is eligible to enter regardless of whether she is at the time a taxpayer, owes at the very least, the following ten duties: (1) duty to participate in a health care jurisdiction; (2) duty to uphold her own health; (3) duty to protect the health of others; (4) duty to seek and access healthcare responsibly; (5) duty of truthfulness; (6) duty of compliance; (7) duty of inpatient conduct; (8) duty of recovery or maintenance; (9) duty of research participation; and (10) duty of citizenship. Grounded in the common good and the common need, these duties are moral duties only and Evans acknowledges that they are potentially unenforceable. Their

---

48   Moreover, contrary to what has been argued at length by both Keown, J. ((1997), Restoring Moral and Intellectual Shape to the Law after *Bland*, *Law Quarterly Review* 113, 481) and Finnis, J.M. ((1993), *Bland*: Crossing the Rubicon?, *Law Quarterly Review* 109, 329), the act/omission distinction provides a perfectly robust legal and moral basis for the House of Lords decision in *Bland* to the effect that the removal of life-prolonging treatment no longer operating in the best interests of a patient will not give rise to a charge of murder or manslaughter against the patient's doctors, notwithstanding the fact that the removal has been effected with the specific purpose of bringing about the patient's death. From a legal perspective, while the *mens rea* element of the offence may be satisfied, the *actus reus* is not, for without the existence of a positive duty to act there is no relevant breach of duty and thus no culpable conduct. From a moral perspective, the doctor is merely withdrawing her existing interference with the laws of nature, whereby she had been artificially keeping alive a patient who would otherwise have died, and allowing the patient to die from her underlying condition. See further McGee, A. (2005), Finding a Way through the Legal and Ethical Maze: Withdrawal of Medical Treatment and Euthanasia, *Medical Law Review* 13, 357.

49   Margaret Brazier would appear to be the only legal scholar to date to have written about the issue: Do no Harm.

purpose is rather to encourage patients to act responsibly in respect of their own good, and considerately in respect of the good of both other patients and carers, so as to maximize the effectiveness and efficiency of the health care system overall.

Draper and Sorrell would go further than Evans as regards the enforceability issue.[50] Focusing on the ethical duties of patients to promote their own health, to follow good medical advice, and not to use health services casually, they would argue that patients who breach such duties may, in certain circumstances, be regarded as disentitling themselves to further treatment. Indeed, they would place a further ethical duty on patients to release from their obligations to treat those doctors whose sound medical advice they choose to ignore. Concerned only to lay the foundation for the general argument that patients have their own ethical responsibilities, Draper and Sorrell touch upon, but do not develop in detail, the highly controversial question of whether a patient's contribution to their ill health through the adoption of an unhealthy lifestyle, should be precluded from accessing certain medical treatments. The classic example would of course be the smoker who develops lung cancer and who refuses to stop smoking. As noted by Brazier, this debate demands several papers of its own.[51]

Even the Department of Health has started to openly engage with the idea of patients having certain duties, for it is notable that its recently published NHS Constitution for England includes a specific section entitled 'Patients and the public – your responsibilities'.[52] The duties listed are very general ones relating to such matters as treating NHS staff with respect, keeping appointments, following prescribed courses of treatment and participating in important public health programmes such as vaccination.

As the only lawyer to have waded fully in to the patient responsibility discourse, it is perhaps not surprising that Brazier has gone beyond the purely ethical analysis and has considered whether patients might legitimately be made subject to certain legal duties, breach of which would expose them to potential legal liability.[53] By way of example, she explores the possibility that, through the implementation of a general duty to act to avoid preventable harm, the victims of diagnosed genetic diseases might be treated as legally obliged to warn relatives of the risks to which they might also be exposed.

Given the clear ethical and legal difficulties raised by each of these questions, it is fortunate that, for present purposes, it is not necessary to enter properly into any of the relevant debates. For all that is required here is support for the basic proposition that patients have ethical obligations to consider the rights and interests

---

50   Draper, H. and Sorrell, T. (2002), Patients' Responsibilities in Medical Ethics, *Bioethics* 16, 335.

51   Do no Harm, p. 399.

52   *The NHS Constitution for England*, published on 21 January 2009, at p. 9. Available at <http://www.dh.gov.uk/en/Healthcare/NHSConstitution/index.ht>, accessed 22 January 2009.

53   Do no Harm, at p. 399.

of others when making requests for treatment, and that these ethical obligations may be used to legitimately qualify the concept of autonomy in demand for treatment scenarios. The foregoing discussion demonstrates that, at the very least, there is a prevailing school of thought which interprets patient autonomy as incorporating patient responsibilities and which expressly advocates the placing of limits on the autonomy principle.

From a philosophical perspective, the work of O'Neill may also usefully be referred to here. In her highly influential monograph *Autonomy and Trust in Bioethics*,[54] O'Neill denounces the standard individualistic account of autonomy as being antithetical to the maintenance of relationships of trust. To the extent that mutual trust between doctor and patient is to be regarded as central to any ethically adequate practice of medicine, O'Neill advocates the adoption within bioethics of a new theory of autonomy that actively promotes trust. Referred to as 'principled autonomy', this new version of autonomy is founded in Kantian philosophy. Often wrongly interpreted as setting out a conception of individual autonomy, O'Neill argues that, on the contrary, 'Kantian autonomy is manifested in a life in which duties are met, in which there is respect for others and their rights, rather than in a life liberated from all bonds.'[55] The essence of 'principled autonomy' is that it obliges patients to take responsibility for their choices, and to consider the rights and interests of others.

Fully endorsing O'Neill's doctrine of principled autonomy, Girrat and Gill argue that medical ethics should always be set within the context of relationships and community. '[I]f patient individualistic autonomy is to be the sole criterion for decision making, the patient doctor relationship is reduced to that of client and technician'.[56] Brazier, too, cautions against the dangers of moving towards a consumer model of medicine:

> If medical integrity has no ethical value, medical ethics itself becomes irrelevant. If doctors and nurses become mere service providers obliged to deliver what is ordered, whatever their own ethical values and at whatever cost to them, we can chuck Beauchamp and Childress on to the remainder pile. Doctors simply supply the goods. Compensation is available for sub-standard goods. Outrageously bad medical practice will be punished by the criminal law. Doctors who do not want to supply particular good simply do not ... They no longer have an obligation to care.[57]

---

54   O'Neill, A. (2002), *Autonomy and Trust in Bioethics*, (Cambridge University Press).

55   *Ibid.*, at p. 83.

56   Girrat, G. and Gill, R. (2005), 'Autonomy in Medical Ethics after O'Neill', *Journal of Medical Ethics* 31, 127, at p. 128.

57   Do no Harm, at p. 420.

The Relationship between Patient Autonomy and Dignity

While autonomy may legitimately be qualified in certain medical scenarios against the wishes of patients, most notably as regards demand for treatment scenarios, dignity may not. Only the competent patient has the power to compromise her own dignity interests. Contrary to what some of the critics of *Burke* would appear to suggest, dignity is not primarily of value as a subjective concept. Nor does the application of the autonomy principle necessarily ensure protection of dignity interests. Indeed, where the competent patient exercises her right to self-determination in refusing beneficial medical treatment and thereby choosing to expose herself to unnecessary pain, suffering or distress, there is in fact a negative correlation between dignity and autonomy. It is thus disingenuous to argue that any judicial limitation of patient autonomy signals a devaluation of patient dignity. Obviously, much will depend on the particular meaning attached to dignity in any given context, but certainly in end-of-life scenarios, with which this chapter is exclusively concerned, and regardless of whether the patient is competent or incompetent, the concept of dignity is going to relate essentially to the idea of being free from avoidable pain, suffering and distress. This is certainly the sense in which the concept was used by Mr Burke. Viewed from this perspective, the dignity assessment has to be approached objectively.

While it is unfortunate that the Court of Appeal did not make this more explicit in its decision, it is nevertheless inferentially clear that its approach to the best interests assessment in life-saving treatment cases is predicated upon the core principles of the sanctity of life and patient dignity. The Court held that as long as treatment is providing some kind of medical benefit to the patient, either in terms of prolonging life or of preventing pain and distress, it will be in the best interests of the patient to receive treatment and the doctor will thus have a duty to provide it. The doctor is not therefore free to make his own subjective assessments about the value of an individual life, nor is he allowed to expose a patient to pain and suffering, unless of course it is in accordance with the wishes of the patient. Indeed, the Court of Appeal made it clear that, even at this stage, the competent patient is able to prioritize the importance to them of the sanctity of life, and to ask for non-futile treatment even if it causes pain and distress. If patient wants the treatment, and it is prolonging life, the doctor has to give it, notwithstanding the fact that it will compromise the patient's objective dignity interests. Where competent patients are concerned, the sanctity of life principle may as such take precedence over the dignity principle.

If a patient is incompetent, as she is most likely to be during the final stages of an illness, section 4(5) of the Mental Capacity Act 2005 applies. It provides that in deciding whether or not treatment is in the patient's best interests, the doctor must not be motivated by a desire to bring about the patient's death. The Code of Practice accompanying the 2005 Act sets out that where an incompetent patient has, through an advance directive, expressed the wish to be provided with life-sustaining treatment, then these requests should be taken into account in the same way as requests made by a person who has the capacity to make such decisions.[58] Thus if the patient has made it clear that he or she would value life over dignity, then the doctors would be obliged to provide clinically indicated life-sustaining treatment. If the doctor is not provided with any evidence of the incompetent patient's wishes, then paragraph 5.31 of the Code sets out that, in limited cases, a doctor could reasonably decide to withhold or withdraw treatment on the basis that it would be overly burdensome to the patient. That is, the dignity principle would be treated as taking priority over the sanctity of life. Arguably the reference to 'overly burdensome' treatment is strongly resonant of the common law test of intolerability, whereby a presumption in favour of life can only be displaced by evidence that continued treatment would cause intolerable pain, suffering and distress.[59] The Code also points out that, where there is disagreement about best interests, an application may to be brought to the Court of Protection.

And so, the Court of Appeal decision, operating in conjunction with the Mental Capacity Act 2005, may be said to accord full respect to the importance of the dignity principle and to provide comprehensive legal protection to patients in end-of-life scenarios generally.

Conclusion

Understood properly, the Court of Appeal's decision in *Burke* may be said to represent a victory for both sides. In framing the doctor's positive duty to provide life-prolonging treatment in a suitably qualified manner, the Court of Appeal managed to allay Mr Burke's specific fears as to his own fate, whilst at the same time addressing the more general concerns of the medical profession about being compelled to provide treatment that is not clinically indicated. It is more than unfortunate that Mr Burke has not been allowed to understand the decision in that way, and that he was encouraged to fight on until all his legal options were exhausted.[60]

---

58   Mental Capacity Act Code of Practice, at paragraph 5.34.

59   Whilst it is true that the Court of Appeal rejected Munby J's promulgation of the intolerability principle as the 'touchstone' of best interests, it is submitted that the Court was rejecting the idea that there could ever be one test for the determination of best interests assessments that applied to all health care contexts, rather than the usefulness of the intolerability principle *per se*. See further, McIvor, C. (2006), The Positive Medical Duty to Provide Life-prolonging Treatment, *Professional Negligence* 22, 59, at p. 63.

60   When his leave to appeal to the House of Lords was refused, he brought his case to the European Court of Human Rights in Strasbourg where he failed on admissibility grounds: App. No. 19807/06.

References

Beauchamp, T.L. and Childress, J.F. (1989), *Principles of Bioethics*, (Oxford University Press).

Biggs, H. (2007), 'Taking Account of the Views of the Patient', but only if the Clinician (and the Court Agrees): *R (Burke) v GMC, Child and Family Law Quarterly* 19, 225.

Brazier, M. (2006), Do no Harm – do Patients have Responsibilities too?, *Cambridge Law Journal* 397.

Draper, H. and Sorrell, T. (2002), Patients' Responsibilities in Medical Ethics, *Bioethics* 16, 335.

Dupre, C. (2006), Human Dignity and Withdrawal of Medical Treatment: A Missed Opportunity, *European Human Rights Law Review* 6, 678.

Finnis, J.M. (1993), *Bland*: Crossing the Rubicon?, *Law Quarterly Review* 109, 329.

Foster, C. (2005), Burke: A Tale of Unhappy Endings, *Journal of Personal Injury Law* 2, 293.

Girrat, G. and Gill, R. (2005), Autonomy in Medical Ethics after O'Neill, *Journal of Medical Ethics* 31, 127.

Gurnham, D. (2006), Losing the Wood for the Trees: *Burke* and the Court of Appeal, *Medical Law Review* 14, 253.

Keown, J. (1997), Restoring Moral and Intellectual Shape to the Law after *Bland*, *Law Quarterly Review* 113, 481.

McGee, A. (2005), Finding a Way through the Legal and Ethical Maze: Withdrawal of Medical Treatment and Euthanasia, *Medical Law Review* 13, 357.

McIvor, C. (2006), The Positive Medical Duty to Provide Life-prolonging Treatment, *Professional Negligence* 22, 59.

O'Neill, A. (2002), *Autonomy and Trust in Bioethics*, (Cambridge University Press).

The NHS Constitution for England, published on 21 January 2009 Available at: <http://www.dh.gov.uk/en/Healthcare/NHSConstitution/index.ht>.

Chapter 14

Liberalism and Constraining Choice: The Cases of Death and Serious Bodily Harm

G.R. Sullivan*

Assume a government that wishes to promote and protect the freedom and autonomy of its mentally competent, adult citizens. It subscribes to a form of social liberalism[1] that eschews enforcing any particular version of what makes for a good and moral life. It is committed to a liberal stance on choices made in their private lives by competent adults, even for an agent whose particular choices would be considered self-destructive and life diminishing from a more reflective and prudential perspective. A consistent application of liberal principles would confirm our current freedom to do such things as eat and drink what we like, whatever the consequences for living a long and useful life. Its scope would be extended for other questionable choices, such as taking mind-altering substances in addition to alcohol and caffeine. All forms of consensual sexual activity would be allowed.

But, of course, we do not live in a liberal polity but in a country where the application of liberal precepts is patchy and inconsistent.[2] The fact of the matter is that a significant part of the voting electorate is not consistently liberal or in any sense liberal and is happy to endorse forms of authoritarianism entailing proscription of even the self-regarding/consensual conduct of competent adults. This state of affairs is suboptimal for liberals who take the primary value of liberalism to be the securing of ordered liberty – persons whose political outlook need not be sustained by the social optimism of a Mill, but who, none the less, attach great weight to freedom and autonomy as values in their own right, and

---

* Thanks are due to John Stanton-Ife, Harvey Teff and Colin Warbrick for comments on an earlier draft of this chapter. The usual conditions apply.

1 There are, of course, uncertainties of interpretation associated with the term 'social liberalism'. However there seems no better term to hand to depict a governmental attitude favouring the promotion of choice on the part of adult citizens in the running of their own lives.

2 For instance, the circumstances in which a competent adult can validly consent to the infliction or risk of serious bodily harm and those circumstances where consent to such harm or the risk of such harm is treated as legally invalid disclose no consistent rule-based or value-based system: Simester, A. and Sullivan, G.R. (2007), *Criminal Law: Theory and Doctrine*, 3rd Edition (Hart Publishing), at pp. 696–703.

also as a means of reducing the disutilities commonly associated with coercive interventions in the private lives of competent adults.[3]

We will not revisit yet again the virtues of a liberalism that prioritizes civic liberty. Indeed, the agenda here is very different. We are examining the possibility of legitimate restriction of freedoms rather than their enhancement. Can liberals of a libertarian persuasion,[4] consistently with their liberal values, ever endorse coercive interventions in the private lives of competent adults to prevent or mitigate adverse consequences for particular persons and for the population more generally, arising from certain forms of self-regarding or consensual conduct? In the next section, certain real-life choices on the part of adult, mentally competent agents to endure death or serious bodily harm will be described. Some of these choices seemingly lack any discernible rationale. In other cases a rationale may be present, but seems of no evident value, even as forms of hedonism or the satisfaction of curiosity. In certain of these cases –cannibalism for example – the strongest feelings of revulsion and disgust may be experienced. In other cases – a succession of localized suicides by young people – a protective response may arise.

What can bring together those very different kinds of case, in at least one dimension, is a policy of using public resources to prevent or minimize such conduct. One resource of particular concern to us is recourse to the criminal law either in its purely retributivist guise or when aspiring to use it as a way to deliver forms of utility. But even in cases where there may be a strong intuition that invoking the criminal law may be justified to condemn publicly wrongs and/or to deliver welfare, coercive interventions remain problematic for liberals if the interventions supervene on self-regarding or consensual choices made by competent adults. Three kinds of response are open to the troubled liberal. First, one can consistently argue for freedom of choice whatever 'free-floating evils' go unchecked.[5] Or one can say that even liberals are not bound to accord immunity to

---

3   The views of John Stuart Mill and Joel Feinberg exemplify the versions of social liberalism under scrutiny here. The focus will be on their shared commitment to the maximization of civic freedom, but there is a marked difference of tone in their respective arguments for limiting the use of state coercion to constrain voluntary choices. Mill, J.S. (1859), *On Liberty*, (Oxford World's Classics) is suffused with an optimism favouring the greatest latitude for personal choice as the surest way of increasing the number of good choices made and, in particular, giving greatest practical implementation to the principle of utility. By contrast, Feinberg, J. (1984–1988), *The Moral Limits of the Criminal Law*, (Oxford University Press), in his exhaustive four volume defence of liberal principles has great awareness that persons who fulfil the conditions necessary for voluntary and informed decision-making may nonetheless make imprudent even self destructive choices. While almost invariably taking a pro-liberty stance, the arguments are frequently finely balanced.

4   Of course, in political discourse the term 'liberal' can be used in broader and looser senses to cover persons not necessarily disposed to enhancing free choice.

5   The term 'free-floating evil' is used by Feinberg to designate a morally bad state of affairs but where no one can be said to be aggrieved: (1988), *Harmless Wrongdoing*,

all self-regarding/consensual choices, if in particular instances they are interdicted by other values of equal or greater weight that are also endorsed by a credible version of liberalism that accords due weight to liberty. Or one can leave the liberal tent if at some point the disvalue of the free-floating evil outweighs the value of freedom of choice, accepting that this curtailment of choice cannot be reconciled with a liberal framework.

Choosing Death or Serious Forms of Bodily Harm

Many forms of conduct that liberals would permit, but some versions of authoritarianism would suppress, are readily comprehensible and rational in terms of the motivation of the agent both to persons of liberal persuasion or persons of authoritarian persuasion. For instance, a person with a particular religious belief may think that certain forms of sexual fulfilment should be proscribed and yet still accept positive affinities between forms of sexual expression that he would permit and those he would suppress. He may acknowledge that persons in same-sex relationships may seek similar fulfilments from their sex lives as heterosexual married couples, yet insist that fealty to his religious beliefs entails that only sexual relations in the latter class are legitimate. In cases of this kind, the gap between liberals and authoritarians who take a religiously or culturally constricted view of self regarding/consensual conduct is unbridgeable.

But there are forms of consensual conduct that even a liberal of the most libertarian persuasion may have profound reservations. Certain episodes of extreme sadomasochism may be fully consented to during sexually charged interactions,[6] yet *ex post* reflections on the encounter may give rise to a sense of grievance.[7] More puzzling again perhaps are persons who may choose injury or death without any discernable motivation, beyond the experiencing the event itself. To be sure, the question of motivation must always be explored. The seemingly unaccountable desire to have a perfectly sound limb amputated may, when fulfilled, deliver welfare in terms of restoring the agent to calm and stability.[8] But other choices seem to

---

(Oxford University Press), at pp. 3–33. For instance, Feinberg accepts that gladiatorial contests staged before paying customers are evil events. Yet if the gladiators have given an informed consent to their participation, the consent, for Feinberg, negates a finding of any wrong done to the gladiators even in the event of death or serious bodily harm. The evil 'free-floats' in that it does not substantiate any grievance based claim.

6　As sexual freedom is an important liberty for modern liberals, there must be a strong presumption by such liberals in favour of regarding choices made during escalating sexual interactions as valid choices albeit that the conditions for reflective and prudential decision-making may be far less than optimal.

7　See, for example, *State v Vann* (2004) NW 2D 600.

8　It seems that there is a form of disorder, labelled Body Integrity Identity Disorder. Persons afflicted with the disorder have intense desires to have one or more of their healthy limbs amputated. Amputation can be successful in restoring the patient to calm, whereas if

flow from inscrutable commitments, seem to rest on nothing more than an opting for the act (whatever it may be) of and in itself. A particular decision to commit suicide may from a humanist perspective seem, and indeed be, entirely rational. And yet another suicide may seem in large measure a product of time, place and external influences and not reflective of a stable choice to vacate an untenable life.[9] And even when we can identify a motive for some forms of extreme behaviour, we may be appalled at what it reveals about aspects of the human condition. Some people really do want to be eaten alive and manage to fulfil that appalling destiny.[10] Others agree to do such things as participate in 'extreme fighting' before paying spectators[11] or, again for payment, subject themselves to forms of serial degradation, incompatible with dignity and self-respect.[12]

Even persons with strong commitments to maximizing the personal autonomy and freedom of competent adults, may find those commitments under stress when confronted with tokens of the forms of conduct sketched above. When revisiting one's liberal commitments in the face of such conduct, one move should be treated with great circumspection. In preparing the ground for some form of state coercion, there arises a familiar temptation to assume an agent's mental incompetence in the

---

amputation is refused the patient may resort to extreme and damaging measures to effect an amputation: Horn, F. (2003), Bodily Integrity Identity Disorder, *Social Work Today* February 24; Bayne, T. and Levy, N. (2005), Amputees by Choice: Bodily Integrity Disorder and the Ethics of Amputation, *Journal of Applied Philosophy* 22:1, 75. Bayne and Levy argue strongly that amputation operations should be permitted as of right in the absence of any legally recognized form of insanity. However, as the desire for an amputation stems from a form of fixation rather than any rational objective, a welfare rather than a rights-based foundation for the legitimacy of such amputations is more cogent. Therapeutically, an amputation may be indicated, but the issue is essentially about the best way forward in terms of the patient's welfare rather than acceding to any right of the patient to insist on an amputation for whatever reason. In other words, the relief of distress emanating from some pathology/disorder is essential to legitimate the removal of a healthy limb. On that view, cases of Bodily Integrity Identity Disorder fall beyond the concerns of this chapter where the focus is on self destructive choices by competent adults.

9   A case in point seems to be a cluster of adolescent suicides in the town and area of Bridgend, South Wales. Although there were issues of unemployment and social deprivation there was evidence of peer influence and imitative behaviour. There is good reason to think that some of the young persons who died by their own hand did not suffer from conditions which would have allowed civil commitment under mental health legislation: *The Sunday Times*, 27 January 2008.

10   Armin Meiwes and Bernd Brandes, German nationals, made contact through an internet chat room, an encounter culminating in Meiwes eating bodily parts of Brandes prior to the latter's impending death. This macabre event, including the killing of Brandes, was seemingly consensual: *The Guardian*, 4 December 2003.

11   Extreme or 'cage' fighting is now an open, commercial activity in the United States and can be viewed on satellite/cable channels available in the United Kingdom.

12   The international pornography industry systemically requires its workers to simulate or participate in procedures of the most abasing and humiliating kind.

light of the choices she has made, rather than scrutinize the agent's actual mental and volitional capacities.[13] For example, it is all too easy to say something like: 'Why should she want to kill herself? She has got everything she could possibly want. She can't be herself'. And the speaker may be absolutely correct. The agent may be suffering from a severe, endogenous depression. Invocation of civil powers of detention under mental health legislation may be entirely in point. The coercive intervention may prove entirely beneficent. The agent successfully re-engages with family and friends and is grateful that she was prevented from taking her own life. Only those increasingly isolated polemicists who deny the reality of all forms of mental illness[14] would question the legitimacy of such coercive interventions.

By contrast, take three young men who have agreed to play Russian roulette. There is no existential despair here, just thrill seeking and macho acting out. To be sure, they have been drinking and may not have agreed to play the game at an earlier point in the day. However, were any one of them for sport to use the revolver on a non-consenting third party, he would be held fully accountable under the criminal law.[15] Therefore there is no warrant for saying he is not fully accountable for what he does to himself. But many liberals, including this liberal, would want to stop this game and would interpret the current criminal law in a way that allowed state intervention to do so.[16] But what moral warrant do we have to intervene in this way and is the colour of right that we claim a departure from our liberal beliefs? And if we disallow Russian roulette, what other self-regarding/consensual conduct of competent adults would we also coercively curtail?

Freedom of Choice: Mill and Feinberg

What does a commitment to liberalism imply for the legitimate regulation by the state law of very harmful yet self-regarding/consensual conduct engaged in by

---

13   *People v Samuels* (1967) 58 Cal Rptr 439 contains a plain example of this kind of thinking. An issue arose as to whether V had consented to a whipping by D, an issue on the face of it difficult to resolve because V could not be traced. The matter was resolved by the Court of Appeals as follows: 'It is a matter of common knowledge that a normal person in full possession of his mental faculties does not freely consent to the use upon himself of force likely to produce great bodily injury', at 442.

14   Such as Thomas Szasz and the late R.D. Laing.

15   Even if D was heavily intoxicated he would still be liable for crimes of violence such as manslaughter or malicious wounding which do not require proof of a specific intent: Simester, A. and Sullivan, G.R. (2007), *Criminal Law: Theory and Doctrine*, 3rd Edition (Hart Publishing), at pp. 633–636.

16   That would not necessarily be straightforward. Following the recent decision of the House of Lords in *Kennedy* [2008] UKHL 38, it is unlikely that any self-inflicted harm would be regarded as causally influenced by any of the other players. Some forms of self-harm may constitute the common law offence of maim, but not in circumstances such as these. Doubtless police could break up the party by invoking breach of the peace.

competent adults? Is there any scope for such regulation? The classic answer, indelibly associated with John Stuart Mill, is that a liberal state should not interfere with the conduct of a competent citizen unless and until that conduct causes or threatens to harm third parties. A paternalistic or morally coercive criminal law is emphatically disavowed. Although Mill's famous essay[17] is rightly celebrated as a vindication of civic freedom as a public good in its own right, one cannot overlook its context or its time. Mill did not concern himself at all with the destructive and negative aspects of human nature. Indeed much of his essay is devoted to the second-order gains that maximizing freedom will bring. He anticipates that many routine and traditional forms of conduct not conducive to the maximization of welfare will be consigned to history. The expansion of state education for both sexes and the power of good examples would encourage a predominance of positive life choices on the part of citizens, increasing individual satisfactions and the general welfare. A major preoccupation of Mill was to persuade us that a liberal democracy would be functionally better in terms of realizing utility than a democracy organized on different lines. What is notoriously vague in Mill's account is the content of the famous harm principle – with what specific restraints it imposes on the interactions of citizens as between themselves. In particular, there is no sustained discussion of the role of consent, in what circumstances, if any, an inflicted harm loses its character as a harm, or at least as a ground of complaint, if a competent adult has consented to suffer it.

These lacunas are addressed at exhaustive length by Joel Feinberg in his four-volume treatise *The Moral Limits of the Criminal Law*.[18] First, he seeks definitional clarity as to what constitutes a harm. In the briefest of terms, harm for Feinberg is any event which entails or threatens a setback to the interests of the agent.[19] Many such events – carelessly falling down one's stairs and breaking a leg – are indubitably setbacks, but have no implications for the criminal law. The criminal law is implicated only when we can say that the event which harmed the agent is a wrong done to the agent – a wrong which warrants the public condemnation of the wrongdoer under the criminal law. It is in the realm of what constitutes a criminal wrong that the prime importance that Feinberg accords to the consent of the harmed agent emerges. For our purposes, we can encapsulate without distorting Feinberg's account if we say that the fully informed, voluntary consent of an adult, mentally competent agent precludes any finding that the wrong consented to will constitute a criminal wrong inflicted on the agent. If we are sure that consent of this character is present, there seems no limit to what may be consented to. So if D, a fight promoter, were to propose to V that he should fight E to the death in a gladiatorial contest for the entertainment of paying spectators, under Feinberg's

---

17   (1859), *On Liberty*, (Oxford World's Classics).

18   Feinberg, J. (1984–1988), *The Moral Limits of the Criminal Law*, (Oxford University Press).

19   Feinberg, J. (1984), *Harm to Others*, (Oxford University Press), at pp. 30–36.

scheme of things, neither the promoters, the fighters nor indeed the spectators should be found guilty of any criminal offence.[20]

Feinberg proposes one important supplement to the harm principle not discussed by Mill, namely the offence principle.[21] To illustrate, suppose D, our fight promoter, decides to drum up publicity for his grisly spectacles by arranging a free gladiatorial contest to be performed 'spontaneously' in some public place before non-volunteer members of the public. Obviously, many unwitting observers may be shocked and revolted by the spectacle. Some may suffer harm, but others in the class of those shocked and offended will live lives that go as well or as badly as before the unwelcome spectacle. Nonetheless, for Feinberg, it is appropriate for the criminal law to protect persons from such public offence. The public dimension should be emphasized. Persons who are aware that certain practices such as extreme yet consensual violence occur in the private realm may, as a consequence of this knowledge, be burdened with feelings of indignation and disgust, arousing strong pro attitudes towards suppression of the activity by the criminal law. The presence of such emotions, however pervasive, however strong, does not trigger Feinberg's offence principle. For him, private lives should be left to be lived freely, whatever disapproval is aroused by private choices.

The importance of the offence principle to the Feinberg schema is that a wrong of proper concern to the criminal law may occur without harm. An agent may be deeply offended by offensive public events, but even in the most fleeting sense will suffer no setback to any of her legitimate interests. If the event is public and sufficiently gross, the perpetrators of the event are fit subjects for condemnation and punishment. But as with harms, consent defeats any ground of complaint. V, from curiosity, may go to the cinema to watch a sexually explicit film. She may be enraged and disgusted by what she sees, but she has not been wronged. The importance of consent to Feinberg's version of the harm and offence principles is to allow that there can be setbacks to the legitimate interests of the agent, or gross offence caused to third parties, but without any ensuing wrong. The notion of wrong is central to his kind of criminal law based on liberal principles, leaving what has been called 'grievance morality'[22] as the only form of morality suitable to be enforced by the criminal law. A wrong to an individual must occur before any question of taking the further step of criminally proscribing the conduct instantiating the wrong arises. For Feinberg, at least in his first considered account

---

20 The example of the gladiatorial contest, originally put by Irving Kristol, was found very troubling by Feinberg who accepted that it tested the dispensing power of consent to the limit. He considered that a society that tolerated such spectacles would diminish the quality of its civic life. However, he did not offer any final conclusion on whether such an event should attract criminal liability: Feinberg, J. (1984), *Harm to Others*, (Oxford University Press), at p. 80.

21 Feinberg, J. (1985), *Offence to Others*, (Oxford University Press).

22 Postema, G. (2005), Politics is about the Grievance: Feinberg on the Legal Enforcement of Morality, *Legal Theory* 11, 293.

of the entailments of the liberal position, any consent meeting the requirements sketched above, precluded any finding that an agent, even if harmed, had been wronged. The absence of any wrong entails the absence of any warrant to punish the agent consenting to the harm and any other agents who may inflict or facilitate the harm.

Resting content with the classic, liberal commitment to maximize choice and refrain from regulating the content of the choices made by competent adults has powerful attractions. Resort to the criminal law should be a governmental option of last resort. As Mill so persuasively argued, example and persuasion can be the least costly and most effective forms of influencing for the good the conduct of others. Even if an argument can be made for some form of state regulation of some self-regarding choices, there are less coercive and damaging forms of intervention than the criminal law, such as taxing or licensing self-destructive forms of behaviour. Even if Mill's utilitarianism would allow him in theory to dispense with the requirement of some form of wrong to an agent as a necessary condition for criminalization, should there be a sufficiency of offsetting welfare, he was acutely aware of the limitations of the criminal law as a mechanism for social progress. For Feinberg, there is no connection, conceptual or contingent, between utilitarianism and liberalism. His is a rights-based version of social liberalism, with the freedom and autonomy of adult citizens at its heart. He has no time for the pursuit of welfarism through the criminal law. The criminal law must be restricted to the punishment of wrongs. If V has consented to the event that has harmed him, he has not been wronged by it. Because of this seemingly unyielding stance, his later equivocal responses to some challenges to his position based on examples of 'free-floating' evils are of particular interest.[23]

A free-floating evil may be brought into being by an event or state of affairs that on particular versions of substantive morality is to be strongly condemned, but where, on Feinberg's version of liberalism, there has been no violation of the rights of any agent. He found particularly troublesome Irving Kristol's paid gladiators and Derek Parfit's cases of malevolent conceptions.[24] The force of these examples brought the concession from Feinberg that in principle a case for intervention by the criminal law had been made out. However, the nature of the justification for the intervention is left unresolved by Feinberg, and in particular,

---

23   Feinberg's original position was that the harm and offence principles constituted the boundaries of the legitimate criminalization of conduct – (1984), *Harm to Others*, (Oxford University Press), at pp. 6–7 – yet in his final account of his liberal position he conceded that certain instances of immoral conduct were arguably within the bounds of legitimate criminalization notwithstanding the consents of the relevant parties: (1988), *Harmless Wrongdoing*, (Oxford University Press), at pp. 321–323.

24   Feinberg, J. (1988), *Harmless Wrongdoing*, (Oxford University Press), at pp. 300–330. Malevolent conceptions are situations where a woman chooses for reprehensible motives to conceive and bear a child aware of a very high probability that her child will be severely deformed and live a very limited human life.

the question whether such interventions can be accommodated within liberalism, or can only be endorsed under some non-liberal rubric.[25]

It will be argued below that in the case of some free-floating evils a strong *prima facie* case can be made for state intervention, including through the means of the criminal law. We will seek to resolve whether such interventions can be reconciled with liberalism or, alternatively, whether a defensible case can be made for a non-liberal ground of intervention.

Inalienable and Unwaivable Rights

An attempt to reconcile liberalism with coercive interventions in the matter of choices made by mentally, competent adults is based on the claim that human beings have some core inalienable rights/dignity interests which are transgressed even if the agent consents to the act/event which violates his rights. In other words, the inventory of rights, of even competent adults, includes certain rights which are beyond the power of the agent to vacate. Should D's conduct violate a right of V falling within that category, he will perpetrate a wrong against V. Accordingly V will have a grievance against D despite V's consent. Consequently, the criminalization of D's conduct is compatible with a liberalism which confines recourse to the criminal law to circumstances where V has been wronged by D.

As alluded to above, to test the limits of liberal tolerance, Irving Kristol offered the example of two gladiators, who on payment are prepared to fight unto death in a spectacle to be performed before paying spectators. The example troubled Feinberg because he thought the conduct involved was detestable on any defensible account of human needs and aspirations.[26] Yet if we assume freely given and informed consents on the part of the gladiators, neither wrongs the other when fighting on these ghastly terms. Logically the same applies to the promoter, who profits most from the event, and the spectators who provide its *raison d'être*. There is great intuitive appeal in finding the wrongdoing lies with the promoter and spectators, rather than with the wretches whose life options are so limited that a chance to earn money in this fashion is something to be taken. But we can only do that consonantly with liberalism if we place the fighters in some special category of the weak and vulnerable. If the fighters are mentally competent adults, that move

---

25   In the case of malevolent conceptions, Feinberg was prepared to allow criminalization beyond the limits of the harm principle on the ground that such cases would be very rare and hence unthreatening to his overall schema. As for the gladiators, he accepted that the consent of the participants did not diminish the wrongness of the fighting yet their consent left the participants without a grievance. He came to no firm conclusion on criminalization, but agreed that a legislature could in principle ban such events, presumably as an exception to the harm and offence principles.

26   See n 23 above and associated text.

is blocked by core commitments of liberalism. There is free-floating evil, but no wrong based on a violation of the rights of the fighters.

Gerald Postema argues that liberals can deal with such events as gladiatorial contests without compromising their liberalism to any degree.[27] He advises against resort to the category of free-floating evils. His position is that if we intervene through the criminal law in circumstances where no claim can be made that a third party has been wronged by the agent whose conduct will be punished, we are subscribing to some form of legal moralism. We would have to say in order to justify criminal liability that anyone involved in any capacity with such things as gladiatorial contests puts themselves in a very bad moral light and that of itself warrants state punishment.[28] On this moralistic approach no distinction could be drawn, at least in terms of the imposition of criminal liability, between fighters, promoters and spectators.

If, in a case like the gladiators, we wish to suppress the activity by focusing on the harm that has or will be done to them without resorting to any notion of free-floating evils, there are, for Postema, two routes that can be taken. We can invoke paternalism and say we intervene to prevent them from harming themselves. As we will discuss critically in more detail below, a paternalistic/welfarist approach also dispenses with the need for any wrong done to a third party on the part of anyone considered eligible for punishment and has (illegitimately) been interpreted by courts to license very hard treatment of persons ostensibly under protection.[29] Alternatively, we can respect all mentally competent adults as autonomous individuals, but compatibly with that respect insist that all persons have certain inalienable and unwaivable rights. He contends that while liberals must respect the choices of individuals, they must not make a fetish of choice. Choice and autonomy are matters of great importance for liberals, but so is the personhood of individuals. He notes that Feinberg would not permit choices for slavery as slavery involves a denial of personhood and is therefore incompatible with a fundamental tenet of liberalism.[30] Postema builds on the notion of personhood and maintains that it entails some bundle of inalienable rights that cannot be waived by consent. If one or more of those rights are violated by a third party, the wrong is not vacated by any consent of the right holder to the violation. Regarding the gladiator example, Postema takes the view that to induce or facilitate even voluntary participation in

---

27   Postema, G. (2005) Politics is about the Grievance: Feinberg on the Legal Enforcement of Morality, *Legal Theory* 11, 293.

28   *Ibid.*, at pp. 295–297.

29   The majority judgements of the House of Lords in *Brown* [1994] AC 212 invoke paternalistic concern for persons at risk of injury during sadomasochistic activities, yet draw no distinction in terms of criminal liability between agents and patients. A paternalist would have to make a rather forced reliance on general deterrence to square this state of affairs with paternalism.

30   *Op cit.*, n 26 at p. 317. Mill, too, considered that liberals could not endorse a choice to become someone's slave.

such a brutal public spectacle violates the inalienable and unwaivable rights of the fighters.[31]

Essentially, his position is that the choices of agents may result in outcomes incompatible with the fundamental values that liberalism protects. When that is so, the consents of even fully competent adults are no longer sovereign, and other values may supervene. One difficulty with his position is to resolve which rights belong in the class of inalienable rights. Postema explicitly declines to engage with this question on the ground that he is merely establishing the cogency of the claim that a class of unwaivable and inalienable *rights* exists, a task distinct, so he claims, from making an inventory of rights that fall within the class.[32]

If one were to consider the question of what rights may be considered inalienable and unwaivable, a very strong candidate member of the class would surely be the right to life – the key and seminal right in any scheme of rights. But an inalienable and unwaivable right to life is difficult to square with any version of liberalism that values respecting choice in supremely important matters. A right to life, considered as a right which an adult right holder may dispense with at any time and for any reason, (including participation in a gladiatorial contest) fits snugly within libertarian liberalism. That said, many persons who would consider themselves liberals would be uncomfortable with permitting wholly untrammelled choices on the part of agents in the matter of waiving their right to life or, for that matter, the right not to be seriously harmed. The difficulty is in reaching some *via media* between free choice and the strictures of legal moralism and paternalism from within the resources of liberalism. Merely establishing the plausibility of the bare existence of a class of inalienable and unwaivable rights does not complete that task.

An attempt to put some content in the claim that an agent may be wronged despite consenting to the intervention that is a necessary constituent of the wrong can be found, respectively, in the work of Antony Duff[33] and Meir Dan-Cohen.[34] Their common starting point is uncontroversial. Human beings, by dint of the fact that they are human beings, are entitled to dignity and respect. Their argument moves from that to a further claim that a lack of respect may be shown to an agent despite his free consent to the treatment that instantiates the lack of respect and disregard for dignity. Such conduct will wrong the agent notwithstanding his consent. If the wrong is sufficiently grave, recourse to the criminal law to punish the wrongdoer may be warranted.[35] So here we have, if only in the broadest of terms, unwaivable rights in the form of rights possessed of us all to dignity and respect and criminal wrongs perpetrated against competent, consenting adults.

---

31   *Ibid.*, at pp. 317–318.

32   *Ibid.*, at p. 312.

33   Duff, R.A. (2002), Harms and Wrongs, *Buffalo Criminal Law Review* 5, 13.

34   Dan-Cohen, M. (2000), Basic Values and the Victim's State of Mind, *California Law Review* 88, 759.

35   Duff, *op cit.*, n 33 at pp. 39–44; Dan-Cohen, *ibid.* at p. 770.

It may readily be agreed that to treat all human beings with dignity and respect is to give no more than is due. And there may frequently be broad agreement when a lack of regard for a person's dignity and respect has been shown regardless of the consent of the person disrespected. Dan-Cohen's assertion that a happy slave is but an example of a 'paradigm of injustice' would receive broad assent. So too might Duff's contention that voluntary gladiatorial contests involve 'dehumanization or degradation perpetrated by the gladiators on each other and by the spectators on the gladiators and on themselves'.[36] But disagreement is also likely to arise. Duff's remark about gladiators would, with suitable adaptation, be used as a text by persons who wished to ban boxing. By contrast, followers of boxing would report sincerely the respect they had for the courage and skill of many professional boxers. Duff and Dan-Cohen at one time disagreed with each other as to which side of the dignity/respect line fell the controversial decision of the House of Lords in *Brown*.[37] Duff supported the decision in that case to criminalize sadomasochistic sex. For him, the facts were indicative of treatment amounting to a disregard of the dignity and respect of the participants in the sadomasochistic orgy.[38] It is not clear whether he at one time thought all the participants, whether sadists or masochists, were equally culpable for showing lack of respect to all other participants or only persons in the former class were culpable in that regard (in so far as the participants can be placed into classes on this or any basis). If all participants are to be considered justly convicted of crimes, his position in functional terms amounts to legal moralism as he makes no appeal to paternalistic concerns. For Dan-Cohen, criminalization on facts such as *Brown* was unwarranted. If one took into account the narratives and procedures of controlled forms of sadomasochistic sex, then there was full regard for the dignity and humanity for all the participants by all of the participants.[39] This is a view that Duff now shares.[40]

As it happens, I agree with Duff that arranging gladiatorial contests should be criminal and with Dan-Cohen that sadomasochistic sex of the non-volatile kind involved in *Brown* should be made lawful. Where I part company is finding much help in reaching these conclusions from ruminations on dignity and respect. It is perfectly possible, as will be argued below, to proscribe certain forms of conduct engaged in by competent, consenting adults without holding that to engage in the conduct to be made criminal is to lose dignity and respect. We may anticipate that such an opinion may be difficult to square with liberal commitments. After all, for liberals, the coercion of competent, consenting adults is to show lack of regard for their dignity.

---

36   *Op cit.*, n 33 at p. 39.
37   [1994] AC 212.
38   *Op cit.*, n 32.
39   *Op cit.*, n 33 at p. 777.
40   Duff, R.A. (2007), *Answering for Crime*, (Hart Publishing), at p. 131.

The Argument from Freedom

A major theme of modern liberalism is the idea of autonomy – freedom of choice as an end in itself. If this is played by the book, the emphasis is on the capacity and circumstances attendant on the agent's choice and not on the kind and quality of choices made. A common criticism of this separation of the capacity of the agent for choosing, and the things she might choose, is that the choosing agent is presented in a socially abstracted form. The focus on volition, knowledge and comprehension may leave out of account powerful cultural and situational influences on what choices the agent may make. If proper regard is had for cultural and social factors, we may find that there may be a distance between what an agent may overtly choose and what that agent truly wants. Such considerations are particularly in point for adolescents and young adults who have attained the age of consent. Peer pressure to make destructive choices may be intense. Constraining the range of choices available to such persons may, paradoxically perhaps, increase rather than reduce their freedom by eliminating options they would prefer not to have, ensuring a better fit between overt choices and settled desires.

Arguments to this effect have been accepted in principle by some liberals. In certain instances it may transpire that a legal restriction on a form of activity can enhance rather than diminish practical freedom. Proscribing certain forms of ostensibly consensual conduct which may lead to serious harm may enlarge the freedom of members of a class who might otherwise be socially constrained to engage in the activity with its attendant risks. The illegal status of the activity will make easier the position of those minded to resist the social conventions, inducing participation therein, and over time may well change those social conventions. An example frequently used to make this form of argument is duelling. Before the practice was made unequivocally illegal, members of those classes who considered themselves obliged to observe the honour code would feel constrained by the code to accept the challenge of a duel, even if their true inclination would result in refusing the challenge. After duelling became legally proscribed, it became possible to reject a challenge without loss of social standing. The change in the law, although restrictive in its terms, was in its function liberating as it increased the ratio of choices which comported with the true wishes of members of the affected classes.[41]

The argument can be adapted to those who, for instance, practice sexual masochism. If we can speak of masochists as members of a class, it seems

---

41 Feinberg accepted that the banning of such socially enforced activities as duelling would not rest on a paternalistic rationale should the legislature be seeking to remove constraints on the majority of the population: 'When most of the people subject to a coercive rule approve of the rule and it is legislated ... *for their sakes* and not for the purpose of imposing safety or prudence on the unwilling majority ("against their will") then the rationale of the rule is not paternalistic.' Feinberg, J. (1986), *Harm to Self*, (Oxford University Press), at p. 20.

a plausible assumption that most members of that class would prefer sexual encounters which did not involve the infliction upon themselves of serious bodily harm. As the law stands now, sadomasochistic activity is tightly constrained – the harm inflicted must be something less than actual bodily harm, otherwise criminal offences will be committed.[42] Relaxation of the law on the lines proposed by the English Law Commission – allow valid consent to harm up to the level of actual bodily harm but continue to rule invalid consent to anything more severe[43] – would seem, on the lines of this argument of imposing restraints to advance freedom, a balanced and liberal proposal, which, if enacted, would enlarge freedom. But if the reform were ostensibly more liberal by proposing to allow valid consents for serious bodily harm, we might end up by constraining freedom. Agents who would prefer to keep the levels of violence down in their sexual encounters might, under a more permissive dispensation, find themselves pressurized by their sexual partners to accept more violence than they truly want. This might also lead to additional losses from the other direction. Persons who might be willing to engage in masochistic encounters under a more constrained regime might decline to do so at all because of the risks inherent in a more permissive environment.

Judged from a consistent liberal perspective, there are severe difficulties with the argument based on enhancing freedom by imposing restraints. First, it is at its core an empirical argument and often the true facts will be elusive. When duelling was finally abolished in England there may or may not have been a collective sigh of relief from the duelling classes. Doubtless, some were relieved to see the back of this macho burden, but others (how many?) may have sincerely regretted the passing of the old ways.[44] By the same token, even Jeremy Clarkson may have secretly welcomed the legislative compulsion to wear a seatbelt. If unattached to a robust duty to ascertain the true state of the facts, this form of argument from freedom can be too easily deployed to suppress freedom. Take drinking alcohol, for example. There is no doubt that young people may come under considerable peer pressure to drink excessively. Without that pressure, there would be more choices for sobriety, less violence and less sickness among people under 30. Furthermore, a significant number within the class socially constrained to drink excessively will become addicted to alcohol and lead less free lives and, in many cases, shorter lives thereafter. Arguably then, one would increase freedom by raising the age for the legal consumption of alcohol to, say, 30. But who can possibly say what such a change in the law might bring about in terms of enhancing 'true' freedom? For many, a legal drinking age of 30 would be uncomfortably close to a repeat of the US prohibition experiment.

---

42   *Donovan* [1934] 2 KB 498; *Brown* [1994] 1 AC 212.

43   Law Commission Consultation Paper No. 139 (1995), *Consent in the Criminal Law*, at paras. 4.46–4.53.

44   For the changing attitudes to duelling during the late eighteenth and early nineteenth centuries see Andrew, D. (1980), The Code of Honour and its Critics, *Social History* 5:3, 409, at pp. 420–431.

The second difficulty with the freedom arising from the restraint line of argument is that it addresses the freedom of persons within a class – freedom in aggregate – whereas the perspective of the modern liberal is the choices of the individual. Of course, individual choices are made in family, cultural and social contexts, but modern forms of political liberalism would change their nature and form if aggressive legislative programmes were adopted seeking to advance freedom and autonomy by overriding family, cultural and societal influences such as, for example, insisting that children should leave home at 18, in order to make their own independent way.[45]

As matters now stand, a person of 18 is free to stay at home even if the home/cultural environment places the strongest strictures on such things as the consumption of alcohol and the choice of life partner. Equally, a child of 18 can leave such a home, drink alcohol and date whom they like. These freedoms, active and passive (in some cases acquiescence), may turn out well or badly in the various individual instances. That freedom may turn out badly for some is a price entailed by any consistent adherence to liberalism.

But how far down should this hands-off attitude be allowed to go? It is disquieting to think of persons of 16 (the age of sexual consent) having the freedom to choose forms of sexuality involving the intentional infliction of serious bodily harm. Even more disquieting is the thought of a young person of 16 left free to decide to die and seek assistance to that end. If we wish to support the current proscription of such choices in a manner consistent with liberalism, we must use something other than the argument from freedom and from inalienable rights. Indeed, if we wish to justify the proscription of such choices, we may have to go beyond liberalism.

Legal Moralism

Anyone broadly in sympathy with the classic liberalism of Mill and its modern, rights-based reinterpretation by Feinberg, should in principle reject two forms of justification for criminalization decisions, namely legal moralism and paternalism.

Legal moralists maintain that certain forms of immorality warrant punishment at the hands of the state simply on the ground of the agent choosing and doing something sufficiently wrong in moral terms. Prominent legal moralists have taken a particular interest in proscribing certain forms of sexuality,[46] but all forms

---

45   Here lies, of course, one of the main tension points of modern liberalism. The emphasis on the freedom and autonomy of individuals while refraining from prescribing any template, however general its terms, as to legitimate modes of life, will leave undisturbed ways of life inimical to the exercise of freedom and autonomy.

46   Perhaps the best known essay defending legal moralism is Devlin, P. (1965), *The Enforcement of Morals*, (Oxford University Press), and is widely regarded as an attack on legislative proposals to decriminalize homosexual acts.

of immorality are grist to the mill.[47] Harm to non-consenting others is neither a necessary nor sufficient condition for judgements that forms of conduct should be made criminal. The immorality that licences state punishment is never solely a function of the consequences that may arise from the conduct at issue. Indeed, for certain legal moralists, most notably Kant, consequences play no part in the moral assessment, which is confined to the movements and the will of the agent. What the agent wills and does may, for a legal moralist, put the agent in such poor moral standing that expiation of her wrong can legitimately take the form of public stigmatization and punishment.

Mill, with his utilitarian outlook, summarily rejected legal moralism. For him, the criminal law should be based solely on the harm principle: the immorality or otherwise of the harmful conduct was not directly in point. Herbert Hart, working in the same utilitarian tradition, offered a more nuanced account of the overarching rationale of the criminal law.[48] He defended Mill's view that the reduction of harm was the defining purpose of the criminal law and that state punishment was unwarranted if not linked to harm reduction. Yet he allowed moral considerations a secondary role in the distribution of punishment, to mitigate the unfairness of a system of punishment based solely on a utilitarian calculus.[49] But he was steadfastly at one with Mill in rejecting the claim that immorality *qua* immorality provides a sufficient justification for criminal punishment, as his famous exchange with Patrick Devlin so emphatically demonstrates.[50]

We do not find the same opposition to legal moralism in the writings of Joel Feinberg. His liberalism is non-consequentialist, rights-based liberalism. He is as concerned with the question of whether the agent has perpetrated a wrong on a third party, as with the question of whether the agent's conduct has caused or threatened a harm to the third party. A harm which does not also constitute a wrong against the person harmed is not a candidate harm for criminalization. For Feinberg, the fact that conduct is immoral is a consideration in favour of its criminalization.

---

47   In theory, a legal moralist could make the immorality of a given token of conduct a sufficient condition for its criminalization. But at least among legal moralists who do not tether the content of their moral codes to religious texts exclusionary principles are put in place. Devlin, it will be recalled, thought that only immoral acts which would arouse the 'intolerance, indignation and disgust' of juries were properly subject to criminal sanction. This psychological reaction test for the legal enforcement of morality makes Devlin a moral relativist because what act tokens evoke such responses will change over time. I am grateful to John Stanton-Ife for making this point.

48   Hart, H. (1965), *Law, Liberty and Morality*, (Oxford University Press).

49   For an argument that Hart's attempt to find some foothold for morality in the criminal law is incompatible with harm reduction as a primary aim see Galligan, D. (1981), The Return to Retribution in Penal Theory, in Tapper C.F.H. (ed.), *Crime, Proof and Punishment*, (London: Butterworths).

50   *Law, Liberty and Morality* was, of course, written by way of rejoinder to Devlin's advocacy of legal moralism, views subsequently elaborated and defended in *The Enforcement of Morals*.

But for the most part, it is never a decisive consideration.[51] The immorality of the conduct is necessary, but not sufficient; it must additionally cause or threaten harm or offence. But his offence principle steers very close to pure legal moralism. Without resorting to explicit examples, we can readily think of behaviour that threatens us with no harm, but which we would prefer not to see in either public or private settings, things that would revolt and disgust us. But there must be something else before such behaviour constitutes the wrong of causing offence to others, even in the public settings where the offence principle applies. It is no accident that the examples which Feinberg uses to illustrate his offence principle predominantly feature public episodes of sexual incontinence. The essential aggravating core of such conduct is that it flouts *normative* constraints on what is considered appropriate behaviour in public.[52] As no setback to the interests of those offended is required, for Feinberg a harmless breach of a moral prohibition applicable to public settings may constitute a criminal wrong in its own right.

Once that is clearly understood, the difficulty caused to Feinberg by Kristol's gladiators is more readily understood. What exercised Feinberg was the immorality of such contests for commercial gain – the fact that such contests create 'evil in our midst'. He conceded that the case for criminalization was strong. But as he could not bring such contests within grievance morality he desisted from offering any final conclusion on the matter.[53]

Feinberg was well advised not to desert his liberalism under the flag of legal moralism. Hart's elegant and effective attack on the legal moralism of Devlin pinpoints the vitiating difficulty of making public and secular judgements of right and wrong sufficient of themselves to resolve criminalization decisions. There is simply no conceivable way of grounding such judgements, save for attempts to assess the state of majoritarian moral opinion about the conduct at issue, with all that entails for the freedom and security of minorities. Interestingly, Hart, as we shall see in the next section, would have no difficulty in proscribing gladiatorial contests under the rubric of paternalism, something that Feinberg strongly opposes.

The cultural roots of legal moralism remain strong. It receives succour from religious beliefs and from authoritarian populism. It receives more sophisticated support from cultural theorists/moral relativists who insist on respect for all forms of cultural difference, including practices and customs which place very severe curtailments on personal autonomy. It may dress itself in the clothing of paternalism/communitarianism, although, properly understood, the core commitments of legal moralism are very different. The day of legal moralism is far from done.[54] But it remains something that liberals should oppose.

---

51   Feinberg, J. (1984), *Harm to Others*, (Oxford University Press), at p. 323.

52   See further Alexander, L. (2005), When are we Rightfully Aggrieved?, *Legal Theory* 11, 325, at pp. 330–332.

53   See n 23 above and associated text.

54   Dworkin, G. (1999), Devlin was Right: Law and the Enforcement of Morality, *William and Mary Law Review* 40, 927.

Paternalism

Paternalism, a problematic term, represents a problematic cluster of ideas for a liberal, most particularly the idea that the state and its agencies may know better than an adult, competent agent where her best interests lie, and may even resort to the criminal law to enforce that judgement. A paternalistic intervention through the agency of the criminal law which is focused on the best interests of the person to be punished must rest on the following assumptions:

1. There may be a negative variance between an agent's best interests and the agent's chosen conduct.
2. In certain cases state intervention is warranted in an attempt to secure the agent's best interests as against her present inclinations.
3. If effective state intervention can only be achieved through the coercive resources of the criminal law, the criminal law may be resorted to.
4. There is sound reason to think that recourse to the criminal law in this instance will further, rather than setback, the best interests of the coerced agent.
5. If there is no sound reason to think that recourse to the criminal law in this instance will further the best interests of the coerced agent, the agent may yet be subject to criminal punishment as a deterrent example to persons who, left to their own devices, would act in a manner at variance with their best interests.

Furthering the best interests of persons by subjecting them to criminal punishment is highly problematic. In the majority of instances, the only plausible claim about best interests will be based on individual deterrence – a claim, say, that if we, say, punish her possession of drugs now she may not use them in the future and her life will go better in consequence. The sheer implausibility of many such speculations with regard to particular agents will drive the apologist for paternalistic interventions to dubious claims about populations rather than individuals. It will be said of the drug laws, for instance, that the proscribed status of drugs deters their use among the general population, thereby increasing general welfare; in other words, a deterrent effect reinforced by the punishment of those individuals who were insufficiently deterred. Directly, we will address the arguments for and against paternalism as a matter of principle. But should anyone be persuaded that paternalistic interventions are in principle acceptable, it should be a revisable stance at the mercy of the facts. A paternalism that does not deliver welfare to individuals who are coerced, or to populations more generally, is dysfunctional (and will frequently be a cover for legal moralism).[55] And as

---

55   The speeches of the majority in *Brown* [1994] 1 AC 212 make frequent but unfounded references to the dangers arising for persons who engaged in the sadomasochistic sex at issue in the case (the prosecution could not produce evidence that any of the participants

the facts are frequently a matter of conjecture, the empirical foundations of any paternalistic claim should be sceptically scrutinized. Such scrutiny is particularly in point for claims of beneficence based on general deterrence.[56]

An advocate for paternalism need not subscribe to any substantive conception of the good life. He can begin his argument on the basis of the undeniable fact that certain conditions reduce the returns from almost all forms of life, whether chosen or imposed, which, all things considered, deliver certain forms of value. There are many such conditions – life-threatening and debilitating diseases; chronic addiction to drugs and alcohol; serious and painful injuries; loss of vital limbs or organs and so on. And then there is the foundation of all forms of value, life itself. If as a matter of deliberate choice a given agent proposed to dispense with her life or contract one or more of these life-diminishing conditions for no discernible reason or for a reason that would generally be judged trivial or transient, a paternalist might take it as sufficient warrant for preventative intervention even in the case of an agent of the age of consent and seemingly normal deliberative capacities. The same would not apply for agents who risk their lives or risk contracting these life-reducing conditions as the necessary concomitants of other, lawful activities.[57] But even in these cases, a paternalist would allow a trade-off between the freedom of the agent and the risk of serious setback to the agent's best interests, with no necessary bias in favour of freedom.

In confronting paternalism, liberals are rightly concerned that to condone coercion of an agent, even in cases presenting the most plausible circumstances for benign intervention, will allow too much scope for majoritarian suppression of individual choices. In postmodern, multicultural societies, the insuperable difficulties of reaching a societal consensus on even minimalist versions of a good life that should be promoted and protected by the state, argue strongly for protecting the self-regarding choices of competent adults and maximizing the realm of the private. Freedom of choice is particularly in point for sexuality, given the importance of sexual fulfilment for the living of non-ascetic lives and the dire consequences for competent adults of publicly stigmatizing and punishing their free, self-regarding sexual choices.

Feinberg's form of liberalism allows no concessions to paternalism. He makes room for what he calls 'soft' paternalism, a move, which when examined, makes no concession to 'hard' paternalism.[58] If a choice that an agent proposes to make may seriously set back her long-term interests, we can require more than the normal indicia of consent and use a heightened procedure to ascertain whether she has given a fully informed and free consent. For choices with drastic consequences,

---

required medical or surgical attention or had acquired an infection). There are also several passages where the activities are condemned *per se*.

56   See Walker, N. and Padfield, N. (1999), *Sentencing: Theory Law and Practice*, (Oxford University Press), Chapter 8.

57   Such as mountaineering or racing cars.

58   Feinberg, J. (1986), *Harm to Self* (Oxford University Press), at p. 133.

we might even insist on consent in writing, independent witnesses, cooling-off periods, etc. We may be astute to find a mistake or ignorance about the facts or find forms of compulsion. But this, ultimately, is a matter of process and not substance. Consent remains sovereign. Above all, there is no closed feedback loop between the weirdness/destructiveness of the choice and negative conclusions about the agent's decision-making capacities. We are not allowed to say of any choice that she may make that no rational agent would choose that and therefore we must assume she lacks the capacity for choice. Rather, we must say that if she has attained the age of consent, is free to deliberate and has an adequate capacity for ratiocination, she is free to choose whatever she wants provided she harms no one but herself and causes no offence to others.

We will test Feinberg's liberalism against paternalistic claims for the two categories of case we have identified. The first category is where the agent chooses death or to endure serious bodily harm for no discernible reason or for a reason judged trivial and transient. Examples within the category would be suicide in the context of group activity and mutual support; consensual cannibalism; extreme forms of sadomasochism; engaging in sex in order to contract a serious form of STD; amputation of limbs for sexual reasons. The common thread is serious harm which is consented to and intentionally inflicted. At the risk of some conceptual looseness, included in this category are activities such as Russian roulette, where the entire point of participation (if no collateral betting is involved) is to run a risk of death or serious injury with no purpose beyond the experience of the risk. In other words, the risk of death or serious harm is constitutive, not ancillary.

The second category of case concerns agents who take risks of serious harm up to and including death as a concomitant of some goal or aspiration beyond the experience of risk. This will include persons who are averse to the risk involved as where a couple strive for a pregnancy through sexual intercourse aware of the risk that one of the partners may contract an STD from the other, but hoping such an eventuality will not arise. It will also include parties who create a risk in order to intensify an experience, such as choosing a difficult route up the rock face or intensifying a sexual experience by risking asphyxiation, yet aiming to avoid injury or death. The common thread for the second category is risking serious harm but not wishing/intending to be harmed.

Both categories will be discussed in sequence to see if any act tokens coming within one or other of these categories give rise to strong intuitions favouring the proscription of self-regarding/consensual conduct. It will be argued that to intervene on the basis of such an intuition cannot be squared with any coherent version of liberalism. A consistent liberalism is attainable only at the cost of a completely libertarian stance towards self regarding/consensual conduct.

The discussion proceeds on certain assumptions. We assume that the subjects to be discussed are persons who have reached the age of consent (what should be the age of consent for certain forms of dangerous or destructive interactions is an important topic not discussed here) and are not afflicted with any form of disability undermining of deliberative capacity.[59] A defect of deliberative capacity is not to be inferred solely from the fact that the agent has chosen a form of conduct which will cause or threaten to cause serious harm to her. What constitutes a valid consent is taken to be a gender-neutral question.

Choosing Death or Serious Bodily Harm

There are well-documented instances of persons who consent to the infliction of death or serious bodily harm upon themselves, either as some form of experience that seemingly has no purpose beyond the event itself, or as a constitutive part or precursor to sexual or other bodily sensations. Persons may have sex in order to contract a significant STD.[60] As we have noted, adolescents and young persons may choose to die at their own hand as part of some cult activity.[61] These instances of choices for death and/or serious harm are far from exhaustive. It is not possible to estimate the number of persons who either inflict or accept death and serious bodily harm in these and other circumstances. The internet facilitates contacts and the formation of mutual support groups between persons inclined to inflict/accept serious bodily harm in sexual and other forms of encounter.[62]

In all parts of the United Kingdom it is a criminal offence intentionally to inflict harm amounting to actual bodily harm or something worse except in self-defence, the prevention of crime and making lawful arrests and in some vaguely defined cases of necessity.[63] We may note in passing that those who consent to harm may be liable alongside the perpetrators of the harm as accomplices and conspirators.[64] Although the punishment of active and passive participants in violent sexual

---

59   What may constitute a disability undermining deliberative capacities is a developing field. Persons may possess certain genetically determined biases impairing the ability to make decisions comporting with the agent's own conception of her best interests. For an accessible discussion see Trout, J. (2005), Paternalism and Cognitive Bias, *Law and Philosophy* 24, 393.

60   Dean, T. (2008), Breeding Culture: Barebacking, Bug Chasing, Gift Giving, *Massachusetts Review* 49, 80; Crossley, M. (2004), Making sense of 'Barebacking': Gay Men's Narratives, Unsafe Sex and the 'Resistance Habitus', *British Journal of Social Psychology* 43, 225.

61   See n 8 above.

62   Every conceivable depravity seems catered for. The *Armin Meiwes* case (see n 10 above) brought to light the existence of websites and chat rooms given over to cannibalism.

63   The intentional infliction of serious bodily harm is criminal even in the case of contact sports – *Barnes* [2005] 1 WLR 910 – although that, on the face of it, makes all the more anomalous the legality of boxing: Gunn, M. and Ormerod, D. (1995), The Legality of Boxing, *Legal Studies* 15, 181.

64   There is a principle that victims of offences however compliant are not to be found the accomplices of the principals who offend against them, yet the principle is confined to

and other consensual encounters can with some contrivance be squared with a paternalistic stance, the susceptibility to state punishment of all participants fits like a glove with legal moralism. The majority judgements delivered in the House of Lords in the leading case of *Brown*[65] are the most prominent examples of modern legal moralism. It is noteworthy that these same judgements contain *dicta* which also justify criminal liability on the facts of the case by invoking paternalism. It is a warning to those such as me who may favour paternalistic interventions in some circumstances how easy it is, consciously or otherwise, to pass off moralism as beneficence.

The English Law Commission has recommended that competent adults should be allowed to consent to bodily harm to the extent of actual bodily harm, but that the infliction of serious bodily harm should remain illegal.[66] There is great intuitive appeal to this position. It would, for instance, enhance sexual freedom by decriminalizing, if you will, normal sadomasochism. If the line were held at restricting valid consent to harm of a lesser magnitude than serious bodily harm, we would be spared the disquieting thoughts which arise from those cases where, in states of arousal, consent has been given to the infliction of serious bodily harm, but where the person harmed subsequently regrets and resents the injury he/she has sustained. It is very difficult for liberals to set aside lightly consents given by mentally competent adults during sexual interactions. Sexual freedom must be a core commitment for social liberals. In the light of that commitment, the disinhibiting effect of sexual arousal on decision-making in the moment cannot of itself constitute a reason for invalidating such consents. And yet it may be thought a wholly *laissez faire* approach is problematic where the long-term effects of the decision driven by immediate gratification are likely to be dire and a matter for regret. A general rule of thumb that invalidated consents to death and serious harm would cater for other cases which prompt similar responses. A game of Russian roulette might seem a good idea at 1.00 am, but some of the willing participants might be very glad in the morning that the key to the locked gun cupboard could not be found. The same applies to more reflective decisions. An adolescent, destabilized by some intensely experienced disappointment, might join a suicide club.[67] He might later be glad that his 'suicide buddy' was arrested before he could deliver to him the wherewithal to end his life.

If some form of coercive intervention is considered warranted in these kinds of case, it is very tempting for anyone wishing to retain their liberal credentials to find some flaw in the consent at issue. But that will not do. For instance, many sexual interactions are subsequently regretted. But unless the circumstances

---

cases where the victim is a member of a limited, defined class, such as persons under the age of consent: *Tyrell* [1894] 1 QB 710.

65   *Op cit.*, n 54.

66   *Op cit.*, n 42.

67   There are many active websites and chat rooms where the orientation is to support and assist the intention to commit suicide.

involved coercion, intoxication or deception as to the nature of the act, the agent's regret concerns what he/she *chose* to do, even when the choice was made in a state far removed from optimum conditions for sensible decision-making. And the same applies even for drastic decisions, such as to end one's life. The World Health Organization estimates that worldwide there is circa a million suicides each year,[68] a figure that experts in the field consider a considerable underestimate.[69] Focusing on adolescents and young adults, studies consistently establish that a significant number in this group who choose to end their lives are legally competent decision-makers in as much as there is no psychosis and no state of clinical depression.[70] Studies and clinical reports also establish that a high majority of persons in this class who are diverted from suicide, sometimes coercively through broad interpretation of mental health legislation, and receive appropriate support, live through their suicidal tendencies and recover their equilibrium.[71] Yet if they had succeeded in taking their lives, it would have been an act based on what they wanted at that point in time. What drives decisions to intervene is the conviction that some things are just plain wrong and should be stopped (legal moralism) or that even agents that in legal terms are considered competent may not know their own best interests (paternalism). Interventions cannot be squared with liberalism, or at least a liberalism that makes freedom and autonomy core and non-trumpable values.

Consenting to Risks of Serious Harm

The previous category of cases – persons who choose to have death or serious harms inflicted on them – are important in terms of testing the limits of liberalism, yet involve a relatively small percentage of the adult population. The category under discussion now – taking a known risk of death or serious harm in pursuit of some other goal – is far more common. The most frequent instance would be engaging in sexual acts aware of the risk of contracting some form of serious STD, and we will focus the discussion on cases of this kind.

Until very recently, English law took a very illiberal stance on the permissibility of running risks of harm in sexual encounters. A combined reading of the decisions in *Clarence*[72] *and Brown* implied that if the harm to be risked in the encounter amounted to actual bodily harm or anything more serious, any consent to the risk,

68   World Health Organization (2004), *Suicide*.

69   Qin, P., Agerbo, E. and Mortensen, P. (2005), Factors Contributing to Suicide: The Epidemiological Evidence from Large Scale Registers, in Hawton, K. (ed.), *Prevention and Treatment of Suicidal Behaviour*, (Oxford University Press).

70   Hawton, K. and Rodham, K. (2006), *By Their Own Young Hand: Deliberate Self-harm and Suicidal Ideas in Adolescents*, (Jessica Kinsley Publishers).

71   *Ibid.*, Part Two: Prevention and Treatment of Self- Harm in Adolescents.

72   (1888) 22 QBD 23.

however voluntary and well informed, was invalid. Consequently, a person acting with a relevant form of *mens rea* who physically harmed his sexual partner could well be liable for an offence against the person. If the person harmed was aware of the risk, but, notwithstanding this, voluntarily entered into the sexual encounter, that person too could be liable for inciting or conspiring towards her partner's offence and be an accomplice in the offence itself.[73]

This unyielding stance towards consent to the risk of sexually related physical injury changed with the decision of the Court of Appeal in *Dica*.[74] In the context of the contracting of HIV status on the part of V following sexual intercourse with D, the court limited the effect of the House of Lords decision in *Brown* (a case concerning sadomasochistic encounters) by ruling that *Brown* was concerned with intentional acts of violence (a question begging characterization), whereas in the instant case the issue before the court was the taking of risks of disease by engaging in non-violent sexual relations. But a limiting interpretation of *Brown* was not the only matter to be resolved. The venerable case of *Clarence* had long been cited as authority for the view that a valid consent could not be given to a risk of an STD. With commendable clarity, the court in *Dica* did not seek to finesse and limit this decision. It straightforwardly ruled that *Clarence* should no longer be followed.

Two examples of what may be termed 'responsible' risk taking were very influential in *Dica*. The examples concerned married couples, respectively a married couple who were having unprotected intercourse despite the infected status of one partner in order to conceive a child and a couple who could not resort to protective measures because of their interpretation of the strictures of the Roman Catholic faith. There is no reason to think the effect of the decision is in any way limited by the salience of these examples in the court's decision to depart from *Clarence*. The departure must be taken to be unqualified; otherwise courts will be forced to make some very invidious distinctions. We should be able to say with confidence post *Dica* that the risk of infection arising from non-violent forms of transgender and same-gender sexual encounters will not criminalize those encounters, provided that the risk of infection was known and consented to by the person infected.

The position is far less clear where the parties to the sexual exchange deliberately create the risk of harm. To enhance the sexual experience, behaviours such as strangulation to the brink of unconsciousness, the ingestion of TCT or behaviours involving fire may be indulged. These cases are not within our first category and therefore not within the compass of the decision in *Brown*: death or injury by asphyxiation, or the inflicting of severe burns are not intended outcomes. Rather, the intention is to intensify the experience by creating a controlled risk, but in the hope that it will not materialize. But neither are such cases obviously covered by the ruling in *Dica* which involved standard sexual exchanges, save for

---

73   See n 63 and associated text.
74   [2004] QB 1257.

the risk of infection. To date, English courts have shown zero tolerance for this form of sexual risk taking. Should a liberal seek to change this stance?

When reflecting on this matter, we may note the ubiquity of permitted risk taking in the United Kingdom. In cultural/legal terms there is typically a sharp distinction drawn between the deliberate infliction of a particular harm and running a risk, even a high risk, of the same harm while pursuing various forms of lawful activity, whether forms of work or leisure. Indeed, certain forms of activity are positively indulged, such as professional boxing, where injuries which seem foursquare within the category of deliberately inflicted harm are characterized as the incidental risks of the activity of trying to score more points (land more blows) than the opponent. There could not be a greater difference in judicial tone and attitude when assessing criminal liability for untoward injury in the context of 'manly diversions of strength and skill'[75] by contrast with cases where injury arises in a sexual context. A stark illustration of this difference can be found in the cases of *Aitken*[76] and Emmet.[77] Both cases involve playing with fire in the most literal sense. The fire game in *Aitken* was, *ex ante*, even more dangerous than the game in *Emmet*: in the former case the injury was, predictably, horrendous, whereas in the latter, merely serious. Yet there was criminal liability for the injury in *Emmet* but not in *Aitken*. Why? In the terms of the law there was a valid consent to the injury in *Aitken* but not in the case of *Emmet*. As both cases involved fully informed and voluntary participation in the dangerous activities, the only variable would seem to be differing judicial attitudes triggered by the different social contexts. In *Aitken* we encounter the bizarre mess games of RAF officers who have dined too well; in *Emmet* we become acquainted with the singular sexual diversions of a soon to be married couple.

There is no form of liberalism which would seek to justify the differing outcomes of these cases. A dominant theme of modern versions of liberalism is the importance of providing the maximum scope for autonomous choices in the living of private lives. The stress is on the authenticity and ownership of personal choices and respect for privacy. One might hope for good, life-enhancing choices, but that is a matter for education and guidance and not state coercion. It is only to be expected that many choices made by individuals will be considered bad and be disapproved of when evaluated against substantive conceptions of good and useful lives. Minority forms of sexual activity may attract strongly negative reactions from persons whose conception of the good life includes rigid sexual codes. It is very important that such reactions are kept in their proper place. Confining ourselves to leisure activities, there are a plethora of sports and pastimes where we permit competent adults to run risks of serious injury and death. There are no reasons congruent with liberalism for excluding consensual sex from this dispensation.

---

75   The characterization of boxing and wrestling given in *Donovan* [1934] 2 KB 498.
76   [1992] 4 All ER 541.
77   *The Times*, 15 October 1999.

Of course, the risk must be the subject of consent. Where there is a high risk of a seriously adverse outcome, we must be sure that a free and fully informed consent was given. That was very much in the mind of the Court of Appeal in *Konzani*,[78] where V became HIV positive as a consequence of intercourse with D. In effect, the court came up with a bright-line rule for such cases. There will be no finding that V has consented to the risk of infection unless informed by D, or some other source, of D's HIV status. That goes beyond findings of consent – it is a substantive rule. Many sexually active persons will be fully aware of the nature and kind of the risks they are running should they choose to engage in unprotected sex. They are in no need of explicit warnings any more than an experienced rugby player needs to be told of the risks he is running each time he takes to the pitch. If liberalism is to hold sway in this category of case, as it should, the presence or absence of consent should simply be a matter of ascertaining the facts.

Conclusion

The version of modern, social liberalism originally expounded by Feinberg in *Moral Limits of the Criminal Law* has, among many virtues, the quality of clarity. The primacy he accords to the choices of competent adults allows the drawing of clean-edged boundaries between the permissible and the forbidden. Although the limits of the harm and offence principles are impossible to state with exactitude, many situations will arise where one can have confidence that neither limit on an agent's choices is in play. For example, consensual sex in private between competent adults would be a sequestered space beyond the reach of any criminal law based on Fienberg's version of liberalism. On the face of it, that seems exactly as it should be. Within the memories of many of us are times lived in when forms of sexuality which nowadays may constitute sources of public identity and social solidarity were publicly vilified and severely punished. It may be timely to reassert the core values of liberalism for sexual freedom, particularly if we now live, as some commentators claim we do, in the 'post-liberal' age. If by post-liberalism is meant further moves away from universalism in political and rights discourse and a greater emphasis on claims-based on membership of discrete groups and communities – the politics of difference – the more important it is to sustain and expand the gains that liberal modes of thought have won for personal freedoms. In that vein, we have advocated further decriminalization of consensual sexual conduct, contending that valid consents should be recognized for sexual relations which are not of themselves acts of violence but which may carry the risk of harm, up to and including death, for one or other of the consenting participants.

By contrast, we have yet to reach any firm conclusions about consensual sexual or other forms of act which involve the direct infliction death of serious violence. Then there are cases of self-harm, such as suicide and the self-amputation of healthy

---

78   [2005] 2 Cr App R 14.

limbs. These are difficult cases, at least on the theoretical plane, for persons who would like to think of themselves as consistently liberal. It is easy to construct examples involving persons of the age of consent who freely choose outcomes that seem dreadful in terms of human flourishing. Yet if the harm or offence principles are not in play despite such outcomes, what warrant has the state to intervene to prevent such things?

Two attempts to win a foothold for such interventions within the conventions of liberalism – the argument from freedom; the argument from inalienable and unwaivable rights – were found unpersuasive. That leaves two other avenues if the possibility for intervention is to be left open: legal moralism and paternalism. The first is to be rejected categorically. Take V, who wishes his sexual partner D to beat him senseless. He should not by that token be taken as a bad person who deserves some form of public remonstration regarding his conduct and desires. That leaves paternalism as the remaining ground for state action in such a case. Paternalism is an uncomfortable word, replete with unwelcome associations. But it has the advantage of highlighting some of the issues at stake. Coercion in the name of paternalism implies, or should be held to imply, a claim that the person coerced will, at least in the long run, have his interests advanced rather than setback by state coercion. The beneficent effects must be sought in the outcomes for the individual coerced. So, using our example, if V is beaten senseless by D and is subsequently convicted and punished as D's accomplice to his offence against the person, there should be no claim of justification for this in the terms of paternalism by pointing to the possibility of a general deterrent effect flowing from V's conviction and punishment. The claim must be that V's own life will ultimately go better if he is publicly denounced and punished as a too extreme masochist or, if preferred, an extreme sadist's willing assistant. We cannot rule out categorically the possibility that V's life might go better as a consequence of his conviction, but there is no cogent reason for thinking that it would.

As protection of V from himself is the object of any *bona fide* claim of paternalism, the criminal law should focus exclusively on restraining the sadism of D. What is known as the rule in *Tyrell*[79] (which holds that where an offence is created for the protection of a vulnerable class of victim, a member of the class cannot be an accomplice in the offence) should be construed to apply to all offences against the person, where the consent of the victim is legally ineffective. It would be perfectly coherent under such a dispensation to find that in our example D offends against V given that V's consent is to be legally ineffective if the harm is death or serious bodily harm. Where harm is self-inflicted – suicide, a do-it-yourself amputation – there seems to be no reason at all to resort to the criminal law in respect of V. (It may be different for D if he advises or assists in V's self-harm.) At most, supportive civil law measures should be contemplated, though effectiveness might require forms of coercion including loss of liberty for preventative purposes.

---

79 *Op cit.*, n 63.

Left to their own devices, people may cause themselves great harm. Most of those harms are quite beyond the competence and resources of state agencies to influence and correct. The case for state intervention is strongest where an agent proposes to do something to herself or have something done to her which threatens to end a life potentially worth living or an immediate, serious and permanent setback to the core interest of her physical health or soundness, with no offsetting gain remotely commensurable with the loss. If there is a freely given consent and no harm or offence to third parties, we must accept that coercive interventions are outside the liberal framework. For some that might not be an insuperable objection, if we can be sure that the intervention will advance the long-term interests of an agent who at this moment in time has opted to be seriously harmed. That is paternalism, better expressed perhaps as communitarian concern for welfare. The only plausible way the criminal law can advance welfare in the kind of case under discussion is to prevent D from causing V's death or causing V serious bodily harm or from preventing D from encouraging or assisting V's self-harm. Where there are very strong grounds for thinking that some form of coercion of V will prevent her death or serious harm, the coercion should take a civil law form, with robust review and release procedures.

References

Alexander, L. (2005), When are we Rightfully Aggrieved?, *Legal Theory* 11, 325.

Andrew, D. (1980), The Code of Honour and its Critics, *Social History* 5:3, 409.

Bayne, T. and Levy, N. (2005), Amputees by Choice: Bodily Integrity Disorder and the Ethics of Amputation, *Journal of Applied Philosophy* 22:1, 75–86.

Crossley, M. (2004), Making Sense of 'Barebacking': Gay Men's Narratives, Unsafe Sex and the 'Resistance Habitus', *British Journal of Social Psychology* 43, 225.

Dan-Cohen, M. (2000), Basic Values and the Victim's State of Mind, *California Law Review* 88, 759.

Dean, T. (2008), Breeding Culture: Barebacking, Bug Chasing, Gift Giving, *Massachusetts Review* 49, 80.

Devlin, P. (1965), *The Enforcement of Morals*, (Oxford University Press).

Duff, R.A. (2007), *Answering for Crime*, (Hart Publishing).

Duff, R.A. (2002), Harms and Wrongs, *Buffalo Criminal Law Review* 5, 13.

Dworkin, G. (1999), Devlin was Right: Law and the Enforcement of Morality, *William and Mary Law Review* 40, 927.

Feinberg, J. (1984), *Harm to Others*, (Oxford University Press).

Feinberg, J. (1984–1988), *The Moral Limits of the Criminal Law*, (Oxford University Press).

Feinberg, J. (1985), *Offence to Others*, (Oxford University Press).

Feinberg, J. (1986), *Harm to Self*, (Oxford University Press).

Feinberg, J. (1988), *Harmless Wrongdoing*, (Oxford University Press).

Galligan, D. (1981), The Return to Retribution in Penal Theory, in Tapper, C.F.H. (ed.), *Crime, Proof and Punishment*, (Butterworths).

Gunn, M. and Ormerod, D. (1995), The Legality of Boxing, *Legal Studies* 15, 181.

Hart, H. (1965), *Law, Liberty and Morality*, (Oxford University Press).

Hawton, K. and Rodham, K. (2006), *By Their Own Young Hand: Deliberate Self-harm and Suicidal Ideas in Adolescents*, (Jessica Kinsley Publishers).

Horn, F. (2003), Bodily Integrity Identity Disorder, *Social Work Today* February 24.

Law Commission Consultation Paper No. 139 (1995), *Consent in the Criminal Law*.

Mill, J.S. (1859), *On Liberty*, (Oxford World's Classics).

Postema, G. (2005), Politics is about the Grievance: Feinberg on the Legal Enforcement of Morality, *Legal Theory* 11, 293.

Qin, P., Agerbo, E. and Mortensen, P. (2005), Factors Contributing to Suicide: The Epidemiological Evidence from Large Scale Registers, in Hawton, K. (ed.), *Prevention and Treatment of Suicidal Behaviour*, (Oxford University Press).

Simester, A. and Sullivan, G.R. (2007), *Criminal Law: Theory and Doctrine*, 3rd Edition (Hart Publishing).

Trout, J. (2005), Paternalism and Cognitive Bias, *Law and Philosophy* 24, 393.

Walker, N. and Padfield, N. (1999), *Sentencing: Theory Law and Practice*, (Oxford University Press).

World Health Organization (2004), *Suicide*.

Index